★

"Dr Leslie Tay is passiona†
Singapore's unique hawke
guide."
—Prof Tommy Koh, Ambassador-at-large

★ ★ ★

"Leslie Tay has done it again! This is the best guide
for serious street food afficionados. Truly the best that
Singapore has to offer the world!"
—Peter A Knipp, *Cuisine & Wine Asia*

★ ★ ★

"Leslie has his finger on the pulse of Singapore's
unique hawker cuisine. This is an essential guide."
—Yukari Sakamoto, author of *Food Sake Tokyo*

★ ★ ★

"Written with passion and dogged determination, this
is the Ultimate Guide to the best hawker foods in
Singapore!"
—Ronnie Tan, chef and owner of Tatsuya

★ ★ ★

"*ieatishootipost* has taken food photography completely
by storm. Leslie's ability to infuse life into every photo
makes good food look even better!"
—William Teo, former Honorary Secretary of The
Photographic Society of Singapore

"Leslie-san is like a samurai food warrior who builds the bridge for world foodies to meet!"
—Hisato Hamada, top restauranteur in Japan

"Leslie doesn't just love great food, he loves great food stories, and nobody talks about these two things with as much authority as he does."
—mrbrown, *mrbrown.com*

"Reading Leslie's stories about food is like reading a love story. Such is his passion for Singapore's favourite foods."
—Benjamin "Mr Miyagi" Lee, *miyagi.sg*

★ ★ ★

"Our hawker stories are a reflection of who we are and that unique facet of Singapore culture is beautifully presented in this book!"
—Tan Chuan-Jin, Acting Minister for Manpower and Senior Minister of State for National Development

COVER & BOOK DESIGN
Foo Siew Huey

EDITORIAL TEAM
Ruth Wan
Sasha Martin
Josephine Tan
Aditi Shivaramakrishnan

National Library Board Singapore
Cataloguing-in-Publication Data

Only the best!: the ieat, ishoot, ipost guide to
Singapore's shiokest hawker food / Leslie Tay.
– Singapore : Epigram Books, 2012.

p. cm.
ISBN: 978-981-07-3780-1 (pbk.)

1. Cooking, Singaporean. 2. Peddlers—Singapore. I. Title.

TX724.5.S
641.595957-- dc23   OCN811550289

First Edition
10 9 8 7 6 5 4 3 2 1

DR LESLIE TAY

ONLY
THE
BEST!

THE IEAT·ISHOOT·IPOST GUIDE
TO SINGAPORE'S SHIOKEST HAWKER FOOD*

*and the best *ieat* guide to durians ever!

EPIGRAM BOOKS / SINGAPORE

Also by Dr Leslie Tay

The End of Char Kway Teow and Other Hawker Mysteries

FOR MY PAPA AND MAMA

CONTENTS

INTRODUCTION

THIS IS A UNIQUE GUIDE TO HAWKER DISHES IN SINGAPORE. EVERY DISH presented here has been tasted and found to be exceptional. It is my ongoing passion to eat and write about Singapore's greatest hawkers. My merry band of makan kakis and I have been eating around the island since 2006. We have nitpicked our way through the good, the bad and the awful. We have savoured the fat, spit out the rest, and then I rave about it on my blog. You won't find any of the bad stuff in this guide. You won't even find the average stuff. No, in this guide, I curated the thousand-plus stalls I've eaten at and present to you only the best! Seriously, why should you want to know about an average nasi lemak, when there is a much shioker version just 10 minutes away?

You will find that I have added little nuggets of information all over the book. These are little stories and facts I have collected over the years through my interaction with the hawkers and they represent a very important part of Singapore's culinary heritage. I hope you will have a few "Aha!" moments reading them.

But wait, there's more! I have also included a very handy durian guide that lists popular durians in Singapore, together with photos and a list of reliable stalls, so that when you go out for durians, you won't come back with lemons! There are also two food trails covering Chinatown and Joo Chiat/Katong, which I have put together with visitors in mind. These neighbourhoods have a great concentration of excellent hawkers, all within walking distance, and would give you a good introduction to Singapore food.

Now, even though we only present you the best, there are some stalls which are "more best" than others. So, we rate them as follows (all ratings are out of 5):

Below 4.0 Did not make it to this book. Nuff said.

4.0 Eat at this stall when you are in the vicinity.

4.25 Shiok! But just lacks that something to give it a 4.5.

4.5 Really Shiok. Even if you live in Pasir Ris and the stall is in Boon Lay, go try it!

4.6 Shioker than Really Shiok, but just shy of an epiphany.

4.75 Moment of epiphany when the earth stops rotating and for one moment in time, you are at peace knowing that you have found what you have been looking for.

4.8 I can't think of how the dish can get any better, but somewhere out there in this big big world, there might just be another dish that can top this. I just haven't found it yet.

5.0 Talk to even the best hawkers who have been making the same dish for 50 years and they will tell you that there is still room for improvement. Perfection can never be reached. It is always another step away.

One final thing. For every dish, I have selected my favourite. Called "Leslie's Pick", these are the stalls that I would introduce to visitors. Most of the time, "Leslie's Pick" would be the stall with the highest rating. At times, I would choose to bring visitors to a stall with a slightly lower rating because that stall has better ambience, better service, or there is an interesting story attached to it. These are places I feel most confident recommending and they should not fail to impress.

So get ready! Armed with this guide book, you are now ready to embark on a culinary adventure to find the Holy Grail of gustatory pleasure. I am well ahead in the journey and I can tell you that it is going to be a wonderful ride. And along the way, remember what I always say: Never waste your calories on yucky food!

DR LESLIE TAY

ieatishootipost.sg

BAK CHOR MEE

BAK CHOR MEE AND MEE POK TAR ARE SIMPLE NOODLE DISHES, BUT THE simplest things are often the hardest to do right. A good quality egg noodle and fresh ingredients are essential. With each mouthful, you should be able to enjoy the aroma of the noodles that has been lightly flavoured by pork lard, with the vinegar cutting through the oil and getting the salivary glands working. I prefer my noodles QQ (al dente), with a firm bite and sufficient curl to give you that serrated feel as you slurp them up. The balance of chilli and vinegar has to be just right, and the combination of pork and sauce really shiok.

DID YOU KNOW?

❶ Bak chor mee is the third favourite dish among Singaporeans, after Hokkien mee and chicken rice. ❷ It can be eaten anytime—for breakfast, lunch, dinner and supper! ❸ The keys to a great bak chor mee are fresh ingredients, great noodles and enough zing from the black vinegar.

LESLIE'S
PICK ★✓

CHIA KENG KWAY TEOW MEE

4.75 I have finally found a mee pok tar that is one head above all the rest, both in taste as well as in the amount of passion going into preparing it. Most ingredients are hand-made by Uncle who has been perfecting his craft for the last 50 years, and his skill shows—from the handmade fishballs, to the pork made from quality pork loin, to the excellent quality prawns and sliced abalone. The homemade chilli sauce is packed with umami from dried prawns and tipoh (dried sole fish), and it is not overly spicy. As for the noodles, they are served perfectly sauced and al dente. Finally, while most fishball soups are made from the water that held the fishballs while they were being formed, Uncle's soup is sweetened with pork bones that have been cooked overnight.

Chong Boon Food Centre • Blk 453A
Ang Mo Kio Ave 10 #01-11 S561453

• 5am to 2pm, closed on Mondays and Fridays • 96446338, 93591838

HILL STREET TAI HWA PORK NOODLE

4.5 This is perhaps the most famous bak chor mee stalls in Singapore, and is perhaps as good as bak chor mee can get! The noodles are really QQ (al dente), the chilli shiok, the lard fresh, and the black vinegar just gets your salivary glands working overtime. Delicious!

466 Crawford Lane #01-12 S190466 • 9.30am to 9pm, closed on 1st and 3rd Mondays of the month

SENG KEE MUSHROOM MINCED PORK NOODLES

4.5 At this stall you will find the famous "clop clop" man, Mr Lee, who throws his bowls and makes a lot of noise as he cooks his wonderful QQ (al dente) noodles—the thin, flat type with excellent eggy flavour. Another thing that stands out is the unique sauce that Mr Lee creates by slicing up the mushrooms, and leaving them overnight to extract the juices before combining them with his secret blend of herbs and spices.

Serangoon Garden Market & Food Centre • 49A Serangoon Garden Way Stall 4

S555945 • 7.30am to 3pm, closed on
Mondays • 84390434

AH GUAN MEE POK

4.5 If tradition is not your thing, try this New Generation mee pok tar, based on Japanese ramen concepts. Here, you can only order mee pok as the owner, Eric, feels that his recipe does not work with mee kia, exactly the same kind of thinking that the Japanese apply to their ramen. You also have the option of adding really good stuff, like scallops, crayfish and fish slices, making this New Generation dish all the more delicious!

69 Syed Alwi Road S207648 • 7am to
9pm, open everyday

AH KOW MUSHROOM MINCED PORK MEE

4.5 The one characteristic of good bak chor mee is freshness of the ingredients, and the piping hot bak chor mee at Ah Kow tastes really fresh. Those who like their bak chor mee with a bit more vinegar will appreciate the unbridled use of black vinegar here, reportedly a special brand of traditional black vinegar from China. They are also generous with the crispy tipoh (dried sole fish)—I simply love the stuff!

Hong Lim Food Centre • 531A Upper Cross
St #02-42 S051531 • 9am to 7pm, open
everyday

132 MEE POH KWAY TEOW MEE

4.5 The Uncle here is the original mee pok man of East Coast, having first started his business at the old Siglap Market almost 40 years ago. Everything from the pork to the prawns is very fresh, and the chilli is rumoured to have buah keluak (Indonesian black nut) in it, which gives it that special smoky, savoury flavour. No wonder this stall was voted the best mee pok stall in the East Coast area by *The Straits Times.*

MP 59 Food House • 59 Marine Terrace
#01-105 S440059 • 7am to 3.30pm,
closed on Mondays and 3rd Sunday of
the month

XING JI ROU CUO MIAN (INNER STALL)

4.25 Located side by side, Xing Ji and Seng Hiang Food

LESLIE'S TIP

Here is the key to cooking great noodles with that al dente, springy texture: the water needs to be on a furious rolling boil. Watch out for this the next time you're ordering noodles!

Stall (next door) have been long-time bak chor mee rivals at Fengshan Food Centre. Xing Ji seems to have a longer queue of people than Seng Hiang. Although Xing Ji's bowl is slightly smaller, the soup is just slightly more tasty, but the difference is so small that unless you ate both stalls' bak chor mee at one go, I doubt you would be able to tell the difference. If you ask me, I would just order from whichever stall has the shorter queue.

Fengshan Food Centre • 85 Bedok North St 4 Stall 7 S460085 • 5pm to 1am, closed on Mondays

SENG HIANG FOOD STALL (OUTER STALL)

4.25 Located side by side, Seng Hiang and Xing Ji Rou Cuo Mian (next door) have been long-time bak chor mee rivals at Fengshan Food Centre. Seng Hiang has slightly more minced pork but tastewise, the noodles of both stalls are similar. I wouldn't be surprised if they shared the same supplier!

Fengshan Food Centre • 85 Bedok North St 4 Stall 8 S460085 • Tuesdays to

Saturdays: 6pm to 5am, Sundays to Mondays: 6am to 1am

MACPHERSON MINCED MEAT NOODLES

4.25 Bak chor mee, if done well, can give you the same feeling of shiokness as a yummy bowl of ramen, at a fraction of the price. This stall's bak chor mee comes close, but for the strong kee (lye water) smell of the noodles. Still, the soup is something to behold. It is a veritable bowl of protein rich broth that is likely to induce gout!

1382 Serangoon Road (Opal Crescent) S328254 • 6.30am to 2.30pm, open everyday

PUAY HENG BAK CHOR MEE

4.25 The noodles here are just right, and have the ability to soak up just the right amount of black vinegar, chilli and mushroom sauce. I also love the way the chilli was made with pounded dried shrimps and crispy tipoh (dried sole fish), designed to create an umami tickle on the tongue. Pity the fish dumplings aren't handmade, but as with all things, bak chor mee is all about

LESLIE'S TIP

If you prefer bak chor mee mai hiam (no chilli), look for stalls that serve this non-spicy version using mushroom sauce and a dash of good quality black vinegar, instead of just tomato sauce. Seriously, why waste your calories?

balance, and Puay Heng's bowl is very much in equilibrium.

Far East Square • 23/24 China St #01-01 S049565 • 9.30am to 9pm, closed on alternate Sundays

TEOCHEW STREET MUSHROOM MINCED MEAT NOODLE

4.25 The mee pok tar here redefines the meaning of chngee (fresh). The uncle will turn aside while cooking the noodles to make some dumplings, then turn back to toss the noodles a few times before moving to the chopping board to slice a few pieces of meat. Though the ingredients are excellent, the noodles and sauce lack a bit of flavour. Yet, this is probably the best value, most elaborate and freshly made bak chor mee that I have ever come across.

Chinatown Complex Food Centre • 335 Smith St #02-23 S050335 • 12.30pm to 9pm, closed on Mondays and Tuesdays

DID YOU KNOW?

Bak chor mee is a uniquely Singaporean dish. While noodles with various toppings exist everywhere, you will not find the same combination of minced pork with stewed mushrooms and crispy tipoh (dried sole fish), laced with a generous dash of black vinegar and chilli anywhere else in the world.

SENG HUAT EATING HOUSE

4.25 A good bak chor mee should taste good even without chilli and this depends on there being a good mushroom sauce and a dash of good quality black vinegar, exactly what Seng Huat does so well. Unconventionally, this stall also uses tomato ketchup to flavour the noodles, but only a small amount so that the taste does not dominate but adds a well balanced complementary tang and sweetness to the noodles.

492 North Bridge Road (opposite Parco Bugis Junction) S188737 • open 24 hours daily

JOO HENG MUSHROOM MINCED PORK MEE

4.0 This is indeed a fine bowl of bak chor mee. The flavours are nicely balanced and you can whiff the eggy aroma of good quality egg noodles with that first mouthful. The texture of the noodles is QQ (al dente). However, the bak chor mee does not really stand one head above the rest.

Ang Mo Kio Market & Food Centre • 628 Ang Mo Kio Ave 4 St 61 #01-86 S569163 • 7am to 2pm, open everyday

LAI HENG MUSHROOM MINCED MEAT MEE

4.0 The ingredients are very fresh, the noodles QQ (al dente) and the sauce well balanced. Also, the crispy tipoh (dried sole fish) is very fragrant. However, there is a

40-minute wait at this stall and for me, the stall's dish does not seem to justify such a long wait.

Blk 51 Lorong 6 Toa Payoh S310051 • 8.30am to 4pm, closed on Wednesdays

PUNGGOL NOODLES

4.0 The hawker is a really nice guy who, having lost his right hand in an industrial accident, has never let his handicap get in the way of making a great bowl of bak chor mee. The highlight of this bowl is the meatballs, which are soft, tender and have a lovely bounciness. However, the noodles and sauce are not the best.

Hainanese Village Centre • 105 Hougang Ave 1 #02-24 S530105 • 7am to 2.30pm, closed on Sundays

NOI'S MUSHROOM MINCED MEAT NOODLES

4.0 If you like your bak chor mee to have a strong vinegar kick and a toothy bite, you will love Noi's. But if you like your ter kwa (pig liver) and prefer QQ (al dente) noodles, you will be disappointed (the liver is replaced with prawns). There are people who will enjoy this stall's bowl of bak chor mee and others who will complain about it. But if I'm around Balestier and hankering for bak chor mee, it's Noi's for me.

588F Jalan Datoh (off Balestier Road) S329899 • 8.30am to 4pm, open everyday

TOM'S CITIZOOM MEE POK TAR

4.0 Tom is a young man who likes mee pok. So he left his engineering career to set up this stall—and it's got great potential! The mee pok here is top quality, sourced from Lau Boon Hong, one of the more reputable noodle makers in Singapore. Tom also tries to make his mee pok special by frying his fish cakes fresh and cutting them into slices, just before serving. Eaten piping hot, the fish cakes are still oozing with juices and the texture is light and bouncy! Another of Tom's innovations is the addition of crumbled fish crackers sprinkled on top of the noodles just before serving. Although I appreciated the crunchy texture, I thought a few slivers of crispy fried tipoh (dried sole fish) would have complemented the dish better.

Blk 57 Lengkok Bahru S151057 • 8.30am to 3pm, closed on alternate Sundays and public holidays • 97420865

DID YOU KNOW?

The noodles used for bak chor mee and mee pok tar do not contain any egg while those used for wanton mee do. That is why wanton mee noodles get a quick dip in water during the cooking process, but not mee pok!

BAK KUT TEH

BAK KUT TEH IS MY PICK FOR THE DISH THAT BEST REPRESENTS SINGAPORE.
It is a dish of heritage and ceremony. The key to an excellent
bak kut teh is the soup. Only four ingredients are required—pork,
water, garlic and pepper. The broth and the meat have to be cooked
separately. For the broth, you need a good amount of pork ribs and
a long slow simmering boil in order to coax all that natural pork
flavour out of the meat and bones. For the meat, it is cooked in a
pot of soup that boils away furiously. The trick is to get the pork to
the stage where it is just cooked, so that the texture is tender and
the meat reverberates when you chew on it. At this point, garlic
and pepper are added and this peppery pork soup is then added
to the slow cooked broth in order to produce a bak kut teh soup
that is slightly cloudy but velvety smooth, with a satisfying pepper
punch at the beginning and a natural sweetness at the end.

LESLIE'S PICK ✓

SONG FA BAK KUT TEH

4.5 **Second generation owner Yeo Hart Pong modified his father's Teochew style bak kut teh recipe to appeal to the new generation, who prefers pork ribs with a fall-off-the-bone texture. Yeo sticks to his father's tried and tested recipe for soup which involves using a particular garlic from China and pepper from Sarawak. I like the soup because it is not overly peppery but nicely balanced with the natural sweetness of pork bones. The modern retro ambience of both branches make them great places to be introduced to bak kut teh. Plus, you can enjoy Pek Sin Choon teas there too!**

---

11 New Bridge Road #01-01 S059383 • 7am to 10pm, closed on Mondays • 6533 6128

UE BizHub East Unit • 6 Changi Business Park Ave 1 #01-38 S486017 • 10.30am to 9.15pm, open everyday • 66948098

OUTRAM PARK YA HUA ROU GU CHAR

4.5 The soup here is very good—robust, but not overly peppery. It has a sweet, savoury taste that comes from boiling the pork bones until they are almost crumbly— that's when all the rich stuff from the marrow gets released into the soup. When I tasted the dish, the ribs were cooked until they were very tender. Frankie Gwee, the owner, is also extremely hospitable. Great bak kut teh with great service to boot!

Tanjong Pagar Complex (PSA) • 7 Keppel Road #01-05/07 S089053 • 6am to 3pm, 6pm to 4am, closed on Mondays • 62229610

OLD TIONG BAHRU BAK KUT TEH

4.5 This bak kut teh soup is smooth, with a satisfying pepper punch at the beginning and a natural sweetness at the end. Here's a tip for you: get to this stall at 11am, when the soup is sufficiently flavourful and the you char kway (fried dough fritter), fresh. And you will be able to get the prized long gu, which are the thicker, more tender pork ribs closer to the backbone.

Blk 58 Seng Poh Road #01-31 S160058 • 6.30am to 9pm, closed on Mondays

TIONG BEE BAH KUT TEH

4.5 Straightforward, no-nonsense bak kut teh that has been around for years. Auntie is over 70 years old and only cooks three pots of soup a day. The pork ribs are simmered in the pot long enough to ensure that the meat is excellently tender, with very well balanced soup that has oomph without being overly peppery. Good old bak kut teh at its best.

588F Jalan Datoh (off Balestier Road) S329899 • 7am to 3pm, closed on alternate Mondays

SIN HENG CLAYPOT BAK KOOT TEH

4.5/4.25 Hokkien version/ Teochew version

At this stall, the Teochew version's soup is sweet and peppery, and a tad darker than the typical Teochew bak kut teh. The Hokkien version is reminiscent of Malaysian bak kut teh, but I found the taste of the herbs a bit too mild. The store also serves yam rice that is flavoured with dried shrimp and yam—this is really nice to eat, even on its own! A traditional pot of gong fu tea is served with your soup.

439 Joo Chiat Road S427652 • Tuesdays to Saturdays: 7.30am to 4am, Sundays: 7.30am to 1am, closed on Mondays

FOUNDER BAK KUT TEH RESTAURANT

4.25 The Uncle did not learn to cook bak kut teh from a master. Instead, he loved eating it so much that he started experimenting and came up with his own recipe! So, he chose the name "Founder" for his restaurant. A former pig farmer, he knows his pork very well and sources only the best for his bak kut teh. The pork ribs are done very well—tender but not overcooked, retaining some bite. The soup is also good—sweet, peppery, and quite light and refreshing.

New Orchid Hotel • 347 Balestier Road S329777 • noon to 6pm, closed on Tuesdays

154 Rangoon Road S218431 • 9am to 3pm and 5.30pm to 10.30pm, closed on Wednesdays

NG AH SIO PORK RIBS SOUP EATING HOUSE

4.25 What is so special about this bak kut teh that made politicians risk potential embarrassment just to get a taste of it at this stall? Both Donald Tsang

DID YOU KNOW?

The light, peppery version of bak kut teh came from the Teochews, while the dark, herbal version, from the Hokkiens. The term "bak kut teh" is Hokkien, but the practice of serving gong fu tea with this dish is Teochew. Hence, bak kut teh was born out of the meeting of the two dialect groups in Singapore.

and Thaksin Shinawatra were publicly spurned at Ng Ah Sio (the former was denied a bowl of this delicious soup because he arrived after closing hours, and the latter made the mistake of arguing with the owner about his food, and got himself thrown out!) The soup here is very enjoyable. It is a robust and spicy, peppery blast, typical of Teochew style bak kut teh.

208 Rangoon Road S218453 • 7am to 10pm, closed on Mondays • www.ngahsiobkt.com

RONG CHENG BAK KUT TEH

4.25 Rong Cheng has opened a new branch, just down the road from its original Sin Ming eatery. Both locations serve very good soup which doesn't contain soya sauce, so you taste more of the original flavour of the pork. Owner Lionel Lim, the son of the founder, has designed the new branch with tea culture in mind. Not only is every table designed to have access to a pot of boiling water and traditional tea sets for you to brew your own gong fu tea, Lionel has also worked with Pek Sin Choon, a tea merchant, to come up with a light tea, called double blossom tea. Its delicate taste is supposed to appeal to the younger generation.

Eng Ho Hup Coffeeshop • Blk 22 Sin Ming Road S570022 • 7am to 4pm, open everyday

Mid View City • Blk 26 Sin Ming Lane #01-114/117 S573791 • 7am to 9pm, open everyday • 96681412

LEONG KEE (KLANG) BAK KUT TEH

4.0 If it is Malaysian style bak kut teh you are looking for, then this is it. The soup was a bit bitter (rather than sweet) the day I tried it, and lacked the oomph you would expect in a good bak kut teh. The pork ribs were very tender though. The real star of Leong Kee is the ter kah (pig's trotters): soft, sticky, sweet and savoury, the fat and tendons simply melt-in-your-mouth—very shiok.

321 Beach Road (Jalan Sultan Gate and Beach Road) S199557 • 11am to 9pm, closed on Mondays

HONG JI CLAYPOT PORK RIB SOUP

4.0 The special thing about this bak kut teh is that it is

LESLIE'S TIP

Ask the hawker to serve you the long gu, the rib cut nearer the backbone. Compared to the pai gu (the part of the rib comprising the rib cage), it is thicker, more tender, and the flavour really develops in your mouth because of the extra bit of fat.

PEK SIN CHOON

Founded in 1925, Pek Sin Choon Tea Merchants currently supplies teas to 80 per cent of bak kut teh stalls in Singapore. Run by fourth generation owner, Kenry Peh, Pek Sin Choon still hand wraps its teas at its Mosque Street shophouse. The original style of wrapping is still followed—there are two layers of paper: the slip of pink paper which forms the inner layer is a throwback to the post-war years when white paper was not easy to get hold of, but there was plenty of pink medicinal paper around! And, the people who hand wrap your tea include Aunties like Madam Lim, who has spent over 50 years of her life packing tea. Amazing! Top marks to Pek Sin Choon for maintaining tradition!

the herbal type which is served in a claypot. The bak kut teh was good, but it didn't have that extra something that would induce me to drive all the way up north just to have it again. All in all, a nice bak kut teh to try if you are around the northern part of Singapore.

Blk 19 Marsiling Lane #01-329 S730019 • 8am to 9pm, open everyday • www.hongji-bkt.com

HENG HENG BAK KUT TEH

4.0 Fancy a $128 bak kut teh? If you are an abalone afficionado or have a craving for abalone, pop over to Heng Heng to order abalone bak kut teh! Or, if you wish for a more affordable meal, just stick with the pork ribs: the meat is nice, with some chew. The soup here

is good for those who don't like their bak kut teh with a peppery kick. It is sweeter, with strong hints of cinnamon and star anise.

107 Owen Road S218914 • 7.30am to 2.30pm, closed on Tuesdays

DID YOU KNOW?

Older folks will insist on the importance of observing the gong fu tea ceremony which accompanies bak kut teh. Take time to make the tea and enjoy a few cups before starting on the soup. A good Chinese tea pairing can elevate the flavour of the soup, just like a good wine pairing for gourmet food.

FIVE BAK KUT TEH TEAS

Here are short descriptions of the five different types of teas usually paired with bak kut teh:

1) XIN CHUN SHUI XIAN (new spring water fairy)—an oolong tea with a smooth aged flavour. The colour is very deep and the tea contains lots of tannin. This is an excellent tea to pair with soup that is more peppery.

2) TIE LUO HAN (iron warrior monk)—one of the si da ming cong, i.e., one of the four famous rock teas from the region of the Wuyi mountain. Pek Sin Choon's version is blended with aged teas to give it a more mellow flavour.

3) TIE KUAN YIN (iron goddess of mercy)—an oolong tea that tends to be a little heavy and unrefined, but it appeals to older folks as they are familiar with its taste.

4) BU ZHI XIANG (unknown fragrance)—a premium tea which costs five times more when it was introduced in the 1960s, this tea is a blend of Wuyi oolong and Anxi tea. This is currently the most popular bak kut teh tea in Singapore, outselling the others 10 to 1. This tea is strong enough to cut through the oil, leaving the palate with a bittersweet aftertaste, which is favoured by seasoned tea drinkers.

5) XIANG JI JI—introduced in the late 1970s, this tea was named after princess Xiang Ge Ge from a popular TV series at that time. This tea is stronger than Bu Zhi Xiang and has more aged teas blended in for a smoother taste. Like Xin Chun Shui Xian, it is a good tea to pair with more peppery soups, and is the most expensive of the five teas.

DID YOU KNOW?

Bak kut teh's origins are closedly tied to Singapore's immigrant history—it was a dish our forefathers ate as coolies to get an energy boost as they did the backbreaking work of carrying cargo off the bumboats into the godowns.

BEANCURD

I LOVE MY BEANCURD SUPER SMOOTH, SOFT AND SILKY. AT THE SAME TIME, beancurd, also known as tau huay, must retain the taste of the soya beans. It should not be too watered down. Beancurd that is freshly made at the stall is always better than a factory made version. The texture of freshly made beancurd is finer and smoother (because the factory made ones are deliberately made stiffer to be able to withstand the trauma of being transported from the factory to the stall). The ones made on the premises are moved very little once the beancurd has set and each vat of freshly made beancurd can optimally last only a few hours, so it has to be eaten fresh. If you want to taste what beancurd used to taste like before hawkers started procuring factory made ones, look out for a machine making soya milk at the stall.

LESLIE'S PICK ✓

WHAMPOA SOYA BEAN AND GRASS JELLY

4.6 **The tau huay in this stall is made with shi gao (gypsum) instead of lactone. While lactone is more forgiving, allowing more room for error, using gypsum requires the skill of an experienced tau huay maker. When you get it right, the tau huay is softer and silkier than the modern lactone tau huay. The day I tried Uncle's tau huay, it had the perfect texture, and disintegrated in the mouth with the slightest pressure. The best tau huay I have had in a while.**

Whampoa Drive Makan Place (Whampoa Food Centre) • Blk 91 Whampoa Dr #01-52 S320091 • 6.30am to 4.30pm, closed on Mondays

BEANCURD CITY

4.5 The texture of the beancurd at this stall is soft and silky. At the same time, it still manages to retain the taste of the beans instead of being too watered down.

133 Jalan Besar (after Desker Road) S208851 • 10.30am to midnight, open everyday

TAN SOON MUI BEANCURD

4.5 This stall is three generations old and was founded in 1966. It has the best beancurd I have eaten in a long while, at only half the price of other famous stalls. The soya bean taste is evident and the texture sublime. It is excellent and ironically, it is one of the cheapest bowls of beancurd around!

Serangoon Garden Market & Food Centre • 49A Serangoon Garden Way Stall 41 S555945 • 8am to 8pm, closed on Mondays

ROCHOR ORIGINAL BEANCURD

4.25 This stall is commonly known as the most famous beancurd stall in Singapore. It was where Anthony Bourdain was taken to taste the best of what Singapore had to offer. I found the beancurd very good, but certainly not the best a beancurd could be. Even though it was silky smooth, it tasted too diluted for me.

2 Short St S188211 • noon to midnight, open everyday

ERYIMIN

4.25 This beancurd is slightly smoother than the beancurd served at Rochor Original Beancurd, which is right next to

TAN SOON MUI BEANCURD

DID YOU KNOW?

Have you tried the latest craze—beancurd pudding chilled in little plastic bowls? The pudding comes in various flavours: almond, honeydew, and even durian! To me, beancurd pudding is easy to do—you can even make it at home. But making quality tau huay requires skill and experience. It also utilises a much smaller amount of chemicals, i.e., gypsum or lactone, compared to the beancurd pudding, which is made from powdered soya bean milk, creamer and gelatine.

it, but the taste is slightly more diluted. The sugar also has a bit more colouring in it. But the truth of the matter is, when I carried out a blindfold test, the beancurds from both stalls were indistinguishable. This just proves that both stalls' beancurds are very similar in taste and texture—in short, just go for the one with the shorter queue!

4 Short St S188212 • noon to midnight, open everyday

BEEF KWAY TEOW

HAVE YOU EVER WONDERED WHY BEEF KWAY TEOW IS CALLED "KWAY TEOW", even though most of the time, you eat it with thick beehoon? There are two types of beef kway teow: the one with thick beehoon in sticky gravy is Hainanese style. The other is Teochew style, with kway teow served with just a dash of sesame oil, soya sauce and chilli. I love my beef slices tender and slightly pink. The soup should be robust and filled with bovine goodness. As for the meatballs, very few places still make their own beef balls, but when they do, you can definitely taste the difference.

DID YOU KNOW?

To make springy beef balls, the meat is not minced, but beaten. In the good old days, hawkers used two metal batons for pounding. Pounding straightens out the protein strands, causing the meat to be springy. The same principle is also used to make springy fishballs.

LESLIE'S PICK ✓

HOCK LAM STREET BEEF KWAY TEOW

4.25 This stall has been around since 1911, and its fourth generation owner Tina Tan gave up her high paying bank job to take over the family business. The sliced beef is very nice and tender. Tina says that the beef is still sliced by hand and no tenderiser is used. The sauce could be more shiok, but because Teochew food emphasises more on freshness, the sauce tends to be a little more bland. Go for the kway teow soup to taste the original Teochew style beef kway teow (see box story).

Far East Square • 22 China St #01-01 S049564 • 10am to 9pm, open everyday • www.hocklambeef.com • 62209290

949 Upper Serangoon Road S534713 • 10am to 11pm, open everyday • 62856119

510 Macpherson Road S368208 • 10am to 8pm, open everyday

EMPRESS PLACE BEEF KWAY TEOW

4.5 The kway teow here is very fragrant and the slices of beef are cooked medium and are very tender. My favourite parts of the dish were the beef and the tendons, which were very pang (fragrant), with an uncomplicated beefy flavour. The soup was also sweet and robust which David, the owner, attributes to having the bones simmer in the soup for over two days. This stall can trace its lineage back to the grandmaster of beef kway teow himself, Tan Chin Sia, founder of Hock Lam Street Beef Kway Teow.

LTN Eating House • 936 East Coast Road S459129 • 11am to 11pm, open everyday

HAI NAN XING ZHOU BEEF NOODLES

4.5/4.25 dry version/soup version The soup version of the dish is wonderfully robust and sweet, and definitely one of the best I have tasted. As for the dry version, I was undoubtedly impressed with the stewed beef tendons, which were so soft, they just melted in your mouth. The beef slices were tender but the beef balls were not handmade, so they did not taste that special. The sauce was good, but maybe because my expectations were too high, I felt that it did not have maximum oomph.

Kim Keat Palm Market & Food Centre • 22 Toa Payoh Lorong 7 #01-06 S310022 • 8am to 7pm, closed on Mondays

HONG HENG BEEF NOODLE KING

4.25 beef kway teow The beef kway teow served here is excellent. The sauce is robust and beefy (though I doubt the sauce is entirely au natural since I did see some powdered beef stock on the shelf). The tendons are to die for. I also loved the generous topping of preserved vegetables, the tartness of which helped to brighten up the whole dish.

Kebun Baru Mall Food Centre • Blk 226H Ang Mo Kio St 22 #01-16 S568226 • 7.30am to 3pm, closed on Mondays • 64524017

THE BEEF HOUSE

4.0 The Beef House sells Hakka style beef noodles that comes with ping pong sized beef balls in a clear soup, accompanied by thin beehoon, kway teow or mee kia. The beef balls are super bouncy, and I suspect that if you drop one by mistake, it would just bounce back up onto the table! They were juicy and had a nice beef flavour—they are made in-house so it is no surprise that I have never tasted anything quite like it anywhere else.

Gar Lok Eating House • 217 Syed Alwi Road S207776 • 8am to 6pm, closed on Fridays

151 Joo Chiat Road S427429 • 8am to 6pm, closed on Mondays • 96654919, 98215463

MR WONG'S SEREMBAN BEEF NOODLE

4.0 This is possibly the only stall in Singapore that sells Seremban beef noodles. The dry version is sweeter than the local version, and I found it quite nice, as I like my food a little on the sweet side. The soup version is also very good, and sweeter than our local version as well, with a very strong beefy aroma. This is good for those who like things sweeter, but might disappoint if you are looking for the beefy umami rush.

Marine Parade Central Market & Food Centre • 84 Marine Parade Central #01-184 S440084 • noon to 7pm, open everyday

BUGIS STREET NGAK SEAH BEEF KWAY TEOW

4.0 The owner here is second generation. The stall started

DID YOU KNOW?

Traditional Teochew beef kway teow does not use thick noodles nor does it come with thick gravy. Flat kway teow is the preferred noodle of choice, while the dry version is served with sesame oil, soya sauce, chilli, salted vegetables and plenty of groundnuts, without the familiar chincaluk (shrimp sauce).

THE CENTENARY BEEF KWAY TEOW

Hock Lam Street Beef Kway Teow is one of the few hawkers in Singapore that can boast it is over 100 years old! Founded in 1911, it moved to Hock Lam Street in the 1920s and this street has since become synonymous with beef kway teow. The father and son team of Tan Chin Sia and Anthony Tan were famous not only for their dish, but also for the heated exchanges they had while manning their stall! In the 1980s, the hawkers where chased off the streets to make way for Funan Centre. Thankfully, fourth generation Tina Tan has taken over at Hock Lam Street Beef Kway Teow, so we can still enjoy its dishes today!

in Bugis and Uncle is friendly and modest, despite his popularity. The soup is robust with a slight tinge of herbs. Drink it hot and it'll be a sure cure for a hazy day. The meat is not overcooked and tender. I especially like the beef, which had a nice beefy taste to it. The tendons could have been a little softer and more gooey.

Lavender Food Square • 380 Jalan Besar #01-28/29 S209000 • 9am to 9pm, closed on alternate Wednesdays

HONG KEE BEEF NOODLE

4.0 Yet another famous beef noodle place! This hawker has been selling beef noodles for 48 years, since his father's time. The original stall was at Koek Street at Cuppage Centre. (For readers who still remember the famous beef kway teow at Cuppage Centre,

now you know where it has moved to!) I liked the dry version served here. The gravy is excellent and the beef succulent. The beef balls are unfortunately bought from a supplier, so they taste quite generic. Otherwise, quite a satisfying bowl of dry beef kway teow.

Amoy Street Food Centre • 7 Maxwell Road #01-42 S069111 • weekdays: 11am to 7.30pm, weekends: 9am to 2.30pm • closed on public holidays • 63231679

LESLIE'S TIP

I always choose the dry version of beef kway teow over the soup version, since with the dry version, I can still get soup on the side. Plus, the dry version has more kick!

ISLAMIC RESTAURANT

BIRYANI

PEOPLE LOOK FOR DIFFERENT THINGS IN A BIRYANI. FOR ME, THE RICE IS OF prime importance, then the meat and the curry. I like the cucumber achar (pickles) to be slightly sweet, so as to contrast with the savoury flavours of the curry. I love my basmati rice light and fluffy, with each grain separate, unbroken, fragrant and aromatic, yet firm to the bite, and not mushy. The springy texture of good biryani rice makes it delicious enough to eat on its own, without any gravy. As for the meat, I love it when the mutton is super tender, aromatic and seasoned just right, with no strong mutton smell.

DID YOU KNOW?

In Singapore, biryani is often called nasi biryani. Being an Indian dish, the Malay word "nasi", which means rice, shows how biryani has evolved to become a Singaporean dish, incorporating some local Malay influence.

LESLIE'S PICK ✓

BISMILLAH BIRYANI RESTAURANT

4.75 **This is the best biryani I have ever eaten. The rice has absorbed so much of the fragrant spices that the aroma lingers in the mouth for quite a while. The mutton is excellent—it is tender and fragrant, and does not have a gamey flavour because the meat is blanched in hot water before being marinated. Amazingly, the rice is quite light, since no oil or ghee is used in the cooking. So you can eat the whole portion without feeling guilty. According to Arif, the owner, biryani should be made by cooking the rice and meat in a pot over a charcoal fire, and also with charcoal on top of the pot as well. This is how he makes his biryani. Arif is a passionate biryani expert (see box story).**

50 Dunlop St S209379 • 11.30am to 3pm, 5.30pm to 10pm, closed on Tuesdays • 93827937

GEYLANG (HAMID'S) BRIYANI STALL

4.75 This is one of the tastiest hawker meals in Singapore! The grains are fluffy, separate and firm to the bite. You can taste the buttery ghee and spices. The mutton is so tender you could separate it with a fork and it would literally dissolve in your mouth. The chicken masala gravy is the real killer—the combination of the gravy with the rice will give you 100 per cent satisfaction.

Geylang Serai Market & Food Centre • 15 Geylang Serai #01-327 S402001 • 9am to 5pm, closed on Mondays • 98310574

BLUE DIAMOND RESTAURANT

4.25 The biryani at Blue Diamond is very good, in that each grain of rice is coated with a very well balanced masala. My mutton biryani was well spiced, and the meat was tender with no gamey flavour. The rice was fragrant and I thought the addition of a hard-boiled egg to the dish set it apart from other biryanis I had tried. If you are mad for masala, this is the place for you!

24-26 Buffalo Road S219791 • 10am to 10pm, open everyday • 62911629

THOHIRAH RESTAURANT

4.25 The rice is nicely done, and I love eating it just by itself without the gravy. Every grain is separate and unbroken. The springy texture is satisfying to the bite, and the cucumber achar (pickles) is also very good. Overall, the rice texture is tops, taste is great but not quite the best.

258 Jalan Kayu (next to the car park) S799487 • open 24 hours daily • 64812009

ALI NACHIA BRIYANI DAM

4.25 This stall is run by ex-butcher turned ex-soccer coach Encik Ali, who happens to be the father of soccer star Rafi Ali. This pak cik is passionate about making a proper dum biryani and furthermore, being an ex-butcher, Encik Ali knows how to handle his meats, so he picks only the best parts of the goat to make his curry. The biryani rice here is light and fluffy, not overpowering, so you can eat lots of it and not feel jerlak (satiated). But the real gem is the super tender aromatic mutton which has been slow-cooked in the rice. The mutton has been seasoned just right such that it does not have that strong mutton smell that puts most muttonophobics off, and it has just the right amount of fats so that the meat is not dry after cooking for so long. The only slight drawback for me was the dhalchat (lentil curry) which could do with a little more oomph.

PSA Tanjong Pagar Complex • 7 Keppel Road #01-16/17 S089053 • 10.30am to 2.30pm, open everyday • 93546363

ALLAUDDIN'S BRIYANI

4.0 The fame of this stall is undisputed, having been in business for over 40 years. Sad to say, Allauddin's fell short of my expectations, as the rice was monochrome in colour, and a little overcooked such that some of the grains were mushy and broken. However, the taste of the biryani was excellent, and the dhalchat (lentil curry) and chicken curry complemented the rice really well.

Tekka Market & Food Centre • 665 Buffalo Road #01-297 S210665 • 10am to 7pm, open everyday

ISLAMIC RESTAURANT

4.0 The Grand Daddy of biryani—this stall has been around since 1911. The grains here are impressive—each grain is almost as long as a lady's manicured fingernail! However, the rice lacked oomph though the mutton was excellent.

745 North Bridge Road S198713 • 10am to 10pm, open everyday • 62987563

DID YOU KNOW?

Some hawkers call their biryani "dum biryani" which means the rice is baked with meat and spices in a large sealed pot. Since all biryani is supposed to be cooked this way, the word "dum" is redundant.

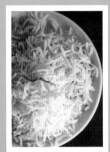

GOING BATTY OVER BASMATI

Did you know that basmati rice can elongate to twice its length when cooked? The Hindi word "basmati" means "the fragrant one" and the fragrance of basmati rice is due to the mutation of a gene called BADH2, which causes the production of 2-acetyl-1-pyrroline, the aroma compound that gives basmati rice, as well as jasmine rice and pandan leaves, its fragrance.

One way to test for true basmati rice is to drop a handful of cooked rice on the floor—the rice should separate like grains of sand. Being low in starch also means that basmati has a low glycemic index, making it suitable for diabetics.

Good basmati rice needs to be aged for two years in order for the rice to dry properly. When dry, the rice should be opaque—a translucent grain means the rice is still young (and "wet"). Having dry grains is key to a great biryani as they readily absorb all the flavours of the spices. If you are wondering why I know so much about biryani, it is not because I am an expert, but because I have been talking to a passionate and dedicated biryani expert, the owner of Bismillah Biryani Restaurant, Arif, who is absolutely batty over biryani!

DID YOU KNOW?

As basmati is an expensive rice, some hawkers use other types of rice and pass them off as basmati. You can't really blame them since the market price for selling biryani is about $3, so most can't afford expensive ingredients. To compensate, they serve a robust masala to boost the fragrance of the dish. Hawkers may also cook their rice and meat separately in order to save time.

While some may prefer their biryani heavy, where the spices hit you like a truck, others (like me) prefer their rice to be light and aromatic, and combine the rice with the masala sparingly, so as to enjoy the light and airy texture of basmati and its natural fragrance which makes real basmati rice special.

BRAISED DUCK

THERE ARE TWO TYPES OF BRAISED DUCK SERVED AT HAWKER STALLS—
the Teochew version's sauce is more savoury and has the consistency of water. The Hokkien version's sauce is sweeter, thick and gooey. When I eat braised duck rice, I don't go for the duck meat, I go for the tau pok (fried beancurd) and the lor (braising sauce). If the stall serves braised peanuts, that's a bonus.

The typical duck used by hawkers is chai ya (lit vegetable duck)—this is the white pekin duck, a breed that grows quickly to reach table size. The ban chai ya (half vegetable duck) has tougher meat and is excellent for braising (since tough meat can withstand a longer braising time, resulting in a more flavoursome dish). However, ban chai ya is much more expensive, so only passionate hawkers use it. Fan ya (rice duck) is even more expensive than ban chai ya, so it is used only on very special occasions.

LESLIE'S PICK ✓

REDHILL LOR DUCK RICE AND NOODLES

4.5 The only braised duck I have ever eaten and found addictive was the one served by this stall. The sauce is perfectly balanced between sweet, salty and umami. Being a Teochew style braised duck, the gravy is watery and it has that hint of blue ginger which is characteristic of Teochew lor (braising sauce). The duck here is really wonderfully tender and juicy, and such a joy to eat. Uncle has been making braised duck for 30 years.

Redhill Food Centre • 85 Redhill Lane #01-79 S150085 • 9am to 2.30pm, closed on Thursdays and Fridays

LIM SENG LEE DUCK RICE

4.5 The duck meat here is moist and tender, and the unique sweet vinegar chilli is the perfect accompaniment. Shiok! Just two problems: the serving of duck meat is small and expensive, and the wait is long during peak periods. I would think twice because of the long queue and the premium price.

38 South Buona Vista Road S118164 • 10.30am to 8.30pm, closed on Sundays • 64759908

HENG GI GOOSE AND DUCK RICE

4.25 This stall is a bit of a legend as Uncle has been selling braised duck for over 60 years. This is the kind of dish that completely ignores the Health Promotion Board's advice to use less oil and salt. If you want to taste Teochew lor (braising sauce) the way it used to be, this is it.

Tekka Market & Food Centre • 665 Buffalo Road #01-335 S210665 • 8.30am to 2.30pm, closed on Mondays

LIAN KEE BRAISED DUCK

4.25 Uncle claims that his lor (braising sauce) is made from 13 herbs and spices! The recipe has not changed for the last 35 years. Everything about his braised duck revolves around his cauldron of braising sauce, which is truly delicious.

Sims Vista Market & Food Centre • 49 Sims Place #01-73 S380049 • 10am to 8.30pm, open everyday

DELICIOUS DUCK NOODLES

4.25/4.0 dry duck noodles/ soup duck noodles
At this stall, I prefer the dry version of duck noodles to the soup version. The former has a super concentrated

lor (braising sauce) and chilli combo that gives the noodles quite a kick. The latter, on the other hand, tastes a little diluted. The meat is nicely done, tender and not too gamey.

Tanglin Halt Market • 48A Tanglin Halt Road #01-23 S148813 • 4am to 2pm, closed on Saturdays

SUM LONG TEOCHEW BRAISED DUCK

4.25 The duck we had was pretty big, allowing the hawker to slice diagonally through the breast, and produce very tender slices of meat. This is Teochew style braised duck, so the lor (braising sauce) is the watery type. Although good, it is not superlative.

Blk 57 Eng Hoon St #01-88 S160057 • Mondays to Fridays: 7am to 8pm, Saturdays: 7.15am to 4pm, Sundays: 7.15am to 3pm

CHEOK KEE DUCK RICE

4.0 The braised duck here is very good. The lor (braising sauce) is Hokkien style: thick, sticky and a little sweet, but the herbs are not overpowering.

East Coast Lagoon Food Village • 1220 East Coast Parkway Stall 29 S468960 • 11am to 10pm, open everyday • 67439755

AH SENG BRAISED DUCK RICE

4.0 This is certainly a good stall to go to for a good Teochew version of braised duck. The lor

(braising sauce) is shiok, the duck is tender, and lots of people rave about it!

Serangoon Garden Market & Food Centre • 49A Serangoon Garden Way Stall 44 S555945 • 11am to 9pm, closed on Sundays • 62888880

AH XIAO TEOCHEW BRAISED DUCK

4.0 The duck meat was a little tough and a tad dry. When I expressed my dissatisfaction, Lao Ban Niang explained that her worker was not as adept at slicing the meat as she was. A second plate was produced—the duck was well sliced, thinner, more tender and juicy. So, if you are patronising this stall, make sure you ask Lao Ban Niang to slice the duck for you!

Geylang East Industrial Estate • 1016 Geylang East Ave 3 S389731 • Mondays to Fridays: 11am to 5pm, Saturdays: 11am to 4pm, closed on Sundays and public holidays • 91098026

DID YOU KNOW?

One quick way to predict if your braised duck is going to be good is to look at the size of the ducks being displayed at the stall. The larger the duck (more than 3kg), the more likely it will be good.

CARROT CAKE

THERE ARE TWO TYPES OF CARROT CAKE (ALSO KNOWN AS chye tau kway)—black and white. As a kid, I preferred black carrot cake, which is cut up into small pieces and fried with an extra shot of black sauce. But now, I prefer the white version because it is a little more sophisticated. With the black version, most of the taste comes from the sweet black sauce, and texture is not really a concern. But with the white version, the flavour profile is more complex. You have the taste of the chye poh (preserved radish), the carrot cake itself and the eggs, each with its own distinct flavour. Then you have the contrast in texture between the crispy eggs and the soft carrot cake. The secret to good white carrot cake is that it must be nice and crisp on the outside, yet soft and flavourful on the inside.

LESLIE'S PICK ✓

LAU GOH TEOCHEW CHYE THOW KWAY

4.5 **The carrot cake at this stall is soft and wonderfully flavoured. One of the things that Peter, the owner, does is to mash the carrot cake into smaller pieces by hand, resulting in an irregular surface to which the egg, chye poh (preserved radish) and fish sauce stick to easily. This ensures that each morsel is covered with yummy umami flavours! Addictive!**

Zion Riverside Food Centre • 70 Zion Road Stall 26 S247792 • Mondays to Saturdays: noon to 2.30pm and 5pm to 11.45pm, Sundays: 10am to 3pm and 5pm to 11pm, closed on Tuesdays

BUKIT MERAH VIEW CARROT CAKE

4.5 Head down to this stall to see what old school carrot cake tastes like. And by old school, I mean that the stall owners actually mill the rice themselves at the back of their stall! The texture of the carrot cake here is very good—soft but not mushy, crispy and chunky. Both the white and black versions are excellent, but if I had to choose, I would say: order both and tar pau (takeaway) the leftovers!

Bukit Merah View Food Centre • 115 Bukit Merah View #01-279 S151115 • 7am to 2pm, 6pm to 1am, open everyday

LIM HAI SHENG COOKED FOOD

4.5 The carrot cake here is very good. Besides steaming its own carrot cake, an interesting method of spraying fish sauce over the carrot cake during the frying process is used. This ensures that every bit of the carrot cake is coated with savoury goodness.

Ang Mo Kio Central Food Centre • 724 Ang Mo Kio Ave 6 #01-09 S560724 • 7am to 10pm, open everyday

MIOW SIN POPIAH AND CARROT CAKE

4.5 This stall serves one of the most visually appealing carrot cakes I have come across. And the taste matches the visuals! Uncle says there is nothing special about his carrot cake apart from his frying technique and the fact that he uses lard which he prepares fresh daily, and mixes it with vegetable oil so that it is not too heavy. Expertly fried, crisp on the outside, soft on the inside, and generous with the fish sauce and the chye poh (preserved radish), this carrot cake gives a great umami-carbo combination that is sure to excite your taste buds!

Lavender Food Square • 380 Jalan Besar #01-04 S209000 • 9am to midnight, closed on alternate Wednesdays • 62928764

CHEY SUA CARROT CAKE

4.25 Like many good carrot cake stalls, Chey Sua steams its own carrot cake in small aluminium bowls which are, apparently, 40 years old! The contrast in texture is what Chey Sua does very well—and the owners achieve this by frying one side to a crisp while leaving the other side only lightly fried. However, I felt that the flavour of the dish lacked a bit of oomph.

Toa Payoh West Market & Food Court • 127 Toa Payoh Lorong 1 #02-30 S310127 • 6am to 1pm, closed on Mondays

CARROT CAKE

4.25 The white version is better than the black version here. The carrot cake is fried till it is nice and crispy. The savoury flavour comes from the secret fish-sauce-based sauce, which has gone through some tweaking, plus the addition of prawns. Overall, a very good white carrot cake, and worth having as part of your hawker feast at Chomp Chomp!

Chomp Chomp Food Centre • 20 Kensington Park Road Stall 36 S557269 • 5.30pm to midnight, closed on alternate Tuesdays

GUAN KEE

4.25 When a stall still steams its own white carrot cake, you should be able to tell the difference since it is not masked by the sauce. However, Guan Kee's white carrot cake is not great. Thankfully, the black version is well worth a try. Uncle fries it till it has all those wonderful caramelised charred bits that are oh-so-heavenly!

Changi Village Market & Food Centre • 2 Changi Village Road #01-02 S500002 • 11am to 11pm, closed on Mondays

HE ZHONG CARROT CAKE

4.25 Like many of the best places to get carrot cake, He Zhong steams its own carrot cake. What makes He Zhong's carrot cake special and different is that you can actually pick up a whole piece with your hand and eat it like a slice of cake. I found the carrot cake to be slightly under salted at first, but the flavour gets lifted to the next level with just an extra dash of fish sauce.

Bukit Timah Food Centre & Market • 116 Upper Bukit Timah Road #02-185 S588172 • 7am to 10pm, open everyday

HENG CARROT CAKE

4.25 The stall has been steaming its own carrot cake at Newton Food Centre since 1971. That's why the texture of the carrot cake is softer and more wobbly than any factory made version. You

SAME SAME BUT DIFFERENT

The birthplace of carrot cake is Chaoshan, China. Known as fried gao guo, the steamed rice cakes are made from rice starch that is made from milling puffed rice. After being steamed, the rice cakes are cut into 4-by-1-by-half inch blocks, marinated in fish sauce and dark sweet sauce, then fried with eggs, fresh oysters and prawns. Chinese BBQ sauce is added and a bit of sugar is sprinkled over the dish just before serving. In Malaysia, there is a dish of fried rice cake called char kway koek. This dish is fried with sweet sauce.

So it seems that different countries have their own versions of fried rice cake, but carrot cake Singapore-style is unique because of the chye poh (preserved radish) and the fact that our version is white! I had always assumed that the white carrot cake came first, then someone added sweet black sauce and the black version was born. But it turns out that carrot cake was black in the early days, then a man called Lau Goh omitted the black sauce and added chye poh, and the White Carrot Cake Revolution was born!

can see the strips of radish in it. The carrot cake is fried till crispy on the outside, while moist and soft on the inside. It is very tasty, but not the best since they avoid the use of lard.

Newton Food Centre • 500 Clemenceau Ave North #01-28 S229495 • 6pm to 1.30am, open everyday

SENG KEE CARROT CAKE

4.0 This is a next generation carrot cake! It is crispy on the outside, yummy on the inside, 2cm thick, not as oily as other renditions of carrot cake, and with real carrots which contain Vitamin A! Lovely for your stomach and for your eyes!

Bukit Timah Food Centre & Market • 116 Upper Bukit Timah Road #02-182 S588172 • 7.30am to 11pm, closed on Thursdays

DID YOU KNOW?

Hawkers rarely serve excellent versions of both black and white carrot cake. Usually, either the black or white version is stellar, and the other one, average.

CHAR KWAY TEOW

MY PERSONAL TEST FOR A GOOD CHAR KWAY TEOW IS WHETHER I CAN FINISH the whole plate. I hardly do this nowadays, but if I do, then the char kway teow must be really shiok! Good char kway teow must be fried with good lard: crispy, crunchy and oh-so-savoury, good lard delivers that knockout punch. Secondly, the hawker must control his fire well and the timing of the stir-fry must be just right—this will ensure that the char kway teow comes out with the right texture every time. The noodles have got to be lively and smooth when you slurp them up. When fried well, char kway teow really hits the spot.

DID YOU KNOW?

The quality of char kway teow depends largely on the frying skills of the hawker. The ingredients—kway teow, eggs, sweet sauce and cockles—are simple. Hence, there is no way to hide poor frying skills.

LESLIE'S PICK ✓ ★

HILL STREET CHAR KWAY TEOW

4.75 I have not found any plate that can surpass this uncle's plate. This char kway teow is the real deal. The texture and taste is absolutely fabulous, plus the owner, Mr Ng, uses a liberal amount of crunchy sweet towgay (beansprouts) and koo chai (chives), which culminates in an explosion of tastes and textures in your mouth. Is this as good as char kway teow gets? So far, for me at least, it is.

Bedok South Market & Food Centre • 16 Bedok South Road #01-187 S460016 • noon to 4pm and 6pm till he runs out of food, closed on Mondays • 90421312

GUAN KEE CHAR KWAY TEOW

4.5 This uncle has been frying char kway teow for over 40 years. In 2002, he was crowned the Champion Char Kway Teow Man by Mediacorp. I must say he really lives up to his title! His kway teow is slippery and lively, something that is made possible by the generous use of freshly prepared pork lard. Lively, savoury kway teow that leaps into your mouth with good wok hei (breath of wok) flavour!

Ghim Moh Market & Food Centre • 20 Ghim Moh Road #01-12 S270020 • 9.30am to 2.30pm, closed on Mondays and Fridays

HAI KEE TEOCHEW CHAR KWAY TEOW

4.5 This uncle has been frying char kway teow since 1967, and he fries each plate individually, hence the long queues at his stall. The taste of the char kway teow here is just right. It has got that savoury flavour mixed with a tinge of sweetness, and just the right amount of fish sauce. This is classic char kway teow fried with passion.

Telok Blangah Crescent Market & Food Centre • 11 Telok Blangah Crescent #01-102 S090011 • 5pm to 10pm, closed on Sundays

LAI HENG FRIED KWAY TEOW

4.5 A good char kway teow hawker is able to toss the kway teow sufficiently for the noodles to be infused with wok hei (breath of wok) aroma, yet maintain a slippery and moist surface. When you get your plate of char kway teow that has been fried by the old man at this stall, just give it a good whiff before tucking in, and you will know what I mean.

Shunfu Hawker Centre • Blk 320 Shunfu Road #02-20 S570320 • 11am to 8pm, closed on Mondays

MENG KEE CHAR KWAY TEOW

4.5 Here is a stall worth spending some of your calories on! This stall is manned by a father and daughter team, and from what I hear, unlike a lot of other stalls where the "old hand" is still the champion, the father has been quite successful in imparting his skills to his daughter. I haven't had the father's version, but the daughter's version was so good that I finished the whole plate— definitely a high Satisfaction per Calorie (S/C) rating!

Wei Xuan Eating House • 22 Havelock Road #01-669 S160022 • Mondays to Saturdays: 10.30am to 7pm, Sundays: 10.30am to 4pm

OUTRAM PARK FRIED KWAY TEOW MEE

4.5 During the frying process, Uncle adds a blend of fish sauce, soya sauce and other ingredients from an old plastic bottle. At this point, he cannot be disturbed because he is counting the number of squirts: 42, the same number that explains the meaning of life, the universe and everything! No wonder this char kway teow is so addictive!

Hong Lim Food Centre • 531A Upper Cross St #02-17 S051531 • 6am to 4.30pm, closed on Sundays and public holidays

SHENG CHENG CHAR KWAY TEOW

4.5 This uncle has been frying char kway teow for 40 years! It is sweet and fragrant, and the pork lard is crunchy and savoury. Uncle is one of the few passionate hawkers who still shucks his own cockles!

Blk 132 Jalan Bukit Merah S160132 • noon to 10pm, closed fortnightly on an ad hoc basis

DAY NIGHT FRIED KWAY TEOW

4.25 This stall serves up yet another "finish the whole plate" version of char kway teow. When it is piping hot, the kway teow is quite wet, but quickly settles into a nice consistency. The kway teow is lively and leaps off the chopsticks easily into the mouth. Everything is coated with a magic combination of sweet sauce, lard and charred kway teow flavour. Shiokalicious!

Bukit Merah Central Food Centre • Blk 162 Bukit Merah Central #02-29 S150162

DID YOU KNOW?

There has been a decline of good char kway teow stalls in Singapore, with few next generation hawkers stepping up to take over the ladles of the old hands. The dish is perceived to be unhealthy and the fear of contracting Hepatitis A from eating partially cooked cockles has put another nail in the coffin.

• 10am to 8pm, closed on alternate Thursdays • 96404870

NO. 18 ZION ROAD FRIED KWAY TEOW

4.25 The hawker at this stall has been around since the days when John Travolta had a really cool hairstyle and a prominent chin. This is one good looking, dare I say sexy, plate of char kway teow. It is slippery and lively. Next time I order though, I'm asking for more wok hei (breath of wok) flavour and more dark sauce.

Zion Riverside Food Centre • 70 Zion Road Stall 17 S247792 • noon to 2.30pm, 6pm to 11pm, closed on alternate Mondays

DONG JI FRIED KWAY TEOW

4.25 Not your classic char kway teow, Dong Ji's char kway teow is more like a fusion between the Penang and Singapore versions of char kway teow. The kway teow is lively, and I like the way it sticks momentarily to your lips as it leaps off the chopsticks into your mouth. It is different from the usual and very enjoyable!

Old Airport Road Food Centre • 51 Old Airport Road #01-138 S390051 • 8am to 2pm, open everyday

ANG MO KIO CHAR KWAY TEOW

4.0 This stall sells a wetter-than-usual version of char kway teow. Uncle here manages to infuse a nice smoky flavour to the kway teow, making the dish more alluring. But I felt that the texture of the kway teow could have been livelier.

724 Ang Mo Kio Ave 6 #01-28 S560724 • 11.30am to 8pm, open everyday

HENG HUAT FRIED KWAY TEOW

4.0 A healthy char kway teow? Heng Huat has been frying his char kway teow this way for 20 years. He started adding vegetables because he felt the dish tasted better that way. This char kway teow is enjoyable even without the lard, and the vegetables will definitely soothe your conscience.

Pasir Panjang Food Centre • 121 Pasir Panjang Road #01-36 S118543 • noon to 10pm, closed on Sundays and public holidays • 97355236

DID YOU KNOW?

There are two types of yellow noodles in Singapore: one for soup dishes and the other for fried dishes, like char kway teow. The soup noodles will be too tough and have a strong "kee" smell if you fry them.

CHICKEN RICE

TO ME, GOOD CHICKEN RICE NEEDS A WINNING COMBINATION OF (1) soft, white voluptuous, succulent chicken meat, the type you can really sink your teeth into, and smooth, silky skin with a lovely gelatinous layer underneath; (2) fragrant rice, each grain coated with savoury chicken broth or chicken oil, not mushy, but full of texture and flavour; (3) chilli sauce with "kick"—not too sweet, and lime juice should be used instead of vinegar; and (4) fragrant drizzling sauce, usually a mix of sesame oil and soya sauce. It is difficult to find stalls that come up tops in all four categories of chicken, rice, chilli and drizzling sauce. Hawkers tend to excel in only one or two categories. Heaven is a piece of chicken thigh with chilli, ginger and thick soya sauce. Put it in your mouth and POW! Cool tender flesh, crunchy skin, smooth gelatine, tangy, spicy, savoury and gingery flavours all combine to give that SHIOK feeling!

LESLIE'S PICK ✓

TIAN TIAN HAINANESE CHICKEN RICE

4.6/4.5 chicken/chilli sauce **When you are as famous as Tian Tian, you are bound to have complaints when the chicken rice does not meet up with the high expectations. So it was with trepidation that I taste-tested the chicken rice, but it passed with flying colours! Tian Tian manages to get that wonderful layer of gelatine under the skin, even though the chicken is cooked through to the bone, with the flesh still wonderfully tender. The chilli sauce is quite shiok and very different from other stalls: the secret is that they use lime juice instead of vinegar!**

Maxwell Road Food Centre • 1 Kadayanallur St #01-10 S069184 • 11am to 8pm, closed on Mondays • www.tiantianchickenrice.com

443 Joo Chiat Road S427656 • 10.30am to 10pm, closed on Mondays • 63459443

FRAGRANT SAUCE CHICKEN

4.6 ginger vinegar chicken The ginger vinegar chicken really caught us all by surprise. The ginger and the vinegar complemented each other perfectly. Go with your friends, order both, and have a second order of the ginger vinegar chicken—yes, it is that good. (This stall is also recommended for soya sauce chicken.)

QS269 Food House • Blk 269B Queen St #01-236 S182269 • 10.30am to 8pm, closed on Thursdays

BOON TONG KEE (KATONG)

4.5 From the rice to the chicken to the chilli, though no item stands out, everything works together in harmony. The pickles that come with the chicken add a bit of zing to the whole experience. The ginger sauce, a little on the sweet side and very fragrant, is one of the best.

199 East Coast Road (opposite Holy Family Church) S428902 • 11am to 10pm, open everyday • www.boontongkee.com.sg • 64781462

TONG FONG FATT (GHIM MOH)

4.5 The chicken here is delicious. It is tender and the skin is very slippery and smooth. The secret sauce here really sets it apart from the rest—I was told that 12 ingredients go into making the sauce. The rice too is excellent, and I like the sweet aftertaste which we Teochew say is very "karm karm".

Ghim Moh Market & Food Centre • 20 Ghim Moh Road #01-49 S270020 • 10am to 8.30pm, open everyday

FOOK SENG GOLDENHILL CHICKEN RICE

4.5/4.25 chicken/chilli Fook Seng has excellent chicken, but it may not be for everybody because Chef Ronnie has the audacity to undercook his chicken a little. This is so that the flesh is slightly pink and as he puts it, it is about 95 per cent cooked. The flesh is very tender and juicy, certainly one of the most tender around and only a very light drizzle of sesame oil is necessary to bring out the full flavour of the meat. The rice was good but did not seem to have enough flavour though the texture was good. I liked the chilli very much—it had the right amount of zing, without being agonising. The use of fresh lime instead of vinegar also adds a lot of value to the condiment, as does the layer of chicken oil shimmering on its surface.

Blk 37 Jalan Rumah Tinggi #01-415/417 S150037 • 8am to 4pm, open everyday • 97773318

HAINAN CHICKEN RICE BALL

4.25 The rice balls here are moulded really tight, and you will be able to taste the smoky salt flavour at the end. The chicken is done very well, though it is rather standard. The uncle here likes to drizzle dark soya sauce over the meat, instead of the light soya sauce gravy that most other stalls use.

Shin Boon Hwa Food Centre • 43 Jalan Besar (Dickson Road) S208804 • 8.30am to 9.30pm, open everyday

NAN XIANG CHICKEN RICE

4.25 This is one of the few stalls that still fries its rice before cooking, and you will appreciate the extra fragrance and texture that set it apart. The ginger has a saltiness that goes well with the chicken, and if you love hot chilli, wait till you try their chilli sauce made from chilli padi and lime juice. The chicken is good, though much the same as any other good chicken rice stall around.

Whampoa Drive Makan Place (Whampoa Food Centre) • 90 Whampoa Dr #01-21 S320090 • 11am to 10pm, open everyday

DID YOU KNOW?

Authentic Hainanese chicken must not be put into cold water after cooking nor hung because that would drain out all the precious juices. The chicken must be an old mother hen which has laid two eggs (not one, not three, exactly two!) and it must be served plain.

NAN HENG HAINANESE CHICKEN RICE

4.25 The people at Nan Heng insist on using chickens that are over 2kg in weight and never soak their chickens in ice water, hence making them more flavourful. They also don't ever hang their chickens, thus making sure that all that precious, tasty chicken oil stays on the skin and flesh of the chicken. Nan Heng provides not only a more artisanal take on chicken rice, but also one that hits all the right combination of notes on my tastebuds.

Bukit Merah Central Food Centre • Blk 163 Bukit Merah Central #02-28 S150163 • 11.30am to 8.30pm, closed on Sundays • 62736993

FIVE STARS CHICKEN RICE

4.25 This is one of the best versions of kampung chicken rice I have tasted. The

DID YOU KNOW?

The term "kampung chicken" is a misnomer because these chickens are not raised in a kampung at all. They are a different breed brought in from France. Our local white broilers take about 30 days to grow to table size, and spend their whole life in the dark. The kampung chicken, on the other hand, has orange feathers and takes 84 days to grow to maturity.

chicken is tasty and Five Stars always manages to get that layer of gelatine under the skin, which makes up for the lack of fats. What I was really impressed with was the drizzling sauce—the boss, Mr Li, told me that the secret of the sauce is that they brew it themselves from soya sauce, with added soya beans and rock sugar. It has a wonderful floral aroma and synergises perfectly with the chicken. In addition, the rice here is very good—flavourful and not too oily. The texture was perfect, with each grain easily separated and whole.

6/7 Cheong Chin Nam Road S599732 • 10am to midnight, open everyday

191/193 East Coast Road S428897 • Mondays to Saturdays: 4.30pm to 1.30am, Sundays and public holidays: 11.30am to 2pm • 67775555

419 River Valley Road S248318 • 11am to 5am, open everyday

HENG JI CHICKEN RICE

4.25 chicken The chicken at this stall has a very nice savoury flavour. The rice is a bit of a disappointment, as the flavour is only so-so. The chilli sauce is a bit surprising and unique in that it is exceptionally sweet.

Chinatown Complex Food Centre • 335 Smith St #02-131 S050335 • 3pm to 9pm, open everyday

TIAN SHUI CHICKEN RICE

4.25 The chicken is tender and lively, and is perfectly complemented by flavoursome oyster sauce. The chilli is bright and citrusy, and has a spicy kick that is not prolonged so that you don't go away with a mouthful of heat. However, the rice is dry and doesn't stand out. A bonus: they have great, crunchy chicken feet in a nice sauce that is excellent!

Tanglin Halt Market • 48A Tanglin Halt Road #01-21 S148813 • 9am to 8pm, closed on Mondays

WEE NAM KEE HAINANESE CHICKEN RICE

4.25 The rice tastes quite rustic and has enough flavour without being too oily. The chicken meat here is tender and juicy, but not particularly voluptuous. Still, it is good for those who enjoy their tender chicken but are concerned about the increasing convexity of their waistline.

Novena Ville (opposite Novena Church) • 275 Thomson Road #01-05 S307645 • 10am to 12.30am, open everyday

YEO KENG NAM (TRADITIONAL) HAINANESE CHICKEN RICE

4.25 chicken The chicken here is quite shiok. It's the plump and juicy, city dwelling (as opposed to kampung), voluptuous and sexy type of chicken that I prefer. And the chicken has managed to retain a lot of its "chickeny" flavour since the stall owner here makes it a point not to soak the chicken in ice water for too long as that tends to wash away all the natural oils and juices. You can just about make out the nice bits of jelly on the surface of the chicken. Also recommended: Hainanese pork chop.

8 Braddell Road S359898 • 10.30am to 10pm, open everyday • 62854261, 62854153

562 Serangoon Road S218178 • 11.30am to 11pm, open everyday • 62991128, 62990218

DID YOU KNOW?

You might think that poaching chicken for chicken rice is as simple as dunking it into hot water. Anyone can cook a chicken, but not everyone can get it right. Being able to get a layer of thick jelly under the skin is an art that differentiates the really good chicken rice hawkers from the mediocre ones. The best hawkers also take the trouble to use lime juice instead of white vinegar for their chilli. Another sign of a serious hawker is the provision of minced ginger and a good quality dark soya sauce.

SIN KEE FAMOUS CHICKEN RICE

4.25 This is a good chicken rice, though not head and shoulders above the rest. The rice is good, the chicken is good, and the chilli is good. The owner specifically says that his chicken rice is Cantonese style, so he doesn't use any ginger in the preparation of the rice or the chicken.

Blk 38 Commonwealth Ave #01-02 S149738 • 11am to 8pm, closed on Mondays

CHIN CHIN EATING HOUSE

4.25 This place has been around since 1934, starting off as a kopi and toast place, then graduating to serving other dishes in 1959. Although it closed down when the owners migrated overseas, we are lucky that Chin Chin reopened a few years back to serve chicken rice to a new generation. The chicken rice here is Cantonese style, with the skin being ultra smooth. Showered with fragrant sesame oil and soya sauce, it is irresistible! I especially like that the chicken has no strong "farmy" flavour. Also recommended: chap chye, sliced fish with bittergourd and Hainanese pork chop.

19 Purvis St S188598 • 7am to 9pm, open everyday • 63374640

YET CON HAINANESE CHICKEN RICE

 Good chicken rice in a nostalgic setting. Founded in 1940, this shophouse restaurant is patronised by so many elderly Hainanese men enjoying their cups of kopi and kaya toast, you might think that you have walked into a Hainanese clan meeting! Yet Con stubbornly sticks to the age old Hainanese recipe of making chicken rice—as a result, the chicken skin is dry, not very fat and has a very strong "chickeny" flavour. The flesh is cooked to the bone, so it is a bit tough, but flavourful. In traditional Hainanese style, no soya sauce is added to the chicken. I personally found the taste of the chicken too "farmy" for me, but I loved the rice which had a great texture and was very savoury. Also recommended: chap chye and Hainanese pork chop.

25 Purvis St S188602 • 10am to 10pm, open everyday • 63376819

TAO XIANG KITCHEN

4.0 white chicken The chicken from this stall is quite unique in that it is cooked in a salty broth that has been flavoured by dried scallops. So, the chicken absorbs all the salty umami as it cooks! Quite a refreshing difference from your normal chicken rice and well worth the trip to try it.

10E Sixth Ave #01-01/02 S276474 • 8.15am to 8.30pm, open everyday

CHINESE ROJAK

IF YOU DESCRIBED THE INGREDIENTS OF ROJAK TO A WESTERNER I AM sure he would not want to eat it. Seriously, does fruit salad dressed with a sauce made from fermented prawns sound delectable? Not only that, you get to eat it with a blackened duck egg that smells of urine. But to Singaporeans, rojak is yummy. It is all about a well balanced, sweet, savoury, tangy, spicy sauce with crumbly, moist ground peanuts coating you char kway (fried dough fritter) that has been freshly toasted or grilled over charcoal. It might not look good, but if you get rojak with freshly toasted you char kway, really flavoursome prawn paste and freshly roasted ground peanuts, it is just heavenly!

LESLIE'S PICK ★✓

KAMPONG ROJAK

4.5 The you char kway (fried dough fritter) here is fresh—it is grilled over charcoal till it is slightly charred so you get it crispy on the outside while the inside is still fluffy and chewy. The rojak is really addictive. I usually finish all the you char kway, then pick up all the peanuts bit by bit until I clean up the entire plate.

East Coast Lagoon Food Village • 1220 East Coast Parkway Stall 9 S468960 • 10am to 11pm, open everyday

LAU HONG SER ROJAK

4.75 One word that separates the good from the great: passion. This is what makes Uncle fry and grind his own peanuts, get only the best hae kor (fermented prawn paste) from Penang, and make his own chilli paste. The rojak is freshly toasted and served with a thick, fragrant peanut sauce by the side. The sauce is as good as rojak sauce can be. Only thing is: there's an hour long wait, but who am I to argue with that?

Dunman Road Food Centre • 271 Onan Road #02-14 S424768 • 4.38pm to 1.38am, closed on Sundays • 63466519

HOOVER ROJAK

4.25 This is a very good rojak. They have a special machine which mixes the hae kor (fermented prawn paste) with their special blend of ingredients, and the sauce is excellent. They also have jellyfish and century eggs. However, their you char kway (fried dough fritter) is not grilled and they use dry and tasteless commercially ground peanuts, so no top marks.

Whampoa Drive Makan Place (Whampoa Food Centre) • 90 Whampoa Dr #01-06 S320090 • Mondays and Wednesdays to Saturdays: 10.30am to 9.30pm, Tuesdays: 10.30am to 6pm • 90214593

SOON HENG SILVER STREAM ROJAK

4.25 The balance between sweet and sour is perfect and the hae kor (fermented prawn paste) is very good. Though the stall is generous with the peanuts, I found them dry. Commercially ground peanuts just cannot compete with freshly prepared (fried and ground) peanuts. However, this generous plate of rojak, that includes cuttlefish, comes with an affordable price tag and is well worth the try!

HDB Hub • 480 Toa Payoh Lorong 6 #B1-23 S310480 • 11am to 8pm, open everyday

KAMPONG ROJAK

TOA PAYOH ROJAK

4.25 This stall is so popular that it has a queue numbering system, like those found in clinics. The reason it takes so long to get your order is that the hawker insists on charcoal-grilling every you char kway (fried dough fritter) before it is cut up and mixed with the sauce. The tau pok (fried beancurd), you char kway and Penang hae kor (fermented prawn paste) are all excellent. While the peanuts are a bit dry (they do not grind their own but get from a special supplier), they are acceptable after being mixed in with the sauce. Another thing that is noteworthy: the uncle has an heir apparent in line, so we will get to savour this rojak for another generation.

Old Airport Road Food Centre • 51 Old Airport Road #01-108 S390051 • noon to 8pm, closed on Sundays

DID YOU KNOW?

Hae kor (fermented prawn paste) is made from belacan, which is made of shrimps that have been left out to rot. The rotting process degrades the protein and releases glutamates, hence giving dishes a boost of naturally occurring glutamates (the natural form of MSG). There is only one undisputed source of good hae kor, and that is Penang.

CHYE KEE CHWEE KUEH

CHWEE KUEH

CHWEE KUEH MEANS "WATER CAKE" IN TEOCHEW. IT IS SO CALLED BECAUSE of the little dimple in the middle, where water collects after steaming. I suspect that the Teochews created chwee kueh as an excuse to eat chye poh (preserved radish). Indeed, to me, chye poh is the star of the dish. Chye poh may be cheap, but good chye poh can give you as much of an umami rush as aged Parmigiano Reggiano. Moreover, it is the chye poh that makes our version of chwee kueh uniquely Singaporean. It is addictive because radish is one of the richest sources of naturally occurring glutamates, just like hae kor (fermented prawn paste), salted eggs and parmesan cheese. Glutamates excite the umami receptors on your tongue and give you that savoury sensation, which is why MSG makes everything taste so good.

LESLIE'S PICK ★✔

CHYE KEE CHWEE KUEH

4.5 Uncle makes his chwee kueh from rice flour, freshly milled from broken rice grains, right in his stall! He tells me that he used to work in a chwee kueh factory before venturing out on his own. The ones he used to make in the factory had tapioca flour in the recipe. The chwee kueh from this stall tastes like rice, but with a smooth, pastey texture. The chye poh (preserved radish) topping is different from the usual ones—it is less oily, with a very dry, chewy texture, which I really liked.

89 Pipit Road #01-129 S370089 • 6.30am to 3pm, open everyday

GHIM MOH CHWEE KUEH

4.25 The chwee kueh here is a glimpse of what chwee kueh was like in the past. The topping is different—it is kiam pang (salty and savoury), as opposed to the usual sweet and savoury. It takes a bit of getting used to, but I have learnt to appreciate it after I found out this was the traditional taste.

Ghim Moh Market & Food Centre • 20 Ghim Moh Road #01-31 S270020 • 6.15am to 6.30pm, open everyday • 64626017

JIAN BO SHUI KWEH

4.25 I really like the texture of this chwee kueh—it is so soft that you could basically eat it after removing both upper and lower dentures. The texture sets it apart from all the other chwee kueh I have eaten, because they still mill their own rice flour! The tasty fried chye poh (preserved radish) is amazing, and they are very generous with the sesame seeds so the dish is very pang (fragrant) indeed!

Tiong Bahru Market & Food Centre • 30 Seng Poh Road #02-05 S168898 • 6.30am to 10.30pm, open everyday • 90223037

BEDOK CHWEE KUEH

4.0 Everyone who frequents Bedok Interchange Food Centre knows this stall. The texture of the chwee kueh is very smooth and the chye poh (preserved radish) is sweet and savoury. Shiokalicious! This chwee kueh stall has now expanded and opened up many stalls islandwide.

Bedok Interchange Food Centre (New Upper Changi Road Food Centre) • 207 New Upper Changi Road #01-53 S460207 • 7am to 11pm, open everyday

GHIM MOH CHWEE KUEH

SHUI KWAY

4.0 I can't decide if I like the texture of the chwee kueh at this stall. The texture is more pastey than what I'm used to and Auntie says this is to give more bite and substance to the cakes. The chye poh (preserved radish), on the other hand, is really good! It's not too salty, not too sweet and Auntie augments the savoury flavour with dried shrimps. Best of all, she drains the chye poh topping well so there is hardly any oil, so you can afford to indulge a little.

Sembawang Hill Food Centre • 590 Upper Thomson Road #01-16 S574419 • Mondays to Saturdays: 6am to 1.45pm, Sundays: 6am to 10am

DID YOU KNOW?

In the old days, chwee kueh was made in clay moulds and hawkers milled their own rice. Aluminium moulds were then introduced in the 1970s when the National Environment Agency deemed clay moulds to be unsanitary as any cracks in the clay moulds could harbour bacteria. Some hawkers insist that clay moulds make better chwee kueh, while others appreciate aluminium moulds as clay moulds are fragile and tend to break easily.

CRAB

WITH THE HUGE VARIETY OF FRESH CRABS AVAILABLE IN SINGAPORE, it is difficult not to have irresistible cravings for crabs. During the *ieat* Crab Fests, which I organised in 2009 and 2011 at Chin Huat Live Seafood Restaurant, we feasted on a global array of crabs— Tasmanian King crab, Dungeness crab, Red Alaskan King crab, Cromer crab, Snow crab, the locally-found Swimmer crab, Sri Lankan crab and Indonesian crab. My favourite crab dish is crab beehoon. Beehoon is excellent for absorbing all the flavours and with the crab roe mixed in, the gravy has this extra oomph!

DID YOU KNOW?

According to the polls on my blog, chilli crab continues to hold the pre-eminent position of popularity, with 49.6 per cent of the vote, followed by black pepper crab (30.2 per cent) and salted egg crab (20.2 per cent).

LESLIE'S PICKS ✓

SIN HUAT SEAFOOD RESTAURANT

4.6 crab beehoon Undoubtedly the best place for crab beehoon in Singapore—the best I have ever tasted! The beehoon is neither too dry nor too wet, and is wonderfully soaked in the flavours of the crab, ginger and a mysterious but addictive stock.

659/661 Geylang Road (junction of Geylang Lorong 35) S389589 • 6.30pm to 1am, open everyday • 67449755

ENG SENG RESTAURANT

4.6 black pepper crab Strangely addictive, the sauce of the black pepper crab is slightly sweet and not overly spicy. As Goldilocks would say, "It is just right!". It is so shiok that you might find yourself eating more crabs in one sitting than you ever have before.

247 Joo Chiat Road S427502 • 5pm to 10pm, closed on Wednesdays • 64405560

ROLAND RESTAURANT

4.5 chilli crab Roland's mother, Madam Cher Yam Tian, is the inventor of chilli crab. Her traditional recipe is lighter than what most people are used to, which lets you appreciate the sweetness of the crab better. The modern version has a sauce chock full of crab roe and is possibly the best I've had in years!

89 Marine Parade Central #06-750 S440089 • 11.30am to 2.30pm and 6pm to 10.30pm, open everyday

CHIN HUAT LIVE SEAFOOD RESTAURANT

4.5 golden sauce Sri Lankan crab My personal favourites here are the golden sauce Sri Lankan crab and the salted egg Dungeness crab. Chin Huat serves a dry version of salted egg crab and it strikes a balance of crispy, sweet and savoury that is very addictive. Also recommended: geoduck.

105 Clementi St 12 (Sunset Way) #01-30 S120105 • 11.30am to 2.30pm and 5.30pm to 11pm, open everyday • 67757348

OCEAN KINGDOM SEAFOOD RESTAURANT

WESTLAKE

4.25 black pepper crab The black pepper is ground very fine and then fried in butter to give it a smooth, creamy texture. The crabs are delicious and the dish is excellent. If you're already there, be sure to sink your teeth into some of their signature kong bak pau as well!

Blk 4 Queen's Road #02-139 S260004 • 11am to 2.30pm and 6pm to 10pm, open everyday • 64747283

OCEAN KINGDOM SEAFOOD RESTAURANT

4.0 A small family run restaurant, Ocean Kingdom owner David says his family has been in the fishing industry for generations, and they really know their seafood. I would suggest ordering the steamed blue swimmer crabs—while these are not as meaty as mud crabs, the flesh of fresh blue swimmer crabs is excellent and these crabs are just as sweet, if not sweeter than mud crabs, and cheaper too. Also recommended: live fish, live scallops and crispy brinjals with curry pork floss.

382 Joo Chiat Road S427622 • 12 noon to 2.30pm and 5pm to 11pm, open everyday • 63420382

MATTAR ROAD SEAFOOD BBQ

4.0 The old couple here operates a tiny stall selling all kinds of seafood, and the chilli crab is supposed to be legendary. Unfortunately, the chilli crab did not

HOW IT ALL BEGAN

Madam Cher Yam Tian is the inventor of chilli crab. Her son's restaurant, Roland Restaurant, continues to sell her version of chilli crab today, and this is her story:

In the 1970s, Madam Cher and her husband lived in an attap house along Upper East Coast Road. Her husband, a policeman, would catch crabs from the beach. Being Teochew, she would simply steam them, but one day, her husband asked her to cook them differently. So she stir-fried the crabs in tomato sauce. Her husband then suggested adding some chilli, and a Singaporean institution was born. Everyone encouraged her to sell her dish, so, in 1950, she began selling chilli crab from a roadside pushcart.

By 1956, Madam Cher had progressed from a pushcart to a little shack that was lit by a hurricane lamp. Since there were coconut palms along the beach near the shack, her husband called the place Palm Beach Seafood. By 1963, they had expanded to a simple zinc-roofed building and it was around this time that chilli crab was quickly becoming a national dish.

Madam Cher's version is not as rich as what we are familiar with today, because no eggs are added to the sauce. The idea of adding eggs and sambal came from the owner of Dragon Phoenix Restaurant in the 1960s.

DID YOU KNOW?

Crab beehoon was invented by Danny of Sin Huat Seafood Restaurant. This cze cha restaurant is widely recognised as the Gold Standard for crab beehoon. It started with a casual request from a customer to combine hor fun with crab since he did not want to have to order both dishes separately. Thus, crab beehoon was born!

meet my expectations, for though it was very fresh, the chilli sauce did not quite do it for me.

Old Airport Road Food Centre • 51 Old Airport Road #01-63 S390051 • 4pm to 11pm, closed on Tuesdays and Wednesdays

CURRY PUFF

THERE ARE TWO TYPES OF CURRY PUFFS IN SINGAPORE, THE MALAY VERSION called epok epok, has a thin, crispy crust and a filling largely made of buttery curried potatoes and freshly boiled eggs, while the Chinese version's crust is thicker, more buttery and more oily. The filling usually contains chicken meat as well as potatoes and eggs. I prefer epok epok because the typical Chinese curry puff is too oily for me, giving me a jerlak (satiated) feeling quickly. Epok epok is much lighter, while not compromising in the taste department.

DID YOU KNOW?

Some say that the term "curry puff" can be attributed to the founder of Polar Cafe, Mr Chan Hinky, who bought an Indian man's curry puff recipe just before World War Two.

TIP TOP CURRY PUFF

4.5 **These curry puffs are exactly like the ones I remember eating as a kid! The crust is nice and buttery, and the filling is fragrant without being overly spicy. There is of course a slice of hard-boiled egg in each curry puff, and finding that tasty chunk of chicken is like finding the toy in a cereal box!**

Hiap Hwa Coffeeshop • Blk 722 Ang Mo Kio Ave 8 #01-2843 S560722 • 9.30am to 9.30pm, closed on Wednesdays

OVEN MARVEL

(formerly known as Delicious Muffins)

4.5 It is very hard to find a curry puff made from puff pastry that is not too oily, but the curry puffs here are great. The puff pastry is thin but resilient, and chock full of buttery potatoes and chicken pieces in light, fragrant curry spices. Definitely one of the best I have come across.

Sunshine Plaza • 91 Bencoolen St #01-51 S189652 • 11.30am to 8pm, closed on the 8th, 18th and 28th of every month • 96361503

EPOK EPOK CENTRAL

4.25 The curry puffs here are excellent—the crust is thin and crispy, and it combines well with the freshly boiled egg and buttery curried potatoes. What is missing is one or two pieces of savoury chicken meat, though it is true that meat is not as common in epok epok as it is in Chinese curry puff. (This stall is also recommended for its nasi lemak.)

Eunos Crescent Market & Food Centre • 4A Eunos Crescent #01-09 S402004 • 7am to 7pm, closed on Mondays • 96958889

KILLINEY CURRY PUFF

4.25 The filling is made with local "Holland" potatoes, which are ideal to be fried with rempah (mixed spice paste) to produce a creamy and spicy sweet filling that goes so well with the thin and crispy crust.

93 Killiney Road S239536 • 7am to 7.30pm, open everyday

SOON SOON HUAT 1A CRISPY CURRY PUFF

4.25 This is where the attractive-looking multi-layered crispy skinned curry puff originated. It was invented 17 years ago by the Teochew Ah Mah at this stall! The curry puffs here are really good—the skin is crispy and thin, more like a Malay epok epok rather than a Chinese style curry puff. The filling is moist, almost as if there was a bit of gravy in it. I quite like the sardine puff as well, which reminds me of the Malay version.

Blk 127 Kim Tian Road #01-01 S160127 • 8am till sold out, closed on Mondays • 68415618

KATONG CHICKEN CURRY PUFF

4.0 Katong Chicken Curry Puff has been around for 30 years and Uncle still uses an old glass bottle as a rolling pin! The filling is moist and not overly spicy, and the crust is crisp but not too buttery. Great as an afternoon snack!

Marine Parade Central Market & Food Centre • 84 Marine Parade Central #01-132 S440084 • 8am to 6pm, closed on Mondays

ROLINA

4.0 Mr Tham is making curry puffs with the same recipe he started with 53 years ago! All the spices and ingredients are still

prepared by hand, and the curry puffs are made fresh daily. What sets these curry puffs apart is the crust, which is somewhere between the thin crust of epok epok and the thicker crumbly crust of Old Chang Kee.

Serangoon Garden Market & Food Centre • 49A Serangoon Garden Way Stall 32 S555945 • 7.30am to 5pm, closed on Mondays

BALMORAL BAKERY

4.0 Balmoral Bakery was previously located at Holland Village before they relocated to Sunset Way. They are still selling the same stuff that they have been selling for the last 40 years. There was a time when pastries in Singapore were an interpretation of what you could get overseas. Here you can find wonderful puff pastry chicken or beef curry puffs. While you are there, remember to pick up their wonderful chicken pies as well!

105 Clementi St 12 #01-06 S120105 • 9am to 8pm, open everyday • 67792064

DID YOU KNOW?

Curry puff evolved from the Portuguese empanada and its crescent shape is significant to Muslims. The Malays call it epok epok, while the Chinese say "kalipok". "Chop chop kalipok" is a Singlish phrase which means "get things done quick smart".

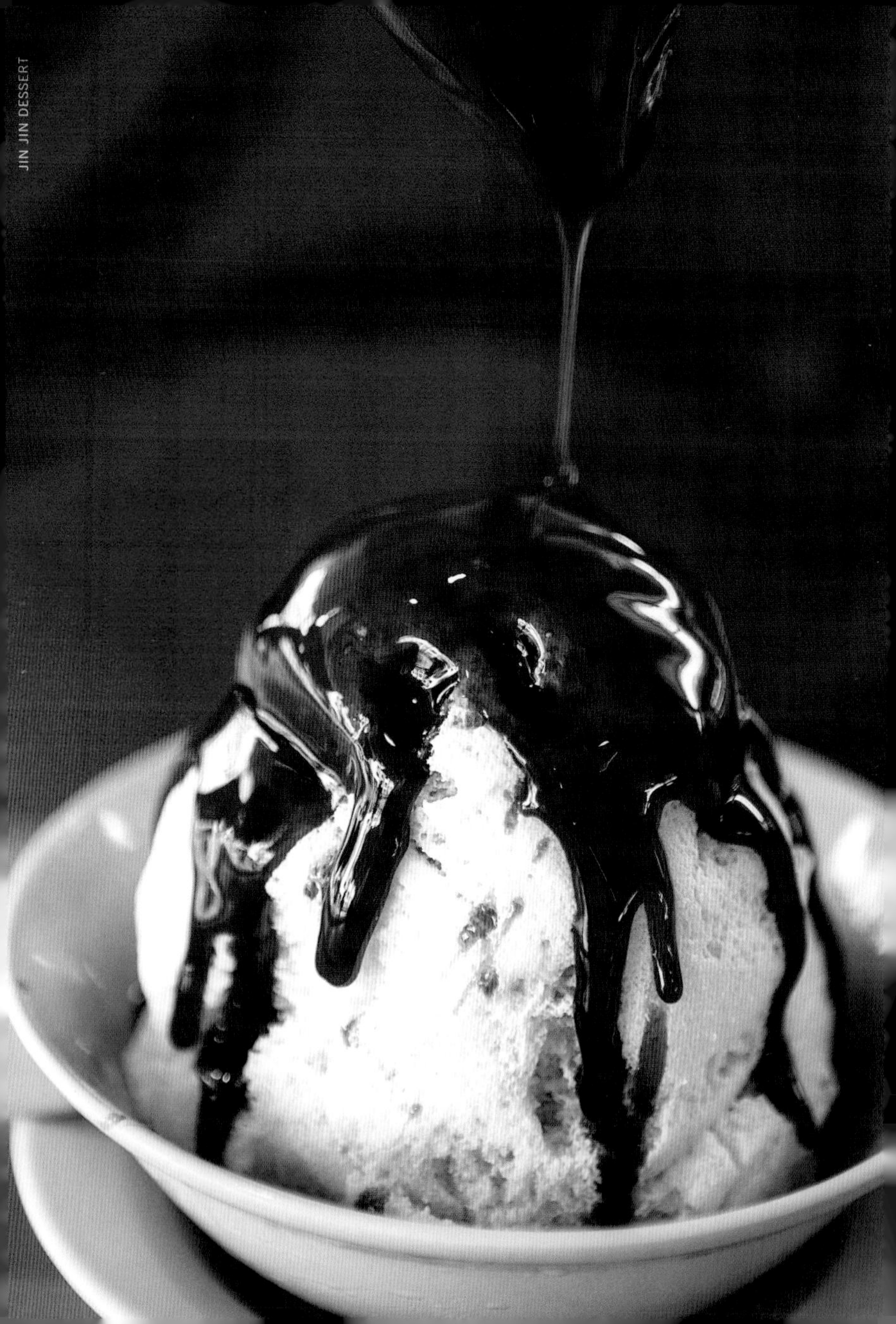

JIN JIN DESSERT

DESSERTS

THERE IS A TREMENDOUS VARIETY OF HAWKER DESSERTS IN SINGAPORE.
The two main categories are: hot and cold. Classic hot desserts
include cheng tng, red bean soup and tau suan. The classic cold
desserts are ice kachang, cendol and cheng tng. Nowadays though,
it seems that the sky is the limit and dessert stalls are offering
anything from mango and pomelo puddings to green tea ice cream!
Although dessert stalls are ubiquitous in every hawker centre,
most of these stalls are the dime-in-a-dozen sort, using pre-bought
or factory made ingredients, producing overly sweet concoctions.
It is rare to find hawkers passionate enough to hand make their
ingredients from quality produce, or who are innovative enough to
bring their dessert dish to the next level of shiokness that will get
me all excited.

LESLIE'S PICK ★✓

JIN JIN DESSERT

4.5/4.25 cendol/gangster ice

Ex-insurance-agent-turned-hawker Calvin Ho serves up one innovative cendol! The gula melaka that is usually drizzled over the dessert has a thick syrupy texture, like the hot fudge in a McDonald's hot fudge sundae. Sensational! The other must-try at Jin Jin is their signature dessert gangster ice. Ho has trademarked the name of his invention. This dessert is a take on the Hong Kong style mango ice dessert, with a scoop of durian puree on top, finished with some condensed milk. If you love durian, you will love this, though I do feel that as a dessert, mango paired with durian is a bit heavy. Also recommended: tau suan.

ABC Brickworks Food Centre • 6 Jalan Bukit Merah #01-20 S150006 • noon to midnight, closed on Wednesdays • 90932018

HOUSE OF DESSERTS

4.75/4.5 lotus suan/tau suan

The tau suan here is very good. The beans are steamed just nice so that they have some bite but still become powdery when you chew on them. The soup is not overly starchy and has a nice caramel fragrance to it. And if you are looking for something a bit more unique, try the lotus suan (ling zhi suan)—the lotus seeds are cooked just right so that they become a nice savoury paste in your mouth when you bite into them. Addictive! Also recommended: ice watermelon and white fungus.

Tampines Round Market & Food Centre • 137 Tampines St 11 #01-02 S521137 • 7am to 5pm, closed on Mondays

DOVE DESSERTS

4.6/4.25 cendol/cheng tng

Lady boss Helen drives all the way to Malacca to procure gula melaka for her cendol. She has also taste-tested several top cendol stalls in Malacca and is confident her cendol rivals the Gold Standard found there. Helen makes this dessert herself, using pandan leaves that pass through a special cendol strainer she bought in Malacca. She also uses freshly squeezed coconut milk and good quality extra large red beans. As for the cheng tng here, I like that Helen adds dried persimmons and dried winter melon strips—great quality ingredients that make up a must-try cheng tng!

Kim Keat Palm Market & Food Centre •
22 Toa Payoh Lor 7 #01-21 S310022 •
Mondays to Thursdays and Saturdays: 11am
to 8pm • Fridays: 11am to 6pm, closed on
Sundays • 92725712

YUE LAI XIANG HOT AND COLD CHENG TNG

4.5 cheng tng This famous stall
has a secret cheng tng
recipe that has been handed down
for three generations and it seems
like no one else has been able to
crack the secret. The cheng tng is
very clear and has got 11 different
ingredients, including some special
ones, like dried persimmon and
dried winter melon strips. The soup
is made from two different troughs:
one trough has got dried longan,
pandan leaves and rock sugar and the
other contains a secret ingredient.
The soup tastes very liang (cooling)
and though you can make out the
sweetness of the rock sugar and the
longan, there is something extra in
there which I cannot put my finger on.

Bedok Corner Food Centre • 1 Bedok
Road S469572 • noon to 8pm, closed
on Mondays

NO NAME CHENG TNG

4.5 cheng tng This stall's cheng
tng could rival the famous
cheng tng at Yue Lai Xiang Hot
and Cold Cheng Tng stall, which
is located nearby. The soup here
is excellent. It is very clear, with a
robust longan flavour. The owner
uses grade A longans from Thailand
and bothers to sort them out, one
longan at a time, to pick out the
ones which are "dirty". The rest of
the ingredients are also impressive—
dried persimmon, winter melon, pong
dua hai (malva nut), white fungus,
sweet potatoes and glutinous rice
balls. Uncle doesn't hold back on
the good stuff!

Blk 69 Bedok South Ave 3 S460069 •
noon to 9pm, open everyday

PEANUTS SOUP

4.5 Yes, in this day and age,
where dessert stalls are
offering a wide variety of desserts,
it takes a really special stall to offer
just three items: peanut soup, red
bean with brown rice soup, and tau
suan. You can add glutinous rice
balls if you like. The peanut soup and

DID YOU KNOW?

If you have tried making cheng tng at home, you would realise it takes skill to ensure the soup is not cloudy, but clear, and still have a strong longan taste. Cheng tng, above all, has to be "cheng", which means clear.

red bean soup were both excellent. The peanuts were fantastically soft and the soup was smooth and full of nutty aroma.

Maxwell Road Food Centre • 1 Kadayanallur St #01-57 S069184 • 7.30am to 4pm, closed on Mondays

XI LE TING

4.25 If you are looking for some old fashioned sweet soups, this is one place to head for. The old lady here makes four items: red bean, white oats, green beans with sago, and cheng tng. They are all very old school, very good and very affordable. Simple, sweet and satisfying.

Commonwealth Crescent Food Centre • 40A Commonwealth Ave Stall 70 S140040 • noon to 10pm, closed fortnightly on Mondays and Tuesdays

ANNIE'S PEANUT ICE KACHANG

4.25 peanut ice kachang At this stall, the mushy red beans are done the way I like them—not overly sweet. But it was the ground peanuts that really impressed me. In this day and age, where these can be easily bought from a supplier, it is heartening to see a tray of freshly roasted peanuts sitting in the stall. This sort of passion for details is what makes the difference.

Tanjong Pagar Market & Food Centre • Blk 6 Tanjong Pagar Plaza #02-36 S081006 •

weekdays: 10.30am to 7.15pm, weekends: 10.30am to 6pm • 81635678

ZHAO AN GRANNY GRASS JELLY

4.0 I like the texture of the grass jelly here. Unlike the factory made versions, that have the consistency of soft agar agar, this stall's grass jelly, also known as chin chow, has the consistency of a nice beancurd, but it is more gelatinous. Soft enough for you to push through the gaps between your teeth. However, it does not really have that strong grass jelly flavour, as if they just watered it down and sacrificed taste for texture.

Golden Mile Food Centre • 505 Beach Road S199583 #01-58 • 11am to 7pm, closed on alternate Sundays

LESLIE'S TIP

There are two ways to serve cendol: with shaved ice or as a soup-drink with crushed ice. I recommend trying the shaved ice version as this allows you to appreciate the different elements of the dish plus the texture of the finely shaved ice as it melts in your mouth. As a soup-drink, everything gets mixed up and you chiefly taste the cold coconut milk with gula melaka.

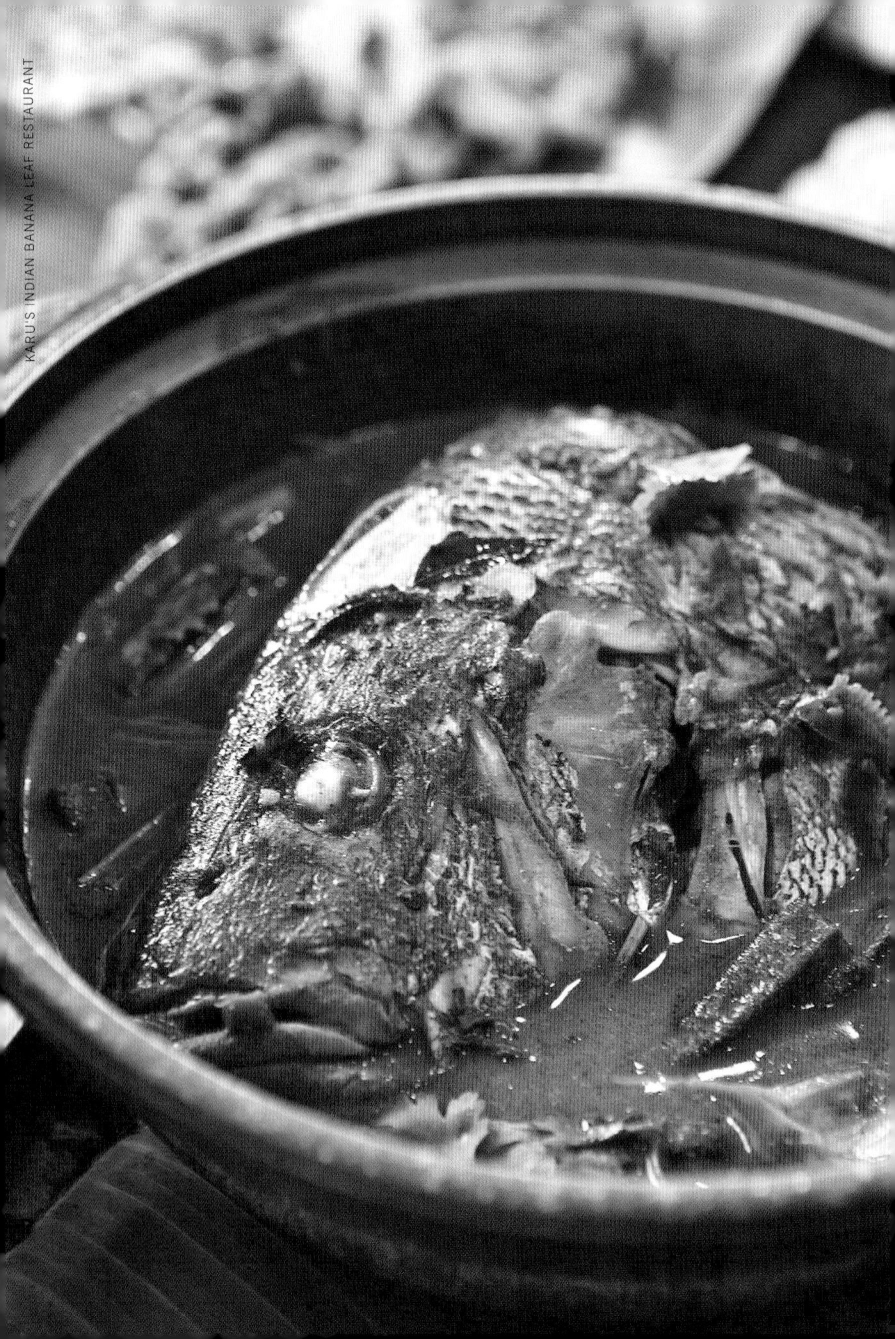

KARU'S INDIAN BANANA LEAF RESTAURANT

FISH HEAD CURRY

FISH HEAD CURRY IS SO FAMOUS AROUND THE WORLD THAT IT REPRESENTED Singapore on MSN's list of 25 things to eat before you die, taking its place alongside the likes of sushi at Tsukiji market, Florentine steak in Italy and Yang Cheng Lake hairy crab. There are two versions of fish head curry in Singapore. In the Chinese version, the fish head is steamed before it is cooked in a curry that has less powdery spices. The Indian version is where the fish head is cooked in a pot of fiery spices designed to make you sweat so that, ironically, you will feel cooler in hot weather.

DID YOU KNOW?

Some say Indian fish head curry was invented by a hawker named Gomez, who used to sell his curry in the Selegie area in the 1950s at Gomez Curry. In his old age, Gomez returned to Kerala, thus explaining why Anthony Bourdain found fish head curry there.

LESLIE'S PICK ✓

KARU'S INDIAN BANANA LEAF RESTAURANT

4.6 This restaurant has been thriving for the last 17 years and is testimony to how food-crazy Singaporeans can be—that they would be willing to travel all the way to Upper Bukit Timah just to eat something good! The curry gravy is deliciously balanced but not quite as fiery as I expected it to be. Also, the fish was tender and moist even though it was cooked directly in the curry. Also recommended: chicken masala, fish and potato cutlet, and masala tea.

808/810 Upper Bukit Timah Road S678145 • 10.30am to 10pm, closed on Mondays • 67627284, 83859511

HOOKED ON HEADS

4.5 The fish head curry here is cooked with a combination of milk and coconut milk so it is not too jerlak (satiated), but still creamy. It isn't overly spicy which suits me fine, though some may find it too mild. The fish is also fresh. If you are not big on fish head curry, like me, this one might just get you hooked on heads! Also recommended: mee siam, green mango salad, prawn paste chicken, mango sticky rice and banana fritters.

Sin Ming Plaza • 6 Sin Ming Road Tower 2 • #01-01/02 S575585 • 11am to 2.30pm and 5.30pm to 9.30pm, open everyday • 64554948

LAU HOCK GUAN KEE

4.5 Every morning, the boss at this stall will scour a few markets looking for ang goli (gold banded snapper) heads. The fish served here is, thus, always fresh. What makes his fish head curry so special is that the boss steams the fish head, brinjal and okra first, then pours the freshly made curry gravy over it, so the fish head is not overcooked, but still tender and moist. The curry gravy is very well balanced, not too spicy nor overpowering, and with the right amount of tang to get those salivary glands going. Also recommended: steamed fish, pork ribs with bittergourd and black bean sauce, and claypot chicken in sesame oil.

328 Joo Chiat Road #01-02 S427585 • 8.30am to 4pm and 4.30pm to midnight, closed on Thursdays • 64404928

PENANG FOOD RESTAURANT

4.5 I was particularly impressed with the assam fish head at this cze cha restaurant. The fish was very fresh and the gravy had a nice balance of sourness that got your salivary glands going but didn't cause you to wince. It is definitely one of the best assam fish heads I have come across! Also recommended: petai, deep fried pork strips and penang char kway teow.

76 Geylang Lor 25A S388258 • 11am to midnight, open everyday • 68413002

GU MA JIA

4.25 The gravy of the assam fish head has a good balance of sweet, sour and savoury that goes well with rice. The extra oomph in the gravy comes from the fact that they cook the fish head in the gravy, so the gravy is infused with the sweetness of the fish head. Though this method of cooking could result in the fish being overcooked, the fish here is cooked perfectly, and the meat is moist and tender. The only complaint is that the fish head was a tad small for the price I had to pay, and there wasn't enough gravy to go around.

45 Tai Thong Crescent S347866 • 11am to 10pm, open everyday • 62852023

SOON HENG RESTAURANT

4.25 The use of spices is less heavy handed than a typical South Indian curry and the addition of coconut in the form of kerisik (dry fried shredded coconut) gives the curry a wonderful flavour. It is sweeter, milder and not as tangy as other fish head curries. However, if you prefer your curry to be fiery and sourish, then this might not give you the endorphin-releasing, sweat-breaking punch you seek.

39 Kinta Road S219108 • weekdays: 10.30am to 8pm, weekends and public holidays: 10.30am to 5pm • 62947343, 62946561, 82884623

KOK SENG RESTAURANT

4.25 The fish head curry is strong on the curry powder without the sourish taste of the Indian version. I feel that you can find better fish head curry elsewhere, though I did finish the whole plate for the fish was quite fresh! Not too bad, but not overwhelming either.

30-32 Keong Saik Road S089137 • 11.30am to 11.30pm, open everyday

DID YOU KNOW?

The Chinese version of fish head curry was developed by Hoong Ah Kong. Arriving in Singapore in 1936, he learnt to cook Indian food to differentiate himself from others. He eventually opened Soon Heng Restaurant—the world's oldest fish head curry restaurant that is still in operation.

FISH HEAD STEAMBOAT

FISH HEAD STEAMBOAT IS ONE OF THOSE DISHES THAT FILLS UP THE stomach, satisfies the palate and clears the sinuses, all at the same time. The secret to making a great fish head steamboat soup is the quality of the tipoh (dried sole fish) that has been added to the broth. Plus, the soup needs to be made from good quality pork and fish bones. The sweetest soups are made from chopped up fish heads, although you can order just fish meat if you prefer.

Nowadays the fish commonly used for fish head steamboat is pomfret or garoupa. But in the old days, the favourite fish for steamboat was the song fish (Asian carp). While song fish is quite big, and contains lots of bits of fish meat to nibble on, it can taste a little muddy. The old people love it, but these days people prefer to have larger quantities of fish meat to feast on, which is why pomfret and garoupa are more popular now.

LESLIE'S PICK ✓

WHAMPOA KENG FISHHEAD STEAMBOAT (RANGOON ROAD)

4.5 **This is a branch of the flagship stall at Balestier Road. Located on a quieter road, it was easier to find parking, while the food was of as high standard as the main stall. They used the same procedure for preparing the soup base, which included adding a pre-packaged mix of herbs. Although there is dried sole fish in the soup, it isn't overwhelming and is nicely balanced with the herbs such that it creates a nice harmony of flavours on your palate.**

116/118 Rangoon Road S218394 • 11am to 11pm, open everyday • 90232854

XIN HENG FENG GUO TIAO STALL (WHAMPOA FISH HEAD STEAMBOAT)

4.6 If you go to Whampoa Market in the evening, you are there for one dish only, as is everyone else: fish head steamboat. You won't find much else available on this stall's menu, except chai buay, if you want some greens, and braised duck wings, if you get there early enough. However, you can choose from garoupa, pomfret or song fish. The boss worked for 17 years at the "granddaddy of fish head steamboat" Nam Wah Chong, before setting up his stall in Whampoa in 1987. The soup is robust and packed with umami, and my dried sole fish was especially fragrant. Expect to wait about 40 minutes and head there early before the food runs out.

Whampoa Drive Makan Place (Whampoa Food Centre) • 91 Whampoa Dr #01-15 S320092 • 5pm to 9.30pm, closed on Tuesdays

WHAMPOA KENG FISHHEAD STEAMBOAT

4.5 I am told that in all, there are 30 ingredients that go into this fish soup, which explains why it is so addictive. Although there is tipoh (dried sole fish) in the soup, it isn't as overwhelming as most places. The soup is nicely balanced with herbs, making it pleasing to your palate.

556 Balestier Road S329872 • weekdays: 11am to 3pm and 5pm to 11pm, weekend and public holidays: 11am to 11pm • 91276550

TIAN WAI TIAN FISHHEAD STEAMBOAT

4.5 Tian Wai Tian started selling fish head steamboat in the early 1980s when I was studying at the nearby St. Andrew's School. Today, they control a steamboat empire with a few branches around the island,

but the one at their original location remains the best, perhaps because the lady boss who started it still works at the shop, keeping an eye on everything. Tian Wai Tian scores for delivering classic Teochew fish head steamboat: plenty of fresh, savoury sole fish and a soup with lots of body, served in charcoal aluminium steamboat pots that are as old as the shop.

1382 Serangoon Road (Opal Crescent) S328254 • weekdays: 5.30pm to 11pm, weekends: 5pm to 11pm • 91722833

NAM WAH CHONG FISH HEAD STEAMBOAT CORNER

4.25 fish soup The fish soup here is your classic Teochew fish soup. The sweetness comes from the fresh fish, which has been sourced from the same supplier for the last 30 years. The umami kick comes from the tipoh (dried sole fish), which makes the soup wonderfully savoury. Overall, the soup is very chngee (fresh).

814/816 North Bridge Road S198779 • 5pm to 1am, open everyday

DID YOU KNOW?

The predominant flavour of fish head steamboat soup comes from the use of tipoh (dried sole fish). This is a classic Teochew style of cooking.

FISH SOUP

DID YOU KNOW THAT THERE IS NO MILK IN MILKY FISH SOUP? THE MILKY white colour is achieved by deep-frying fish slices, then mixing a bit of the oil with a simple ginger stock. Next, the lid is put on the wok and high heat is applied until white smoke starts streaming out from the edges. The ginger stock is then poured over the lid slowly. The combination of high heat, stock and oil causes the oil and water to combine and form a milky emulsion!

Even though I am 100 per cent Teochew, I must admit that I prefer the Cantonese style "milky" fish soup to the Teochew style fish soup which comprises a very clear chngee (fresh) soup made from boiling fish bones, and sometimes, chicken and pork bones. I love it when the hawker gives you lots of fresh, tender fish slices that have no fishy odour. The soup is healthy and sweeter than the milky version.

LESLIE'S PICK ★

JING HUA SLICED FISH BEE HOON

4.75 My first taste of this fish soup was quite a Holy Grail experience. The best thing is that you don't have to pay a bomb for the soup as it comes in individual servings. The only problem is the long queue, even during off-peak periods. Take it from me though, it's worth it.

Maxwell Road Food Centre • 1 Kadayanallur St #01-77 S069184 • 11am to 8.30pm, closed on Thursdays

HAN KEE FISH PORRIDGE

4.5 Healthy stuff can't be tasty right? Wrong! At Han Kee, they start boiling the soup at 5am and it is only ready at 10am. The fish is very fresh, and the meat is firm but still delicate. The soup is really sweet and you can taste the quality and effort that goes into the preparation. For the more adventurous, you can also have fish eyes, head, stomach, roe and the male equivalent of roe. A healthy dish that you can enjoy and still feel that you have done your heart a favour!

Amoy Street Food Centre • 7 Maxwell Road #02-129 S069111 • 10am to 3pm, closed on Sundays

MEI XIANG FISH SOUP

4.5 The soup here is full of "bits", making it slightly cloudy, but really tasty. You get thickly sliced fish and fried battered fish which is quite yummy (though a bit on the salty side). However, the stall owner here is a bit of a Food Nazi. You can only take away food if you bring your own container. Plus, you have to pay for extra chilli.

Berseh Food Centre • 166 Jalan Besar #02-44 S208877 • 11am to 2pm, closed on Saturdays, Sundays and public holidays

YONG LAI FA JI COOKED FOOD

4.5 fish head noodle soup They make everything themselves here, and the soup is made from boiling fish bones and chicken for at least eight hours. They are generous with the fish, which is very fresh. They also add bittergourd to the soup, which is tasty and good for your cholesterol levels.

Circuit Road Food Centre • 79A Circuit Road #01-648 S371079 • 5am to 9pm, closed on Sundays and public holidays

NG SOON KEE FISH AND DUCK PORRIDGE

4.5/4.0 batang soup/pomfret soup One of the few hawker stalls that sells sliced pomfret soup. The fish is super fresh but you

YONG LAI FA JI COOKED FOOD

should request a bit more Szechuan vegetables to give it more kick! The batang soup on the other hand is more potent, and definitely one of the tastiest fish soups I have ever tasted. The stall owner emphasised that the soup stock is prepared from fish bones and old mother hen. They don't use any pork bones.

Aljunied Market & Food Centre • 117 Aljunied Ave 2 #01-11 S380117 • noon to 9pm, closed on Sundays

ICHIBAN FISH SOUP

4.25 Ichiban offers value for money, serving up generous portions of not the more commonly used (and cheaper) dory but a very good, fresh sea bass.

The fish is sliced surprisingly thick and cooked perfectly such that the flesh is tender but firm. Both the fried and fresh versions of the soup are excellent. If you like a clear and light soup, you will especially enjoy this dish. But if, like me, you prefer a soup with plenty of oomph, be sure to ask for the chilli. Rather than the usual sliced chilli with soya sauce, Ichiban's version is more like a chicken rice chilli and has a wonderfully strong calamansi fragrance that goes surprisingly well with the fish.

Seah Im Food Centre • 2 Seah Im Road #01-18 S099114 • 8am to 8pm, closed on Saturdays

HOLLAND VILLAGE XO FISH HEAD BEE HOON

4.25 This is the stall that first started putting XO in fish soup! Ricky, the stall owner, believes in using only the best and freshest ingredients—he brags that he sources his snakeheads (loi he) from Malaysia and only uses top grade MSG that does not give a bad aftertaste. The result is a tasty fish soup with that extra XO kick!

Jumbo Coffee Hub • 19A Dover Crescent S131019 • 11.30am to 2pm and 5pm to 11pm, open everyday • 98331003

PIAO JI FISH PORRIDGE

4.25 The soup did not quite meet my high expectations, but the fish was very fresh and moist. The fact that each bowl was cooked individually meant that Uncle could make sure the fish was not overcooked but maintained its juices. I wouldn't mind eating it again, if not for the long queue and the fact that the smallest serving was $5.

Amoy Street Food Centre • 7 Maxwell Road #02-100/103 S069111 • 10.30am to 3pm, closed on Thursdays

HONG KONG STREET CHUN KEE

4.0 This is the original Hong Kong Street fish soup. The soup here is good and certainly better than the fish soups you get at your average hawker centres, but I remember it being more shiok in the past.

125 Bukit Merah Lane 1 #01-190 S150125 • Mondays to Saturdays: 11.30am to 2.30pm and 5pm to 11.30pm, Sundays: 11am to 2pm and 5.30pm to 11pm • 62718484, 62728484

HONG QIN FISH AND DUCK PORRIDGE

4.0 This stall is widely held to serve the best Teochew style fish soup in Singapore. The soup was very chngee (fresh), clear, light and sweet. However, the fresh fish slices were nothing to rave about. I really liked the tasty fried fish—the seasoned batter perfectly complemented the fish meat, making it really pang (fragrant).

134 Geylang East Ave 1 S380134 • 5.45am to 3pm, closed on 1st and 3rd Tuesdays of the month

DID YOU KNOW?

It takes five to 10 minutes to prepare one bowl of Cantonese style fish soup (due to the time needed to carry out the various steps to produce the milky emulsion). And because every bowl is made individually, you can't ask for more soup without having to wait a while. Nowadays, however, some hawkers take a shortcut and simply add evaporated milk or milk powder into the soup.

FISHBALL NOODLES

IT IS GOOD TO SEE MORE STALLS MAKING THEIR OWN FISHBALLS. THE additives and fillers used in commercially produced fishballs means sacrificing taste for a more bouncy texture. Hawkers use either sai tor her (wolf herring) or yellowtail—the fish meat is first scraped off to form a paste, then beaten till the meat is bouncy. The paste is then moulded into balls and soaked in water. This same water they soak the fishballs in becomes the clear soup which you can enjoy with your bowl of noodles!

Fishballs made with no addition of fillers tend to look big when they are being cooked but shrink in size when they are left in the soup for a while. A man from Chao Zhou, the birthplace of fishballs, told me that the fishballs in Singapore are better than the ones from Chao Zhou! And people from Hong Kong tell me they come to Singapore looking for our fishballs.

LESLIE'S PICK ✓

SONG KEE FISHBALL NOODLE

4.75/4.5 her giao/ fishballs

The second generation stall owner here insists on making his own fishballs. They taste amazing, with the right balance of bounce and taste. Sample the her giao (fish dumplings) which, being handmade as well, are excellent. And check out the chilli, which is shiok because buah keluak (Indonesian black nut) has been added to it. Finally, a warning: the noodles are prepared with a generous amount of lard and fried shallots so this dish can hardly be considered a light, healthy meal.

Blk 75 Toa Payoh Lor 5 #01-354 S310075 • 10.30am to midnight, closed on alternate Wednesdays • 96776979

HUI JI FISHBALL NOODLES AND YONG TAU FOO

4.6 Fishball. Pork lard. Chilli. This stall serves up amazing fishball noodles with super simple ingredients but maximum oomph. The fishballs are small, rustic, with the surface grooved by fingerprints. The pork lard crunches like Twisties, with an addictive taste. And the chilli—it is savoury and well balanced, with the right combination of sweet, salty and spicy.

Tiong Bahru Market & Food Centre • 30 Seng Poh Road #02-44 S168898 • 7am to 2pm, open everyday

ZHONG XING FOOCHOW FISHBALLS

4.5 This stall, which has been around for two generations and used to be at China Street, is faithfully sticking to tradition and making their foochow fishballs from scratch daily. I love biting into the fishball and tasting the burst of savoury pork flavour. Shiok! They also serve addictive meatballs and a very interesting dumpling made of yan pi (pork membrane).

Blk 148 Silat Ave #01-14 S160148 • 7.30am to 5pm, closed on Tuesdays

LI XIN CHAO ZHOU FISH BALL

4.5 The fishballs at this stall were bouncy and very tasty. The other thing to rave about is the chilli sauce. While it is fiery, it does not linger on your tongue such that you need a drink. This stall is a branch of another famous fishball stall at Toa Payoh Lorong 7, which has been around since 1968. The hawker is a second generation hawker determined to stick to the traditional way his father has been selling his famous dish.

ION Food Opera • Orchard Turn Basement 4 S238801 • Mondays to Thursdays: 8am to 10pm, Fridays, Saturdays and eve of public holidays: 8am to 11pm, Sundays: 10am to 10pm

MING KEE FOO CHOW FISH BALLS

4.0 The foochow fishballs here are specially made in a factory, according to a recipe provided by the hawker. The soup is tasty and full of protein precipitate. Great for supper and good value for money too!

Old Airport Road Food Centre • 51 Old Airport Road #01-103 (facing main road) S390051 • 7am to 11pm, closed on Sundays

CITIZOOM MINCED FISH NOODLES

4.0 The fishballs here are some of the best I have tasted. They are substantial and meaty, but at the same time bouncy and you can really savour the taste of the fish. The only let down was the soup,

which could have been more solid. This place also sells shou gong yu mian (handmade fish noodles). For this dish, not only are the noodles made of fish, everything else is either fish or stuffed with fish!

117 Aljunied Ave 2 #01-34 S380117 • 7am to 3pm, closed on alternate Thursdays • 81254883

YONG KEE FISH BALL NOODLE

4.0 The soup here is tasty and clear. The fishballs are excellent, with great bouncy texture. This stall also sells meatballs, which comprise a mix of pork, fish, chillies and spring onions. However, they were not fantastic.

ABC Brickworks Food Centre • 6 Jalan Bukit Merah #01-121 S150006 • 7am to 2am, open everyday

---

DID YOU KNOW?

A foochow fishball is a fishball filled with minced pork. This type of fishball is more doughy than springy to the bite as it has a higher ratio of flour to fish meat. The best foochow fishballs are soft and al dente, while the minced pork is still juicy inside.

HAINANESE CURRY RICE

IF YOU BRING A FOREIGNER TO EAT THIS DISH, HE MIGHT THINK YOU ARE pulling a fast one on him. Curry gravy mixed with lor (braising sauce), then mixed with gooey stewed cabbage does not sound particularly appetising, but trust me, this stuff will definitely hit the G-spot, as in, the Gastronomic Spot. Although the mixing of gravies may sound like a collision of flavours, they go very well together! When you are famished, that bolus of rice and gravy slides down the oesophagus like engine oil on pistons. It's the quick and tasty way to satisfy your hunger pangs. It works at a level that produces an umami bomb. I feel it every time I eat Hainanese curry rice.

With Hainanese curry rice, you really only need three dishes—a good chicken curry, lor bak (braised pork belly) and chap chye (stewed cabbage). Having crispy fried pork is a bonus, but the trinity of Hainanese curry rice dishes must be there.

LESLIE'S PICK

TIAN TIAN HAINANESE CURRY RICE

4.75/4.5 pork chops / lion heads

(pork balls) They don't have just three gravies, they have six different types—chicken curry, seafood curry, special curry, char siew sauce, pork chop gravy and lor (braising sauce). The pork chops here make me really happy, and should be slowly savoured with your eyes closed. The best Hainanese pork chops I have eaten so far and a very satisfying Hainanese curry rice overall. Also recommended: lor bak (braised pork belly).

116 Bukit Merah View #01-253 S151116 • 9.30am to 9.30pm, closed on alternate Tuesdays • 91096732

NO NAME HAINANESE CURRY RICE

4.75 The crispy pork here is really shiok! Unlike other stalls which I have tried, the crispy pork here is so crispy, it is like eating keropok (fish crackers). When you add it to the plate of rice covered with the deluge of curry, lor (braising sauce) and cabbage, it is superlatively heavenly. Also recommended: curry chicken.

40 Beo Crescent S160040 • 6.30am to 3pm, closed on Wednesdays

REDHILL CURRY RICE

4.5 Everything is good! No kidding! Eating here is a Holy Grail experience. The sambal is sweet and savoury, not spicy, and super shiok. The braised pork is one of the best I have ever tasted—it melts in your mouth and the kiam pang (salty and savoury) flavour lingers at the back of your tongue long after you swallow the tasty morsel. And the crispy pork is almost like eating chewy keropok (fish crackers). So satisfying! Also recommended: fish rolls, braised pork and crispy pork.

Redhill Food Centre • 85 Redhill Lane #01-95 (facing main road) S150085 • 10.30am to 9.30pm, closed on Sundays • 96523471

BEACH ROAD SCISSOR CUT CURRY RICE

4.5 At this stall, they use a pair of scissors to cut up all the food and pile it on top of your rice. With the meat in little pieces and the rice smothered with lots of gravy, the dish is effortlessly tasty and superbly shiok!

Lao Di Fang Restaurant • 229 Jalan Besar S208905 • 11am to 3.30am, open everyday

NO NAME, HAINANESE CURRY RICE

LOO'S HAINANESE CURRY RICE

4.5 This stall dates back to 1964! The food here is good because Uncle insists on doing things the traditional way. The pork chops are coated with cream crackers before frying, just like how my Hainanese mother-in-law does it. The killer dish was the curry prawns—it was fragrant and had a natural sweetness that got me lapping it up and thinking of when to go back for more.

Blk 57 Eng Hoon St #01-88 S160057 • 8am to 2pm, closed on alternate Tuesdays

ELEVEN FINGER (EU KEE) CURRY RICE

4.25 If you are near the National Library and are really hungry, this is a great place to satisfy that hunger with some extremely tasty grub.

QS269 Food House • Blk 269B Queen St #01-235 S180269 • 10am to 6pm, closed on alternate Fridays

DID YOU KNOW?

In the good old days, many Hainanese were employed as chefs by both the British and the Peranakans. They got the pork chop idea from the British and adapted curry chicken, babi pongteh (braised pork in salted bean paste) and chap chye (stewed cabbage) from the Peranakans.

HAWKER WESTERN FOOD

THIS IS A UNIQUE GENRE OF WESTERN FOOD. THE HAWKERS USUALLY HAVE Hainanese roots. Many Hainanese men used to work as chefs in British colonial households. Hence, the food cooked is a blend of western style with local cooking. The humble Hainanese pork chop is a fusion dish—it is pork schnitzel seasoned to suit local tastes and served with potatoes and peas. Other hawker western food dishes are typically served with baked beans and chips. In addition, the meats are marinated with a mixture of local sauces, such as, maggi seasoning, soya sauce and MSG.

DID YOU KNOW?

There's a growing number of western food hawkers using western ingredients like basil and tarragon in their dishes. Although this is interesting, it also makes hawker western food lose its unique identity.

LESLIE'S PICK ✓

ASTONS SPECIALTIES

4.75 **ieat Super Burger** This burger is named after a psychologically challenged blogger, yours truly, because I instigated Aston to create this amazing dish. With an XL soft sesame seed bun, freshly chopped sirloin steak patty (200gm, medium done), Astons' homemade smoked hickory BBQ sauce (fantastic smoky, tangy flavour), two slices of cheese and two rashers of streaky bacon (grilled to crispy), a fried egg, lightly battered, crispy fried onion rings, lettuce, tomatoes and mayonnaise, this is easily the best tasting, value for money burger in town. One bite and I feel like a cowboy. Yeehah!

119/121 East Coast Road S428806 • 11.30am to 10pm, open everyday • www.astons.com.sg

WOK INN FISH AND CHIPS

4.6 At Wok Inn, you can get excellent fish and chips at an excellent price. This stall uses the traditional British style batter—made from flour, water and baking powder, forming a light, thin and crispy crust while the fish is moist and succulent. When eating fish and chips, I always look for the bits of uncooked batter in between the fish and the crust—a moist and creamy batter is what sets a really good fish and chips apart from ordinary run of the mill ones.

Toa Payoh Lor 2 Blk 125 S311125 • 11.30am to 9.30pm, closed on Tuesdays • 98976048

DE BURG

4.5 Even though this is a kopitiam burger that you can have with a cup of teh C, I would say that it ranks right up there with all the best burgers in town. The wagyu burger is excellent, though it could be a little cheaper, given that it is located in a coffeeshop. The standard burger is something really worth making the trip for though—the patty is beefy and has just the right texture and bounce with a wonderful charred crust.

Blk 119 Bukit Merah Lane 1 #01-40 S151119 • Tuesdays to Thursdays: 11.30am to 3pm and 6pm to 9pm, Fridays to Sundays: 11.30am to 3pm and 6.30pm to 9pm, closed on Mondays

PRINCE COFFEE HOUSE

4.5 If you are hankering after old-fashioned food, then the address for memory lane is 249 Beach

Road! They still do old favourites like oxtail stew and pork chops served in a signature sauce that hasn't changed over the years. The corned beef and long beans dish is awesomely simple, and simply awesome—I'd be happy to order it with just a bowl of rice. Don't forget to leave with their most iconic takeaway—the chunky, old-fashioned chicken pie. (This stall is also recommended for hor fun.)

249 Beach Road (opposite Park Royal) S189757 • 11am to 9pm, open everyday • 64682088

HAPPY CHEF WESTERN FOOD

4.25 barbecued pork ribs Returning from Sydney after a 15-year stay, the owners started this stall serving interesting items like chicken kiev and pork cordon bleu, which are to Sydneysiders what Hokkien mee is to Singaporeans. The real gem here is the BBQ pork ribs. You get a meaty portion of pork ribs, cooked till the meat can be sucked off the bone, swimming in a lovely tangy BBQ sauce. The BBQ pork ribs are also great value for money. Shiokalicious! Also recommended: chicken kiev.

Tai Hwa Eating House • 466 Crawford Lane #01-12 S190466 • 11am to 10pm, open everyday • 92749591, 96827000, 63980073

WESTERN BARBEQUE

4.0 chicken chops The chicken chop is, without a doubt, the star of the show. The red coloured garlic sauce that they serve is a little sweet, but it goes well with the chicken thigh fillet that was well seasoned, and very tender. The pork chop, on the other hand, is beaten to a pulp, though it does taste alright.

Old Airport Road Food Centre • 51 Old Airport Road #01-53 S390051 • 11am to 11pm, open everyday

WOW WOW WEST GRILL

4.0 The serving of fish and chips is huge—the fish is the size of a ping pong bat and thick too! The bread crumb crust is well executed, crisp and not oily. The other bestselling items are the chicken and pork chops, seasoned with Western herbs. The pork loins are big, and I like the way the meat is pan-fried till there's a nice crust on the outside.

ABC Brickworks Food Centre • 6 Jalan Bukit Merah #01-133 S150006 • 10.30am to 9pm, closed on Sundays

DID YOU KNOW?

The best western food hawkers will make their own demiglace by reducing beef and chicken stock. This sort of passion separates them from run-of-the-mill hawkers!

HOKKIEN MEE

THERE ARE SO MANY ELEMENTS THAT MAKE UP A SHIOKALICIOUS Hokkien mee—crispy, fragrant pork lard bits, melt-in-your-mouth pork belly slices, a very hot wok with an expert hawker who times his frying well. And let's not forget the importance of a rich prawn-based stock. Some hawkers proudly boast they use only sua lor (wild prawns), which are sweeter than farmed prawns. For a good Hokkien mee, the noodles need to be fried till slightly charred and ready to absorb stock. The hawker spends some time frying the noodles before adding the gravy. Everything gets really messy as the noodles are flagrantly swirled around the wok, with rogue bits escaping off the rim. The stock is then added before covering the wok. When the lid is lifted, you are greeted by a blossoming fragrance as the noodles and stock merge to become a familiar yellow-brown gooey mass. With the right timing, the result is absolute magic.

LESLIE'S PICK ✓

GEYLANG LORONG 29 FRIED HOKKIEN MEE

4.75 **Alex See has been frying Hokkien mee for over 40 years and boasts his Hokkien mee is fried in the same style as that of the 1950s. The noodles are very well fried and the lard is crispy. He uses a special charcoal fire wok that allows him to really swirl the noodles around to make sure that every strand gets fair attention.**

396 East Coast Road S428994 • 11.30am to 9.30pm, closed on Mondays

NAM SING HOKKIEN FRIED MEE

4.6 *ieat* readers voted this the best Hokkien mee in Singapore. The noodles and beehoon are served al dente, and taste shiokalicious! The uncle here says there's no big secret to his Hokkien mee—he just uses good prawns and ikan bilis in the stock, and it all boils down to good control of the wok fire. Exceptional!

Old Airport Road Food Centre • 51 Old Airport Road #01-32 S390051 • 11am to about 8pm, closed when Uncle feels tired

HAINAN FRIED HOKKIEN PRAWN MEE

4.6 Unlike a lot of Hokkien mee, which is prepared more like pasta where the stock is added at the end and served really wet, here it is fried until all the wonderful stock is completely absorbed into the noodles. Every mouthful is a delight!

Golden Mile Food Centre • 505 Beach Road #B1-34 S199583 • 11am to 2pm and 3pm to 9pm, closed on Wednesdays • 62946798

TIAN TIAN LAI (COME DAILY) FRIED HOKKIEN PRAWN MEE

4.5 The main characteristic of this Hokkien mee is its gooeyness, which intensifies the crustacean taste of the stock. The noodles were well fried and you can get lard and pork belly strips here as well. The prawns and sotong (squid) serve only as garnishing. Simple and no frills.

Toa Payoh West Market & Food Court • 127 Toa Payoh Lorong 1 #02-27 S310127 • 9.30am to 9pm, closed on Mondays • 62518542, 96717071

CHIA KENG (PREVIOUSLY CHE JIAN) FRIED HOKKIEN MEE

4.5 Truly traditional, this Hokkien mee has got it all—the opeh leaf, the crunchy pork lard, the boiled melt-in-your-mouth pork belly, the cut chilli, and most importantly, a stock made from sua lor (wild prawns), giving it extra sweetness.

Chomp Chomp Food Centre • 20 Kensington Park Road Stall 11 S557269 • 5.30pm to 1am, open everyday

SINGAPORE FRIED HOKKIEN MEE

4.5 The sambal here is very tasty, not overly spicy. The pork lard is one of the best I have ever tasted. Light, crispy and pang (fragrant). The combination of the noodles, chilli and pork lard really made my day!

Whampoa Drive Makan Place (Whampoa Food Centre) • 90 Whampoa Dr #01-32 S320090 • 4pm to 1.30am, open everyday

TIONG BAHRU YI SHENG HOKKIEN MEE

4.25 This stall has been serving up Hokkien mee for more than 40 years. The current owner Uncle Toh took over from his father in 1989. Watch as the thin beehoon is evenly cooked in an extra large wok, swimming in thick gravy. As the finishing touch, the Hokkien mee is topped off with a top secret chilli that is rumoured to contain dried anchovies and prawns. For a truly shiokalicious experience, enjoy your noodles with some perfectly grilled sio bak from Fatty Cheong's in the same food centre.

ABC Brickworks Food Centre • 6 Jalan Bukit Merah #01-13 S150006 • 3pm to 10.45pm or until food runs out, closed on Wednesdays

AH HOCK FRIED HOKKIEN NOODLES

4.25 Perhaps it has something to do with the hawker, whose white hair flies in the wind like a modern day Beethoven, but there is an element of authenticity in his Hokkien mee. Tastewise, it is very good, and the thin beehoon that he uses is very well fried. I was just a little disappointed that there was no pork lard or pork belly, which I think, would have added extra oomph to the dish.

Chomp Chomp Food Centre • 20 Kensington Park Road Stall 27 S557269 • 5.30pm to 11pm

KIM'S HOKKIEN MEE

4.25 Who hasn't heard of the eccentric Mr Tan Kue Kim who wears a gold Rolex and long-sleeved shirt while frying Hokkien mee? Those who like the "thick beehoon, wet style" Hokkien mee will be happy here. The other commendable item is the wonderfully fresh and crunchy lard bits! It could have been even better if the stall had included pork belly and fried the noodles a little more to get all the flavour in.

62B Jalan Eunos S419510 • 11am to 1am, open everyday

ORIGINAL SERANGOON FRIED HOKKIEN MEE

4.25 Anyone from the baby boomer period will remember Mr Neo, the crippled man who used to fry his Hokkien mee while seated over a charcoal fire. Today, the Hokkien mee continues to be very well fried with wok-charred flavour in the noodles. The soup stock is excellent, as well as the prawns, sotong (squid) and pork belly. Unfortunately, the thick beehoon does not have the chewy texture that I enjoy.

556 Serangoon Road S218175 • 4.30pm to 11.15pm, closed on Mondays

SWEE GUAN

4.25 Hokkien mee and satay is my number one, all-time favourite hawker combo and it is a delight to find two really good stalls side-by-side that serve these dishes, as is the case at Sing Lian Eating House. The Uncle behind the famous, original Geylang Lorong 29 Hokkien mee had a few children and today they run their own stalls to carry on their father's legacy. Swee Guan is one of them. Keeping in line with the tradition, the thin beehoon is fried over charcoal and tends to come out a little gooey but full-flavoured. The prawns are also larger and the price a little cheaper than at his other children's branches. Be sure to try Kwong Satay and order their delicious pork belly satay for an authentic Singaporean dining experience.

Sing Lian Eating House • 549 Geylang Road Lorong 29 S389504 • 4.30pm to 11.30pm, closed on alternate Wednesdays • 98175652

YONG HUAT HOKKIEN MEE

4.25 The thick noodles used here are limp and soft. The sauce is pale and has bits of egg in it, so it's not the most attractive. But the taste is good, thanks to the fact that it is fried with pork lard. There was a crunchy, savoury piece in my first mouthful and I was sold immediately. The dish lacks wok hei (breath of wok) flavour, but the stock, comprising three-layered pork, pork leg bones, dried squid, ikan bilis, prawns and rock sugar, scores for potency. The owner took over the stall from his father who had been around since 1949.

125/127 East Coast Road (junction of Joo Chiat Road) S428810 • 8am to 8pm, open everyday • 96301370

YANG ZHOU

4.25 The Uncle at Yang Zhou is quite an expert. He swirls the noodles around the wok and avoids breaking them unnecessarily, which makes sense, as you want to enjoy slurping the long strands of noodles with a pair of chopsticks rather than spooning them into your mouth. His technique produces a Hokkien mee with excellent texture, and the gooeyness of the gravy covering each strand of noodles is almost perfect.

40 Beo Crescent #01-16 S160040 • 10am to 8pm, closed on Fridays • 62730429, 97400653

SIMON ROAD FRIED HOKKIEN MEE

4.0 I have grown to love Hokkien mee which is fried with thin beehoon till the gravy is absorbed and the noodles have crisp little brown bits full of that charred crustacean flavour. Sadly, not many hawkers fry this way any more as it is rather time-consuming. But Uncle here has recently resumed frying with pork lard after 13 years of not doing so. For a plate of Hokkien mee that truly hits the spot, order both wet and dry versions and mix them together. The gravy contrasts nicely with the flavourful noodles. I also recommend visiting when Uncle is not too busy so he can cook your noodles till they are fully fried. Or order takeaway and enjoy your Hokkien mee at home, after the noodles have had enough time to rest and absorb the wonderful stock.

941 Upper Serangoon Road (corner of Simon Road and Upper Serangoon Road) S534709 • noon to 11pm, closed on Mondays • 98202888

THYE HONG

4.0 I have observed that most of the famous hawkers around do not just serve good food, but also have distinctive personality and PR skills. Take for instance the Uncle at Thye Hong, who was handpicked to prepare Hokkien mee at the 2008 Singapore Day celebrations in New York and who was part of a delegation to promote Singapore food in California's Napa Valley in 2004. You can't walk past his stall without noticing his floral Hawaiian shirt and straw hat. Uncle even has a unique method for the preparation of Hokkien mee—he adds uncooked prawns to fry together with the noodles. According to him, this imparts extra sweetness to the mee and the prawns are more tender as they are not overcooked. The final product is something to behold, the suitably untidy noodles and the charred black bits in the gravy harking back to the rustic days of pushcart hawkers.

Newton Food Centre • 500 Clemenceau Ave North #01-69 S229495 • 5pm to 1am, open everyday • 96181221

DID YOU KNOW?

Some stalls serve Hokkien mee on an opeh leaf. The subtle, woody fragrance of the leaf is supposed to add to the flavour of the dish. The humble opeh leaf comes from the inner sheath of the bark of the betel nut tree and was used extensively in the good old days to wrap hawker food.

HOR FUN

THE STATE OF HOR FUN IN SINGAPORE IS PRETTY LACKLUSTRE. IT IS ONE
one of those uncelebrated staples that never makes it onto the
recommended list of any cze cha menu. Hor fun is always on the
"in case you don't want to spend more than $5 for your meal" list.
As a result, there aren't many star versions of hor fun out there. My
quest for the ultimate hor fun has two criterion: first, the noodles
must be slightly charred and so tasty they can be eaten on their
own. Finding good wok hei (breath of wok) flavour, which refers to
the slightly charred flavour derived from the breath of a really hot
wok, is very hard these days because some Singaporeans prefer
not to have their noodles charred due to health reasons. The rice
noodles cannot be a matted mass, but must be soft, lively and
smooth. Second, the gravy cannot be ordinary—it must have the
flavour that makes you think, "What the heck did they put in this?"

LESLIE'S PICK ✓

PRINCE COFFEE HOUSE

4.5 It is unusual that one of the best versions of hor fun is not found in a hawker stall, but in a good old Hainanese coffee house! Prince Coffee House was so named because it was first established at Shaw House along Beach Road where Prince cinema was located. After 13 years at Shaw House, they relocated to Coronation Plaza for the next 21 years before relocating back to Beach Road after a young investor came along. The beef hor fun here is excellent. The beef is tender and the sauce irresistible. And the hor fun—that smoky metallic wok hei (breath of wok) flavour is amazing. It is shiok food with retro furniture. The table mats, Pyrex cups and plates are the original ones used in the 1970s! (This stall is also recommended for its hawker western food.)

---

249 Beach Road S189757 • 11am to 9pm, open everyday • 64682008

KONG KEE SEAFOOD RESTAURANT

4.5 sang har hor fun The gravy for the sang har mee is so good that it can go with anything—so pour it over the hor fun too. Best of all, they manage to infuse the wonderful smoky wok hei (breath of wok) flavour into the hor fun. One of the best plates of hor fun I have eaten in a while.

611/613 Lor 31 Geylang S389550 • 11pm to 1am, open everyday • 64438221

CHANGI LORONG 108 FEI LAO SEAFOOD

4.5 The legendary hor fun hawker, Fei Lao (Old Fatty), may have passed on, but his legacy lives on with his nephew helming the wok, trying to emulate everything his famous uncle used to do. The wok hei (breath of wok) flavour of the hor fun is good, and the sauce is tasty. Overall, one of the best hor funs around, even if it is not as legendary as the original.

86 Bedok North St 4 #01-165 S460086 • 11am to 2pm and 5pm to 10pm, closed on Tuesdays • 63464116

NAM SENG WANTON MEE

4.25 The sauce for its special dish, venison hor fun, is addictive and satisfying. However, I was less enthusiastic about the hor fun as it lacked the smoky wok hei (breath of wok) flavour. The owner, Madam Leong, explained that this is because the landlords do not allow them to use a gas stove, so they have to use an electric hotplate which could not produce the wok hei effect. Still, definitely one of the tastiest versions of beef (or rather, venison) hor fun around. (This stall is also recommended for wanton mee.)

Far East Square • 25 China St #01-01 S049567 • 8am to 8pm, closed on Sundays

LORONG 9 BEEF KWAY TEOW

4.25 This stall dishes out one shiok plate of beef hor fun—the sauce is irresistibly tasty and the beef super tender. The smooth, wok hei (breath of wok) flavoured hor fun, combined with the super tender beef in black bean and chilli sauce, is just so shiok!

237 Geylang Lorong 9 S388756 • 4.30pm to 2.30am, open everyday

TECK HIN FRIED HOR FUN

4.25 You can smell the wok hei (breath of wok) while you are carrying your plate back to the table! I love the hor fun and the sauce, but I find the ingredients over

tenderised and lacking in flavour. It would have been perfect had the beef had a bit more bite, and had the prawns been less springy. Otherwise, very enjoyable.

Ghim Moh Market & Food Centre • 20 Ghim Moh Road #01-44 S270020 • 10am to 3pm, closed on Mondays

YUET LOY

4.25 This mom-and-pop cze cha stall dishes out some mean Cantonese-style favourites but is especially famous for its beef hor fun. The tender slices of beef are not overly marinated with bicarbonate, so they retain a good bite. The hor fun itself has that wonderful smoky wok hei (breath of work) aroma, which speaks volumes of Uncle's wok power! Also recommended: homemade tofu with beansprouts, beef kai lan and salted fish chicken.

Chinatown Complex Food Centre • 335 Smith St #02-151 S051335 • 12.15pm to 2pm and 6.15pm to 9pm, closed on Thursdays • 91704152

DID YOU KNOW?

Searing hor fun properly, to get it just burnt, but still soft and slippery, is a skill that differentiates the experts from the wok wannabes. It does not even require pork lard. Simply a hot wok, oil, kway teow, a big fire and lots of skill!

INDIAN ROJAK

A GOOD INDIAN ROJAK CAN MAKE YOU SWAY YOUR HEAD, INDIAN STYLE.
The key to the dish lies in the fiery red gravy, which is actually more fierce on the eyes than on the tongue. Indian rojak gravy is pretty sweet and is thickened with root vegetables. Usually, mashed up sweet potatoes form the base of the gravy, and this is spiked with chilli powder and other spices to give it some kick.

It is getting more difficult to find good Indian rojak in Singapore. Many stalls merely resell items bought from suppliers. So the number of good Indian rojak stalls can be counted with one hand.

DID YOU KNOW?

In Singapore, the sauce for Indian rojak is served separate from the ingredients. However, if you head up to Penang, where the dish is known as pasembur, the sauce is poured over the ingredients.

ABDHUS SALAM ROJAK

4.5 The rojak here is excellent and all items are homemade—the items are freshly fried and crisp, and the sauce tends to be a little spicier than usual. The coconut fritters really stood out, probably because they still use freshly grated coconut to make the fritters every day, so you can really taste the coconut. The vadai is also very good, and has a spicy punch which pairs well with the sauce. The potatoes were slightly undercooked though.

Ayer Rajah Food Centre • Blk 503 West Coast Dr Stall 73 S120503 • 10.30am to 11.30pm, open everyday

SIRAJ FAMOUS WATERLOO STREET INDIAN ROJAK (BUGIS)

4.5 The rojak here was fantabulous. Everything was fresh and the sauce was just perfect. Among my favourite was the vadai, which was crumbly and extremely pang (savoury). When you put it in your mouth, it just breaks apart, releasing the umami flavours of the lentils and spices. Shiokalingam nah! I don't remember the last time I was so excited about Indian rojak!

Albert Centre Market • 270 Queen St #01-120 S180270 • 9am to 7pm, closed last Monday of every month • 81395647

AL MAHBOOB INDIAN ROJAK

4.5 Most of the dough balls and prawn fritters are made on site, and they are excellent as they are freshly fried when you order. The sauce has a nice balance of sweet, spicy and savoury and is highly addictive. If you haven't eaten Indian rojak for a long time, this will make you fall in love with it all over again. (This stall is also recommended for its sup tulang.)

S11 Food Court • Blk 506 Tampines Ave 4 S520506 • 12.30pm to 9pm, closed on alternate Wednesdays • 67882257, 91322080

HABIB'S ROJAK

4.5 The Indian rojak here is excellent, being homemade. Must try items include the egg flour, fish fillet, coconut fritter, crispy prawn fritters, and be sure not to miss out on their potatoes. If there are any flaws, I would say that the sauce could have been a little more spiced up. However, when combined with the fried items, you will forget about it as the flavours just meld

MAHBOOB INDIAN ROJAK

together so well. Certainly worth the drive to the West Coast!

Ayer Rajah Food Centre • Blk 503 West Coast Dr Stall 68 S120503 • noon to 10.30pm, closed on alternate Mondays • 93358528

TEMASEK INDIAN ROJAK

4.25 This stall sells not one, not two, but three types of crispy fried shrimp! The sauce here is very good—hot, thick and rich, but still very well balanced, the kind of sauce that sauce fanatics would talk about. The hawkers here also make most of the items by hand, so you will find the size to be a little larger than elsewhere.

Tekka Market & Food Centre • 665 Buffalo Road #01-254 S210665 • 9am to 9pm, closed on alternate Mondays • 93350957

DID YOU KNOW?

Both Abdhus Salam Rojak stall and Habib's Rojak stall were run by hawkers who named their stalls after their sons when they were still children. Now, the sons have grown up and taken over the stalls, both of which are located at Ayer Rajah Food Centre. Talk about self-fulfilling prophecy and coincidence!

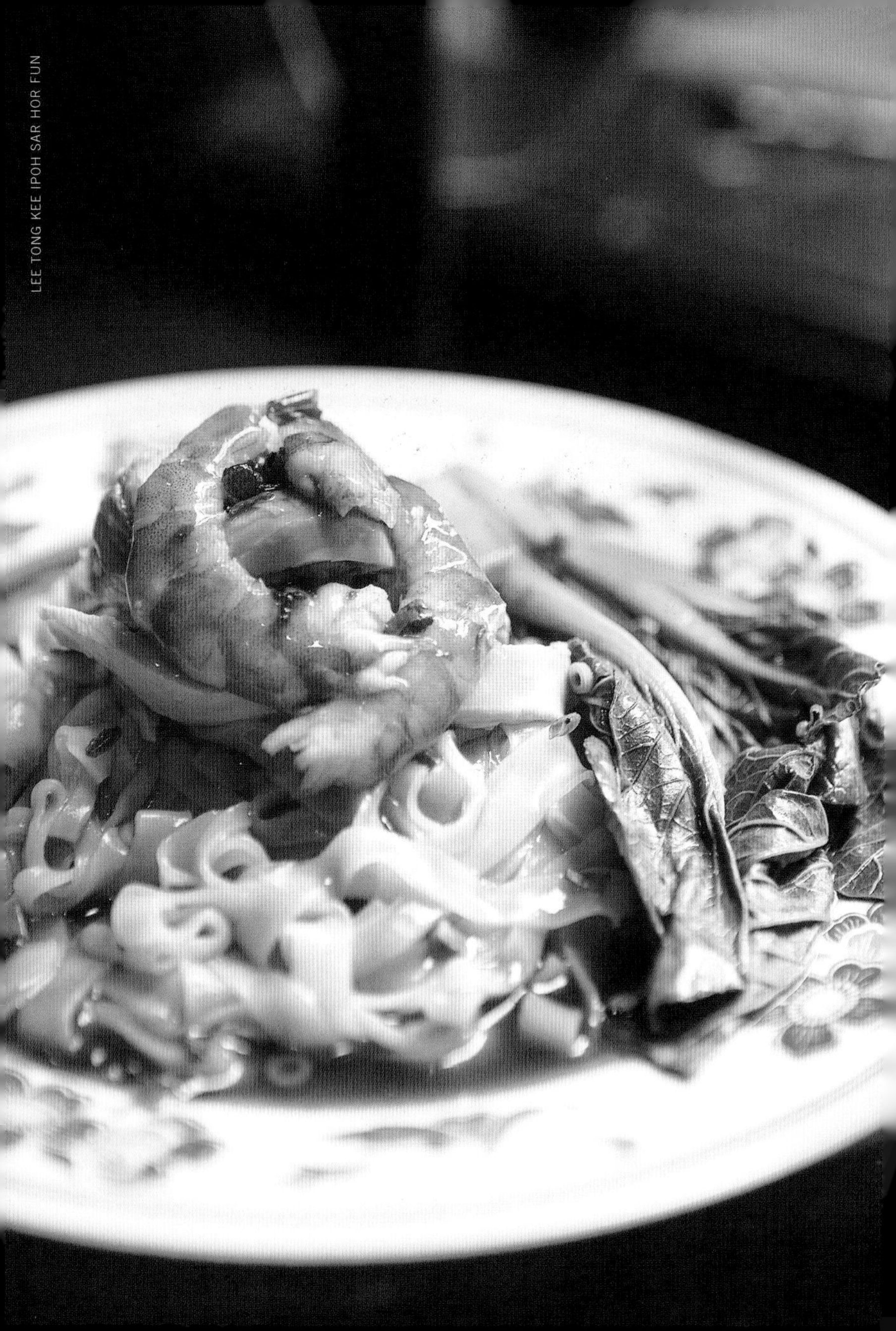

LEE TONG KEE IPOH SAR HOR FUN

IPOH HOR FUN

IPOH HOR FUN IS NOT FOUND IN IPOH. MORE ACCURATELY, THE SINGAPORE version of Ipoh hor fun is not found in Ipoh. The Singapore version is usually served with a brown soya sauce based gravy made from chicken stock. But the Ipoh version is a soup dish, served in chicken broth, making it more like kway teow tng. The Ipoh version of Ipoh hor fun can be found at Old Town White Coffee outlets in Singapore.

What defines Ipoh hor fun is the smooth texture of the thin flat rice noodles. Since the Singapore version is served dry, it is critical that you eat it as soon as it is served, or at least thoroughly mix the noodles together with the sauce before they start clumping up. This is especially important if you are in the habit of taking photos before you eat. Guess how I found this out?

LESLIE'S PICK ✓

WING KEE IPOH HOR FUN

4.6 **This is a seriously enjoyable, tongue-tingling, lip-smacking experience that is worth the trip to the end of Singapore! The hor fun is really smooth and the chicken cutlet is crispy on the outside, and juicy and savoury on the inside. Combined with that shiokalicious sauce, this is the real star of Changi Village Hawker Centre!**

Changi Village Market & Food Centre • 2 Changi Village Road #01-04 S500002 • Mondays to Fridays: 10.30am to 11pm, Saturdays and Sundays: 8am to midnight • 65456425

LEE TONG KEE IPOH SAR HOR FUN

4.5/4.0 ngau lam hor fun/Ipoh hor fun This must be one of the most well-established Ipoh hor fun places in Singapore— Mr Lee started selling his hor fun in 1948 in KL. Later, he left KL to flee from the racial riots, and opened a stall in Tanjong Pagar in 1969. The hor fun here is really smooth and slippery, and though the secret sauce complements the hor fun well, it could have a bit more oomph. I was bowled over by the ngau lam hor fun, which was one of the best versions of this dish I have come across.

278 South Bridge Road S058827 • 10am to 9pm, open everyday • 62260417

SHI HUI YUAN HOR FUN SPECIALTY

4.5 The hor fun is excellent and you can tell from the taste of the gravy that it is still made with much passion. I suspect that they never make a batch of sauce from scratch—there will be some leftover every day, to which they will add new ingredients, and make gravy for the next day. That means theoretically that there might be molecules of stuff in there from 1969! Note that this is celebrity chef Eric Teo's favourite haunt.

Mei Chin Food Centre • 159 Mei Chin Road #02-33 S140519 • 7.30am to 2pm, closed on Mondays and Tuesdays

TUCK KEE (IPOH) SAH HOR FUN

4.5 Tuck Kee has been in business for a long time and it has a loyal following. There are not many places in Singapore where you can find crayfish hor fun and this place is no doubt the most famous. This stall caught my attention with its very reasonably priced crayfish hor fun. The portions are large: a plate comprises two half crayfish and some big prawns. Once you get the dish, mix the sauce quickly so

that it spreads evenly throughout the hor fun strands. I also recommend the sui gao at this stall for they are generous with the prawns.

531A Upper Cross St #02-41A S051531 • 11am to 3pm, closed on Sundays

FUNAN WENG IPOH HOR FUN

4.25 What makes this hor fun stand out is a dollop of specially brewed herbal dark soya sauce, which is added before the hor fun is bathed in the more conventional light hor fun gravy. This gives the hor fun a certain kick you don't get anywhere else, though some might find the herbal taste a little overpowering if they're not big on anything herbal. Otherwise, the hor fun is very smooth, and the tiger prawns a good size.

32 Maxwell Road #01-07 S069115 • Mondays to Fridays: 11am to 9pm, Saturdays to Sundays: noon to 8.30pm, closed on public holidays • www.funanweng.com • 96990498

DID YOU KNOW?

It is said that Ipoh produces the smoothest, silkiest hor fun noodles because of the quality of the water there.

KOPI & TOAST

THERE IS SOMETHING VERY SINGAPOREAN, EVEN VERY PATRIOTIC ABOUT ordering a cup of kopi C siew dai (coffee with evaporated milk and less sugar) and kaya toast. It makes you feel very local. How many of us take pride in bringing our foreign guests for a cup of kopi and teaching them how to order it properly? I find it most interesting to try to explain the meaning of kopi O tid loh (extra strong black coffee with sugar). Honestly, a hot cup of kopi C with kaya toast is the best $3 you can ever spend on afternoon tea.

Although I have an espresso machine at home, when it comes down to it, I will still go back to using the trusty old coffee-stained coffee sock. Call me Ah Beng, call me Ah Peh, call me an anti-barista coffee ignoramus, I don't care. Nothing beats a cup of kopi C (coffee with evaporated milk) brewed in a sock! Smooth, sweet, syrupy and brimming with pang-ness (fragrance)—shiokalicious!

LESLIE'S PICK ✓

CHIN MEE CHIN COFFEE SHOP

4.5 **kopi & raisin buns** Everything about this place is just so original—from the shop interior to their food! They still heat their coffee over charcoal fire and bake their own buns and scones. The buns may not look as glossy as the ones in fancy new bakeries, but they sure taste good. With thick slices of butter, these buns still get me salivating just by looking at them. The kopi here is excellent: full bodied and robust with little acidity. In the morning, the favourites are their custard puffs and luncheon meat buns.

204 East Coast Road S428903 • 8.30am to 4pm, closed on Mondays • 63450419

KILLINEY KOPITIAM

4.75/4.25 kopi/bread According to the *Singapore Book of Records*, the original Killiney Kopitiam is the oldest existing Hainanese coffeeshop, having been around since 1919.

Originally known as Qiong Xin He, the coffeeshop was bought over by Mr Woon in 1993 and rebranded as Killiney Kopitiam. The kopi C is the best I've ever had—it was smooth and very aromatic, with only a slight tinge of bitterness and acidity. Try their fresh bread with butter and kaya first thing in the morning. They are super soft and you can really savour the taste of butter and kaya. To get the best experience, make sure you visit the original shop along Killiney Road!

67 Killiney Road S239525 • Mondays, Wednesdays to Saturdays: 6am to 11pm, Tuesdays, Sundays and public holidays: 6am to 6pm • www.killiney-kopitiam.com

TONG YA COFFEESHOP

4.5 kopi & kaya toast Make sure you order the grade A kaya toast, which has been toasted and re-toasted several times to achieve super crispy and brittle bread that is excellent with the cold butter and homemade kaya. The kaya has that nice pandan fragrance, and is the pale green and lumpy type, which I prefer to the smooth brown version. Though they don't roast their own coffee beans anymore, they still retain their secret blend. Their kopi is fragrant with little acidity, but with a good bitter bite.

36 Keong Saik Road S089143 • weekdays: 11am to 2.30pm and 5.30pm to 10.30pm, weekends: 11am to 2.30pm and 5.30pm to 11pm, closed on alternate Wednesdays • 62235083

YA KUN KAYA TOAST

4.5 Unlike your normal toast, crunching into Ya Kun's kaya toast is almost like eating crackers and kaya, except that you can never get that airy crunchy texture with crackers. The contrast between the light and airy crispy toast, cold butter and sweet creamy kaya is a simple yet extremely satisfying experience. The soft-boiled eggs here are just about as perfect as soft-boiled eggs can be, an amazing feat considering it is done consistently without a thermometer or timer. Although there are many branches, the eggs at the original shop at Far East Square are still the best!

Far East Square • 18 China St #01-01 S049560 • weekdays: 7.30am to 7pm, weekends: 8am to 5pm • www.yakun.com

SENG HONG COFFEESHOP

4.5/4.25 steamed bread/ kopi Not only do they steam their lohti (bread) here, they still boil water in an ancient pot which, I am told, is at least 70 years old! The steamed bread is very shiok, and with the peanut butter, it is one of the best things I have ever eaten. The kopi is thick, full-bodied, creamy and fragrant. It can be a bit on the bitter side, but this can be easily fixed with the addition of evaporated milk.

58 Lengkok Bahru S150058 • 6am to 6pm, closed on alternate Sundays

GOOD MORNING NANYANG CAFÉ

4.5/4.0 kopi/scones & ciabatta with kaya The kopi here ranks as one of the best in Singapore—it is smooth, creamy and fragrant, with very little bitterness and acidity. This place is unique because it is the only place I know of in Singapore where you can get freshly baked scones with kopi and teh C (tea with evaporated milk). My standard order is a teh C kosong (tea with evaporated milk with no sugar) and their signature orange ciabatta with freshly made kaya. You will find me here every Monday at 1.30pm!

Telok Ayer Hong Lim Green Community Centre • 20 Upper Pickering St S058284 • Mondays to Fridays: 7.30am to 7.30pm Saturdays, Sundays and public holidays: 8.30am to 5.30pm

DID YOU KNOW?

"Ah Gong" was the nickname affectionately given to the man who spent 54 years brewing kopi at Killiney Kopitiam. In 2004, Ah Gong returned to Hainan Island and passed on at the age of 86 after having served close to a million cups of kopi (assuming he made 500 cups a day for 54 years, with 2 weeks' break each year).

The Grandstand • 200 Turf Club Road
#01-34a S287994 • 9am to 9pm, open
everyday

RUI XING COFFEE

4.5 **kopi** Uncle tells me that he
gets his own special blend
from a supplier. The kopi was strong,
full bodied, aromatic with little acidity,
and had lots of creamy caramel flavour
from an adequate shot of evaporated
milk. Only here can you find a cup of
satisfaction at 5am in the morning,
and all for 70 cents.

Blk 216 Food Centre • Bedok North St 1
#01-42 S460216 • 3am to 11am, closed
on Mondays

COFFEE HUT

4.5/4.25 **kaya toast/kopi**
The kaya toast is
delightfully light, crispy and crumbly
on the outside but soft on the inside.
The butter is the right consistency
and not overly thick, while the kaya
is fragrant but not sickly sweet. The
kopi is one of the best in the area.
There is that spiciness when the coffee
first hits the palate, followed by the
full-bodied taste of the evaporated

milk and coffee, finishing off with a
lingering aroma at the back of the
throat after swallowing. This stall
also serves buns and French toast.

Berseh Food Centre • 166 Jalan Besar
#02-43 S208877 • weekdays: 7am to
3pm, weekends: 7am to noon • 90108311

ORIOLE COFFEE ROASTERS

4.25 If you want to experience
the ultimate version of a
typical Singapore breakfast, order
the Straits Seven Set here. It comes
with a cup of kopi, made with quality
espresso in a traditional cup complete
with latte art, a pair of 62 degree
sous vide eggs, using farm fresh,
hormone and antibiotic-free eggs, and
homemade kaya on traditional lohti
(bread). Yes, it is more expensive
than the usual, but it is worth it.

10/10A Jiak Chuan Road S089264 •
Mondays to Saturdays: 8.30am to 10pm,
Sundays and public holidays: 8.30am to
6pm • 62248131

LESLIE'S TIP

**For the best soft-boiled eggs ever, visit the original Ya Kun at Far East Square in the
mornings, when Mr Algie Loi makes them. Algie is the tou chiew (master) of making
soft-boiled eggs, controlling water temperature by instinct, while making his eggs
in Milo tin cans!**

KWAY CHAP

IF YOU'RE THE SORT THAT DOES NOT LIKE TO WASTE FOOD, THEN YOU WOULD be very happy with kway chap. Every part of the pig is eaten in this dish, including the rectum, fallopian tubes, small and large intestines, as well as the skin and the meat. Nothing is wasted. When eating kway chap, I look out for good lor (braising sauce)— it must be pang (fragrant). The kway (broad rice noodles) must be smooth. When the kway is served, it must be really hot and look almost transparent.

As for the pork dishes, my favourites are the skin and pork belly. Don't think for a moment that cooking kway chap is just about boiling piggy parts together. The expert hawker knows the importance of timing and often cooks by instinct to produce various offals perfectly cooked!

TONG LOK KWAY CHAP

4.5 The uncle here washes the intestines so meticulously that there is no off-putting flavour. The real killer, however, is the ter kah (pig's trotters). Uncle chops them up before braising them in a special thick spiced gravy till the collagen turns into that sticky slimy goodness that we all love. Definitely shiok and not to be missed!

114 Pasir Panjang Road S118539 • 7am to 3pm, closed on Sundays, Mondays and public holidays

LAO SAN KWAY CHAP

4.5 I never really placed much emphasis on the kway (flat noodles) in kway chap till I had it here, and realised how wonderfully smooth and slurpilicious a good kway can be! The lor (braising sauce) is one of the best I have come across. It has the perfect balance between sweet, salty and savoury, and is rather addictive. The innards are excellent—velvety and tender, without any off-putting stench. The passion that fuels this

wonderful bowl of kway chap lies with the old Uncle who starts preparing at 11.30pm in order to get the food ready for the next day by 6am. He then sells the dishes till 3pm before heading home to sleep for six hours. That's a solid 15 and a half hours of work a day!

Blk 232 Ang Mo Kio Ave 3 S560232 • 6am to midnight, closed on Mondays

TO-RICOS GUO SHI

4.25 The kway chap here is one of the most famous in Singapore as evidenced by the perpetual queue. The flavour of the lor (braising sauce) is very pang (savoury). Uncle tells me that he torches the ter kah (pig's trotters) the day before, leaves them overnight and braises the trotters for only one and a half hours the next morning.

Old Airport Road Food Centre • 51 Old Airport Road #01-135/36 S390051 • 11.30am to 4.30pm, closed on Mondays

BLANCO COURT GARDEN STREET KWAY CHAP

4.0 This is one of those heritage hawker stalls with a sterling reputation. While the kway chap here is good, it's not exceptional. Everything is above average—the lor (braising sauce) is good, and the kway (flat noodles) smooth, but no item stands out.

Serangoon Gardens Market & Food Centre • 49A Serangoon Garden Way Stall 21 S555945 • 8am to 3pm, closed on Mondays

ROXY LAKSA

LAKSA

NOTHING HITS THE SPOT LIKE A GOOD BOWL OF LAKSA. I LOVE MY LAKSA gravy with a lot of hae bee (dried shrimp). You can tell a good bowl of laksa by simply rubbing the porcelain spoon on the bottom of the bowl and sensing the grittiness of the dried prawn shells. Unfortunately, laksa is not the healthiest of dishes, and the no-holds-barred, gimme-your-best-shot versions are usually not something I would recommend for those who have problems with indigestion or cholesterol. That is why I appreciate the more soupy version of laksa, as I can finish a whole bowl without feeling too jerlak (satiated) or unhealthy!

The word "laksa" refers to the rice noodles which we know as thick beehoon. These noodles are used in Penang assam laksa and Singapore laksa, which is why both dishes are termed "laksa" even though they are vastly different.

LESLIE'S PICK ✓

MARINE PARADE LAKSA

4.5 **This is the laksa I grew up on and it is my favourite. There are three outlets—one at Bedok with the signboard: "The Original Katong Laksa Since 1950s, Also Known As Marine Parade Laksa"; one at Queensway with the signboard: "Janggut Laksa, The Original Katong Laksa Since 1950s"; and one at Roxy Square. The business is family run, keeping to the original recipe. The gravy has oomph with enough hae bee (dried shrimp) to give you an umami kick!**

Blk 128 Bedok North St 2 #01-02 S460128 • 9.30am to 5pm, open everyday

Queensway Shopping Centre • 1 Queensway #01-59 S149053 • 10am to 9.15pm, open everyday

Roxy Square • 50 East Coast Road #01-64 S428769 • 9.30am to 5pm open everyday

328 KATONG LAKSA

4.5 The laksa gravy at this stall is still one of the best around, although it seemed even better in the days when Lao Ban Niang was cooking for one stall. Back then, the best part of the meal was finding the minced hae bee (dried shrimp) at the bottom of the bowl. Nowadays, it is minced too finely so you can't really enjoy the grainy bits in your mouth. Nonetheless, it is still one satisfying bowl of laksa.

216 East Coast Road S428914 • 8am to 10pm, open everyday • 97328163

CANTONESE DELIGHTS

4.5 The couple at this stall really knows how to cook a great curry, and the laksa gravy they serve with yong tau foo is just as good. Frankly, I feel that their laksa dishes warrant an entire stall by itself instead of playing second fiddle to the rest of their noodles dishes. Just a note about the chilli: it can be quite salty, so don't add too much before tasting it first.

Hong Lim Food Centre • 531A Upper Cross St #02-03 S051531 • 9am to 3pm, closed on weekends • 91051904

ROXY LAKSA

4.25 Roxy Laksa was an icon in Katong in the 1960s, together with Marine Parade Laksa. It relocated to East Coast Lagoon Food Village when Roxy cinema closed to make way for Roxy Square. The hawker here, Mike Lim, is the grandson of the original hawker. He continues to use freshly squeezed coconut milk, quality spices and sua lor (wild prawns) as he is dedicated to keeping his family's laksa recipe alive. While eating here was not a Holy Grail moment, I loved the citrus scent of freshly squeezed coconut infused with lemongrass, and the fresh chiffonade of laksa leaves, assaulting my olfactory glands. If you wish for more oomph, just add an extra spoon of pounded dried shrimps.

East Coast Lagoon Food Village • 1220 East Coast Parkway Stall 48 S468960 • Mondays to Fridays: 10.30am to 9pm, weekends and public holidays: 8.30am to 9pm • 96302321

BETEL BOX: THE LIVING BISTRO

4.25 laksa goreng Helming the kitchen of this restaurant-cum-museum is veteran chef Uncle Ben, an experienced Nonya-Eurasian chef who used to cook at Casa Bom Vento. The laksa goreng is his signature dish. It is essentially a dried form of laksa. You can think of it as a laksa flavoured Hokkien mee. I really like this dish, and it's certainly worth a trip to try.

200 Joo Chiat Road #01-01 S427471 • 8am to 10pm, open everyday • 64405540

KATONG LAKSA

4.25 This stall at Telok Kurau is the stall that can officially claim to have first registered the name "Katong Laksa". The gravy is nice and savoury, and as good as (some say better than) the other more famous

stalls. It's sure to satisfy your laksa craving!

1 Telok Kurau Road (opposite SPC Petrol Station) S423756 • 8am to 3.30pm, open everyday • 64404585, 98559401

SUNGEI ROAD LAKSA

4.25 The distinct characteristic of this laksa has to be the gravy—it is much lighter than what I am used to, and still has flavour without making you feel jerlak (satiated). The owners here are very generous with the haam (cockles), so lovers of this mollusk will be very happy. If you still want to eat laksa that is cooked with charcoal fire, you better hurry down to this stall which made it to *Newsweek's* 2012 list of 101 best places to eat in the world!

Jalan Shui Kopitiam • 27 Jalan Berseh #01-100 S200027 • 9am to 6pm, closed on the first Wednesday of every month

FAMOUS SUNGEI ROAD TRISHAW LAKSA

4.25 The laksa comes with a very light gravy that is more soupy than grainy, so you can drink a lot of it without feeling jerlak (satiated). That does not mean that the flavour is compromised though. The soup is fragrant and has the savoury sweetness of hae bee (dried shrimp) that I enjoy.

Hong Lim Food Centre • 531A Upper Cross St #02-67 S510531 • 10.30am to 6.30pm, closed on Sundays

THE STORY OF JANGGUT

Marine Parade Laksa was iconic in the 1950s and 1960s as it was where Janggut, the inventor of Katong Laksa, served up his famous laksa. In laksa lore, Janggut is a legend of mythic proportions. He started off as an itinerant hawker plying the Katong and Joo Chiat areas with his amazing laksa dish. He was nicknamed "Janggut" because he had prosperous mole hair ("Janggut" means "beard" in Malay).

In 1963, after being forced off the streets by the government, he began selling laksa at his brother's corner coffeeshop stall, Marine Parade Laksa, at the junction of Ceylon Road and East Coast Road. He did so only on weekends. His unique style of laksa, to be served with a spoon, not chopsticks, became known as Katong Laksa. Unfortunately, Marine Parade Laksa closed in 1978 due to the increase in rental.

Today, Janggut's daughter Madam Ng is serving up her father's famous laksa at Queensway. The Marine Parade Laksa brand has spawned three stalls, with the Queensway branch calling itself Janggut Laksa!

928 YISHUN LAKSA

4.0 This is a good bowl of laksa, but I wouldn't drive all the way to the north to eat it when there are so many good stalls in the east. The first thing I noticed is that the laksa leaves are put into a food processor, so the dish lacks the fresh laksa leaf fragrance you get when the leaves are hand sliced. Perhaps it was just the batch of gravy that day but I didn't get that nice savoury oomph that I look for in a good laksa.

Blk 928 Yishun Central 1 S760928 • 10am to 7pm, open everyday • 97319586

DEPOT ROAD ZHEN SHAN MEI CLAYPOT LAKSA

4.0 This famous laksa stall is also known as the Depot Road Laksa stall. It serves up a no-holds-barred, give-me-your-best-shot kind of laksa that is great for people who are young, but probably not the best for people with cholesterol problems.

Alexandra Village Food Centre • 120 Bukit Merah Lane 1 #01-75 S150120 • 8.30am to 3.30pm, open everyday • 90889203

LOR MEE IS A HOKKIEN DISH THAT ORIGINATED FROM XIAMEN IN FUJIAN province. However, like many of our hawker dishes, even though lor mee has its origins in China, it has since evolved into something unique to Singapore, such that it is nothing like the version you get in Xiamen today.

The beauty of lor mee lies in the contrast of textures. The most prominent is the contrast between the sticky, gooey, slimy sauce and the crunchy, fried bits. For me, the shiokness of lor mee comes from nibbling on the crunchy, salty and savoury fried nuggets of flavoured batter coated in the slimy, sweet, garlicky and sourish sauce. It is not easy to get so many textures and tastes in perfect balance. But when it happens, you have a bowl of gooey goodness to behold.

LESLIE'S PICK ✓

BUKIT PURMEI LOR MEE

4.5 **The owner, Mr Teo, manages to get the many textures and tastes of lor mee in perfect balance. The vinegar here is specially flavoured with a secret blend of spices and this very important condiment gives the lor (braising sauce) a well balanced and rounded taste which coats the whole palate. If you want to make the lor mee extra special, ask Mr Teo for his special stash of pork belly that he prepares for his regulars, and you will get the ultimate bowl of lor mee!**

109 Bukit Purmei Ave #01-157 S090109 • 7.30am to 3.30pm, closed on Mondays

YUAN CHUN FAMOUS LOR MEE

4.25 The lor (braising sauce) here is quite unique— thick, but not as sticky as other places. People with weak chopstick skills might struggle a little to pull the thick and flat noodles up to mix with the sauce! The sauce itself is very flavourful, and the combination of the sauce with the pork belly and the fried prawn cakes is excellent. However, I found the kee smell of the noodles too overpowering, and would have liked more sauce.

Amoy Street Food Centre • 7 Maxwell Road #02-79/80 S069111 • 8.30am till around 4pm when sold out, closed on Mondays and Tuesdays

LOR MEE 178

4.25 The special draw at this stall is the famous shark meat fritters which are added to the lor mee. The lor (braising sauce) is very tasty and they give lots of crispy crunchy stuff that is simply awesome. I also like their crispy meat fritters, which are very pang (fragrant). There are some things I miss though, like the braised pork, ngoh hiang and braised egg.

Tiong Bahru Market & Food Centre • 30 Seng Poh Road #02-58 S168898 • 6am to 9.30pm, closed on Wednesdays

WEI NAN WANG HOCK KIAN LOR MEE

4.0 If you are really hungry and looking for a tasty, affordable meal, head down to this stall and you can have a nice big bowl of lor mee with lots of ingredients! The lor mee tastes quite good—the sauce is not overly thick, and has a sourish tang to it. The crispy fried stuff soaked in the lor (braising sauce) is shiok!

BUKIT PURMEI LOR MEE

Market Street Food Centre (also known as Golden Shoe Food Centre) • 50 Market St #03-03 S048940 • 9.30am to 3.30pm, open everyday

XIN MEI XIANG

4.0 This famous stall is well-known for its fantastic lor mee, and it was sold out the first time I came. I found the ingredients fresh, and the fried snapper was generous. I also loved the black vinegar, which was really smooth and piquant.

Old Airport Road Food Centre • 51 Old Airport Road #01-116 S390051 • 7am to 2.30pm, closed on Thursdays

DID YOU KNOW?

Traditionally, a spice called cao guo (black cardamom) is often used in lor mee, alongside other spices like cinnamon and star anise. Black vinegar and chopped garlic are also served alongside to elevate the flavour of the lor (braising sauce), which is made from braising pork and duck.

NASI LEMAK

GOOD NASI LEMAK NEEDS TO BE MADE WITH GOOD RICE, THE SORT WITH BITE.
You should be able to taste and smell the coconut and pandan leaves emanating from the rice, and the sambal tumis (stir-fried sambal) should be on the sweet side, yet have a wonderful savoury taste that hits the umami spot. The combination of the warm coconut-flavoured rice with appetising sambal tumis is shiok!

There are two camps when it comes to nasi lemak: those who favour the Malay version and those who prefer the Chinese version (perhaps because you can order luncheon meat with this version). Traditionally, the Malay version's rice is cooked in a steamer, also known as nasi lemak kukus. The Malay version uses Malaysian grown rice instead of Thai jasmine rice, which is used by the Chinese version. Malaysian rice tends to be lighter and less sticky, lacking the more chewy bite of the Thai variety.

LESLIE'S PICK ★✓

PONGGOL NASI LEMAK CENTRE

4.5 **Some people say they are overrated, but personally I think Ponggol Nasi Lemak manages to get the basics right. The quality of the rice is very good—it has good bite and its fragrance is accentuated by coconut and pandan. The sweet sambal tumis (stir-fried sambal) goes very well with the rice, and is not overly spicy. If there is anything I would mark down, it would be the chicken wings, which I felt could be tastier.**

965 Upper Serangoon Road S534721 • 6pm to 5am, closed on Thursdays • 62810020, 97805597

238 Tanjong Katong Road S437026 • 5.30pm to 2.30am, closed on Thursdays • 62870020, 63483383

NASI LEMAK KUKUS

4.5 "Nasi lemak kukus" means that the rice has been steamed over water rather than cooked in water. This traditional way of cooking nasi lemak results in rice that has more grainy bite. By the way, the rice is free flow and only costs $1! The sambal tumis (stir-fried sambal) is excellent, and they have a whole series of different dishes you can choose from to accompany your nasi lemak.

908 Upper Thomson Road S787111 • 6pm to 3am, closed on Mondays • 82229517

SELERA RASA NASI LEMAK

4.5 This nasi lemak is so shiok that the Sultan of Brunei gets his embassy to buy it for him when he comes to Singapore! They use basmati rice, which gives a lighter texture, better flavour and beautifully separated grains. The sambal tumis (stir-fried sambal) is equally shiok, and you should not miss the sambal cuttlefish that they offer as an optional side dish.

Adam Road Food Centre • 2 Adam Road #01-02 S289876 • 7am to 6pm, closed on Fridays

CHONG PANG NASI LEMAK

4.25 Chong Pang uses traditional rice that is lighter and doesn't clump as much as jasmine rice. Second generation owner Edmund Lee is not heavy-handed with the coconut milk, and that's good. The chilli is bright and tangy. What Chong Pang does really well are the chicken wings and fried ikan kuning, which are lightly battered and so crunchy.

This is the place to head to if you are hungry in the middle of the night as they close at 7am.

447 Sembawang Road S758458 • 5pm to 7am, open everyday • 96551868

EPOK EPOK CENTRAL

4.25 All I needed was one whiff of the steaming rice to know this nasi lemak would be good. The sambal belacan was very shiok, and on the sweetish side which I feel should be the case with nasi lemak. It also had that wonderful savoury taste of belacan which hits the umami spot. They put in special effort to sandwich the chilli between two pieces of banana leaves for that added fragrance. (This stall is also recommended for its curry puff.)

Eunos Crescent Market & Food Centre • 4A Eunos Crescent #01-09 S402004 • 7am to 7pm, closed on Mondays • 96958889

BOON LAY POWER NASI LEMAK

4.25 There is no doubt that the rice and chilli here are a powerful combination. This is not traditional nasi lemak as they use

Thai rice, which I think is better as it retains moisture better. The soft, moist rice has a wonderful coconut fragrance, and is almost perfect. The chicken wings are fresh, but not particularly impressive.

Boon Lay Place Market & Food Centre • 221B Boon Lay Place #01-06 S641221 • 7am to 3am, open everyday

Blk 474 Tampines St 43 S520474 • 7am to 3am, open everyday

BALI NASI LEMAK

4.0 This place is famous for its black chicken wings— chicken wings coated in a sweet and savoury kecap manis-based sauce (Indonesian soya sauce), which is very shiok. I really like the Hainanese-style curry chicken wings—the gravy is darn shiok and is sure to satisfy your umami craving. The rice is fragrant, though not the best that I have tasted. The sambal chilli is on the sweeter side.

2 Geylang Lorong 15 (Geylang side) S388596 • 6pm to 4am, open everyday

DID YOU KNOW?

The Malay style rice is very light and starchy. It is best eaten cold, wrapped in a banana leaf. The Chinese style nasi lemak uses jasmine rice and is best eaten hot.

RUMAH MAKAN MINANG

NASI PADANG

NASI PADANG MEANS MANY THINGS TO MANY PEOPLE, BUT FOR ME, IT IS all about the chicken korma (Indonesian chicken curry), which is also known as gulai ayam, ayam korma or ayam opor. My parents ordered this for me as a kid, and the first taste of it changed my life forever. The creamy, citrus-coconuty flavour of that non-spicy curry was incredible.

My other favourite nasi padang dish is bergedil (fried mashed potato fritter). I can down half a dozen of these at one go, especially when I have chicken korma gravy to drown them in. Another famous classic nasi padang dish is beef rendang. I have always enjoyed beef rendang with a nice, tender, melt-in-your-mouth texture. However, I was told that authentic beef rendang is supposed to have a bit of a chew, so that the flavour develops in your mouth.

LESLIE'S PICK ✓

RUMAH MAKAN MINANG

4.5 tahu telor & paru belado (beef lung) **The legacy of Hajjah Rosemah and Minangkabau food lives on at Rumah Makan Minang. It is good to know that there is a new generation that will take over the baton. Most of the dishes served here are excellent. The one I always order is the tahu telor (deep-fried tofu), which is superlative. It is served with a sweet sauce, bringing a bit of respite in the midst of the explosion of spices from the other dishes. A plate of rice accompanied by a few dishes will surely hit that gastronomic G-spot! Also recommended: ikan bakar, beef rendang, ayam belado hijau and botok botok. (This stall is recommended for teh tarik.)**

18 Kandahar St S198884 • 8am to 6pm, open everyday • 62944805

HAJJAH MONA NASI PADANG

4.5 My first mouthful of chicken korma at this stall was a Holy Grail moment. The gravy was so full of lemongrass, the fragrance seemed to waft out of my nostrils like the flames of a fire-breathing dragon. From the ayam opor to the beef rendang to the sayur lodeh (mild curry vegetables), you can taste passion and quality in each mouthful.

Geylang Serai Market & Food Centre • 1 Geylang Serai #02-166 S402001 • 8am to 7pm, closed on Wednesdays • 82826902

NASI PADANG RIVER VALLEY

4.5 beef rendang & egg omelette While some may complain that the food here is too sweet, not spicy enough and rather expensive, it certainly doesn't bother me! The quality of food here is very good and the family is so meticulous in food preparation—they even squeeze their own coconut milk! Also recommended: chicken korma and sambal sotong (squid).

54 Zion Road S247779 • 11am to 8.30pm, closed on Mondays and public holidays • 67343383

NASI PADANG SABAR MENANTI II

4.5/4.25 chicken korma & bergedil/beef rendang Although this stall is an offshoot of the original Sabar Menanti, I find the food here better! The chicken korma (called opor ayam here) is shiok!

The beef rendang is dry, with chunks of tender beef coated with a fragrant spicy paste that contains kaffir lime and tumeric leaves to give it a nice spicy citrus flavour.

747 North Bridge Road S198715 • 6am to 5pm, closed on Sundays and public holidays

RABIAH MUSLIM FOOD NASI MELAYU

4.25 If you like sotong (squid) with roe, you will definitely want to make a beeline for this stall. I really enjoyed the peanuts with ikan bilis, as well as the bergedil (fried mashed potato fritter). While the sayur lodeh (mild curry vegetables) was quite average, the assam fish was very good. If you want your sotong (squid) full of roe though, make sure you behave when you are making your orders!

Whampoa Drive Makan Place (Whampoa Food Centre) • 90 Whampoa Dr #01-34 S320090 • 10am to 6pm, closed on Sundays

NO NAME NASI PADANG

4.25 mutton rendang & ayam merah The best dish at this stall is the mutton rendang—the spices are just right and the meat tender. The ayam merah (red chicken curry) has a good combination of sweet and sour, with just a tinge of heat, which suits me very well. Unfortunately, the chicken korma and the sambal sotong (squid) are not up to par.

Khong Guan Restaurant • Blk 49 Stirling Road S141049 • 7am to 5pm, closed on Sundays and public holidays

ISTIMEWA NASI PADANG

4.25/4.0 ayam goreng/ beef rendang, sambal sotong & sayur lodeh The chicken is lightly spiced, tender and juicy on the inside while the skin was crisp and thin like nori sheets (toasted seaweed)—definitely worth the 10-minute wait! The sayur lodeh (mild curry vegetables) was very good, though I must say that it lacked addictive quality. The beef rendang was on the sweet side and very fragrant though the meat was a little tough. The quality of the sotong (squid) was excellent—each one tender and full of roe, but again, the sambal did not have "wow" factor.

DID YOU KNOW?

Beef rendang is so closely associated with nasi padang that most people think it is an indigenous part of Malay cuisine. But it was invented by the Minangkabau, inhabitants of West Sumatra whose capital is Padang. Traditionally, it is cooked for a long time until all dried up and can be kept for a month without refrigeration.

Blk 28 Hoy Fatt Road S151028 • 10am
to 3pm, closed on Sundays • 96301272,
97260239

RENDEZVOUS RESTAURANT

4.25/4.0 sambal brinjal/
beef rendang The
chicken korma was a disappointment,
though the combination of the eggs
and sambal for the sambal eggs
worked remarkably well. The beef
rendang was nice, though lacking
oomph. The best dish was the sambal
brinjal, which was cooked just nice,
striking a balance between the natural
sweetness of the brinjal and the
sambal. The cuttlefish sambal was
very good except that it had spent a
little too long in the bain-marie and
had lost that bounce to the bite. This
place has been around for a long
time and is a nasi padang institution.
However, of late, standards seem to
have dropped a bit.

The Central • #02-72/73 6 Eu Tong Sen St
S059817 • 11am to 9pm, open everyday •
63397508

WARONG NASI PARIAMAN

4.25/4.0 ayam pangang/
beef rendang
Come during lunch and you could be
hard-pressed to find a seat! One of the
most famous nasi padang eateries in
Singapore, the current stallholder is the
third generation owner. He insists that
the stall's traditional padang recipes
continue unadulterated. The ayam
pangang is good—the caramelised,

char-grilled flavour of the spices on the
chicken skin is really shiok, though the
gravy is too light. The beef rendang
is another signature dish here, and is
quite fiery, appealing to those who like
more heat in their food.

738 North Bridge Road S198706 • 7.30am
to 3pm, closed on Sundays and public
holidays

SINAR PAGI NASI PADANG

4.0 chicken rendang & bergedil You
can easily spot this stall by
the numerous awards pasted on the
front of the stall. The food is indeed
delicious—the chicken rendang has
that special oomph. The bergedil
(fried mashed potato fritter) is a little
chunky, moist and savoury on the
inside—just the way I like it.

Geylang Serai Market & Food Centre • 1
Geylang Serai #02-137 S402001 • 9am
to 10.30pm, closed every fortnight on
Mondays and Thursdays

DID YOU KNOW?

A good bergedil (fried mashed potato
fritter) is made from local potatoes
which tend to be buttery and slightly
sweet. These potatoes should be
roughly pounded so that they are still
a little chunky and should be moist
and savoury on the inside.

NGOH HIANG

IT IS HARD TO FIND HANDMADE NGOH HIANG THESE DAYS. WITH THE ADVENT OF commercially made ngoh hiang, most stall owners have opted to be traders instead of chefs. It is even harder to find handmade Teochew ngoh hiang as most stalls sell factory made Hokkien style ngoh hiang. Teochew ngoh hiang uses a lot of water chestnuts in the prawn rolls and water chestnut slices. Teochews also love yam, so they add yam to their pork rolls. Having tasted handmade ngoh hiang, I refuse to waste my precious calories on factory made ones and only support passionate hawkers who make theirs from scratch!

DID YOU KNOW?

The original ngoh hiang comprised five different types of fritters—prawn, pork rolls, pork liver rolls, egg rolls and pork sausage. Others think that the term "ngoh hiang" refers to the five spices that are often added to the liver and pork rolls.

LESLIE'S PICK ★✓

LAO ZHONG ZHONG FIVE SPICE STALL

4.75 At this stall, you can find Teochew Ah Chiks and Ah Sohs busily wrapping ngoh hiang. Of the 10 or so items offered here, only the tofu is bought from a supplier. The heh chor (prawn roll) here is definitely the world's second best (the world's best has not been found yet)! I rate this stall 4.75—what else needs to be said?

Lao Zhong Zhong Eating House • 29 Tai Thong Crescent (corner of Tai Thong Crescent and Siang Kiang Ave) S347858 • 11.30am to 11.30pm, closed on alternate Mondays

CHINA STREET FRITTERS

4.5 Like Hup Kee, another ngoh hiang stall also at the same food centre, this stall serves up traditional Hokkien style ngoh hiang. The third generation hawkers here, two brothers, have been preserving their family recipes which can be traced back to before World War Two. The pork liver rolls, ngoh hiang rolls, guang chiang and egg slices are excellent. The rolls are fragrant and have an addictive quality about them, as do the egg slices. The braised sauce and the chilli are perfect complements.

Maxwell Road Food Centre • 1 Kadayanallur St #01-64 S069184 • noon to 8pm, closed on Mondays • 92386464

HUP KEE WU SIANG GUAN CHANG

4.0 Hup Kee, like China Street Fritters stall which is in the same food centre, serves homemade ngoh hiang. Their ngoh hiang rolls were really tasty, though a tad small. The guan chiang (pink pork sausage) also tasted better than factory made ones. I don't usually go for liver rolls, but the liver rolls here did not have a strong "livery" taste and there was koo chai in them. Overall a good Hokkien style ngoh hiang with a serious chilli sauce to boot.

Maxwell Road Food Centre • 1 Kadayanallur St #01-97 S069184 • noon to 8pm, closed on Mondays

93 WU XIANG XIA BING

4.0 The ngoh hiang is not as spiced up as those in other stalls. It did not have the same kick as a full flavoured, spicy pork ngoh hiang roll, though there is a freshness that is nice. Of the chef's own inventions, one that is worth mentioning is the tofu egg fritters, which are silky soft on the inside. Shiok!

LAO ZHONG ZHONG FIVE SPICE STALL

Blk 93 Food Centre • Toa Payoh Lorong 4 #01-33 S310093 • noon to 9pm, closed on Thursdays

BLANCO COURT PRAWN NOODLES

4.0 When you visit Blanco Court Prawn Noodles, order some ngoh hiang as an appetiser as you wait for your prawn mee to arrive. Prawn mee and ngoh hiang seem to be betrothed since the days they were sold together at the wayang. The crispy prawn crackers here are excellent, as is the guang chiang (pink pork sausage). However, the yam fritters are gummy and the ngoh hiang rolls have little oomph. (This stall is also recommended for its prawn mee.)

243/245 Beach Road #01-01 S189754 • 7.15am to 4pm, closed on Tuesdays • 63968464

FIVE SPICE PRAWN FRITTER

4.0 This is the only stall in Singapore that makes prawn fritters on the spot and their sweet sauce is very special. It is more like the sauce for lor mee rather than the usual pinkish sweet sauce. The ngoh hiang and egg rolls are also more savoury than sweet. Aside from the prawn fritter, which is quite special, albeit very oily, the rest of the items are not spectacular.

Teck Kee Coffeeshop • Blk 5 Tanjong Pagar Plaza #02-04/05 S081005 • 11am to 1pm, closed on Sundays

OYSTER OMELETTE

OYSTER OMELETTE IS A HIGH CALORIE, HIGH CHOLESTEROL DISH, SO WHEN you eat it, make sure that the calories are worth it. This dish has such simple ingredients—it is essentially starch and eggs fried in oil—but skill and experience are required to make the perfect oyster omelette. Some hawkers can get it dreadfully wrong by ruining the consistency of the starch.

The flavour of the dish comes from the eggs, oil, oysters and fish sauce. The texture has got to have the right balance of crispy-starchy, chewy-starchy, sticky-starchy and crispy brown egg bits! A good oyster omelette is crispy on the outside, yet still sticky with a good amount of fried eggs on the inside. That contrast of crispy-ness and sticky-starchiness, together with the contrast of fresh, juicy oysters is out of this world (when it is done right)!

LESLIE'S PICK ★✓

AH CHUAN OYSTER OMELETTE

4.75 The oysters served here are big, juicy and fresh, and the texture of the dish is just perfect. The only thing I can think of that would make the dish even better is if Uncle were to fry it in pork lard.

Kim Keat Palm Market & Food Centre • 22 Toa Payoh Lorong 7 #01-25 S310022 • 3pm to 9pm, closed on Tuesdays

AH HOCK FRIED OYSTER HOUGANG

4.75/4.5 orh neng/orh luak The owner is a Teochew Ah Hia who insists on using grade A ingredients—the best oysters from South Korea, the best sweet potato flour from China, and the best eggs from Swee Choon egg farm. The only thing he does not make is the lard but he gets the best available. The orh neng is better than the orh luak, but both are exceptional and worth trying.

Whampoa Drive Makan Place (Whampoa Food Centre) • 90 Whampoa Dr #01-54 S320090 • noon to 11pm, closed on alternate Wednesdays

CHAO SHAN CUISINE

4.5 oyster omelette I think all oyster omelettes should be fried the way they do it at this stall—like a disc, instead of being fried almost to the point of being scrambled, which is how it is typically done. The eggs and flour are fried to a crisp and the oysters are excellent! Take it with a dash of fish sauce and you are in oyster heaven!

85 Beach Road S189694 • 11.30am to 2.30pm and 6pm to 10pm, open everyday • 63362390, 90046655

OYSTER OMELETTE STALL

4.5 This stall used to be at the corner of Simon Road and Upper Serangoon Road, but moved up the road when that coffeeshop underwent renovations. Mr Lim has been frying oyster omelette for almost 30 years. He picked up the skill while working as a stall assistant when he was 15. The oyster omelette here is super crispy and the accompanying chilli sauce is tangy and shiok. The oysters are small but tasty, and they get a quick flambe that give them a smoky aroma. Very good but beware, this is a cholesterol bomb!

Mee Sek Coffeeship • 965 Upper Serangoon Road S534721 • 4pm to 2am, closed on Tuesdays • 90878457

TONG SIEW FRIED RICE

4.25 The oyster omelette here is a plain omelette topped

with oysters which have been fried in a rather nice chilli paste. Not many places actually make them this way. It's not too oily, unlike the usual orh jian, and is a nice little side dish to order.

Pek Kio Market & Food Centre • 41A Cambridge Road #01-23 S211041 • 11am to midnight, closed on Wednesdays • 96939599

HUP KEE OYSTER OMELETTE

4.0 This oyster omelette is quite well known and the stall has a perpetual queue. I like the fact that the eggs and the sweet potato flour are fried till they are really crispy. The oysters are also plump and taste fresh.

Sing Lian Eating House • 549 Geylang Road Lorong 29 S389504 • 3.30pm to 10.30pm, open everyday

DID YOU KNOW?

There are two versions of oyster omelette: one where there is sweet potato flour added to the starch is known as orh luak or orh jian. The second version is orh neng. Orh neng does not have sweet potato flour and it is wetter than orh luak.

PAU

I AM DELIGHTED THAT THERE HAS BEEN A RESURGENCE OF HANDMADE PAU in recent years, so we no longer have to waste our calories eating factory made pau. Prior to this, I was getting fed up eating poorly disguised protein molasses wrapped in synthetic skin. Good pau must have the rustic homemade feel of thick, soft fluffy skin. The pau maker needs to strike a delicate balance between making the pau look pretty and keeping the skin as thin as possible. The meat in the pau should be juicy and savoury. It helps if the stall roasts its own meat, like char siew, giving it a nice, smoky charred flavour.

LESLIE'S TIP

Most people like to buy paus that look pretty, but sometimes, the best paus are the ugly ones! You know, the ones where the skin is so thin that the juices have soaked through such that when you peel off the paper at the bottom, you are left with a bottomless pau? That bit of skin adhering to the paper is often the tastiest bit!

LESLIE'S PICK ★✓

D'BUN

4.5/4.0 tua pau/curry pau

They sell really interesting pau like curry pau and yuan yang pau. The tua pau (big pau) here is excellent. The meat is juicy and tender, and the flavour accented by the use of coriander, which I feel helps to cut through the oil. The best time to eat the pau at this stall is when they come out fresh from the steamer at 10am, as the juices simply burst out of the pau! Their char siew pau is very popular among their regulars and if you are lucky, sometimes you will get char siew pau with bits of sio bak inside!

358 Joo Chiat Road (junction of Marshall Lane and Joo Chiat Road) S427603 • 8am to 10pm, open everyday

TANJONG RHU PAU & CONFECTIONERY

4.6/4.0 tua pau/char siew pau & yuan yang pau

There is something inexplicable about the taste of the pau here. It is head and shoulders above the rest. The combination of the soft sweet skin and the juicy savoury meat makes my tastebuds resonate with excitement. The pau here is small and can be finished off in two mouthfuls. Thus, one pau is never enough!

Chin Huan Eating House • 7 Jalan Batu #01-113 S431007 • 12.30pm to 8pm, closed on Sundays

389 Guillemard Road S399701 • 12.30pm to 8pm, closed on Sundays

72 Thomson Road S307589 • 12.30pm to 8pm, closed on Sundays

GUANG JI BAO ZAI

4.5 Uncle has been making pau for over 30 years, and it's amazing how fast his hands work. He still roasts his own char siew with a charcoal oven, which is why the filling is so good. It is juicy and sweet, and you can really taste the char-grilled flavour of the meat. The tua pau (big pau) is commendable, but the char siew pau is the real show-stopper.

ABC Brickworks Food Centre • 6 Jalan Bukit Merah #01-135 S150006 • 10am to 10pm, closed on Thursdays

MAN JI HANDMADE PAU

4.5 The tua pau (big pau) here is easily the juiciest pau in Singapore and is chock full of crunchy turnips. There is no egg, and the meat filling is on the sweet side. While the meat could have been more fragrant, the joy of biting into the pau and having the juices trickle down your hands is guaranteed to get most pau lovers excited.

327 Hougang Ave 5 S530327 • 6am to 1pm, open everyday

JOO HUAT PAU

4.5 If you are looking for rustic homemade pau, head to this unassuming little stall. The yellowish pau skin is reminiscent of what Grandma used to make and the pau has a toothy bite that makes it very different from the smooth, spongy version that is sold everywhere. The big pau and tau sar pau are very good, particularly the latter as they make their own red bean paste. Believe it or not, they are still making their dough by hand!

Circuit Road Food Centre • 79A Circuit Road #01-62 S371079 • noon to 11pm, closed on Mondays and Tuesdays • 97558688

HONG HO PHANG HONG KONG PAU

4.5/4.25 fan choy/lo mai kai While the char siew pau was not as fantastic as I had been led to believe, this stall's fan choy is the first which has ever left me thinking about going back to eat it again. The rice was moist and the savoury sweet sauce was a delight on the palate. The vegetarian pau was quite good—the filling was made of turnip and hae bee (dried shrimp), and was a great alternative to meat pau.

5 Telok Kurau Road S423758 • 7.30am to around 4pm, closed on Mondays

TIONG BAHRU PAU

4.25/4.0 char siew pau & siew mai/tua pau Even though this franchise serves up pau that is no longer as great as the "good old days", Tiong Bahru Pau still deserves mention. The distinctive feature of the tua pau (big pau) is the lack of egg. Unfortunately, the skin has become thicker and more dry over the years. Thankfully, the char siew pau is still good and one of the best around— the char siew is very tasty, and still retains that distinctive smoky flavour.

Tiong Bahru Market & Food Centre • 30 Seng Poh Road #02-18/19 S168898 • 7.30am to 9pm, closed on Mondays

DID YOU KNOW?

The pau skin in Singapore is quite unique. You won't find the same type in Japan where they prefer a more yeasty, off white skin with a more toothy bite, the sort that is used by Din Tai Fung. The Hong Kong style char siew pau with the "open flower" on top makes use of yet another style of pau skin.

TEOCHEW HANDMADE PAU

4.25 **tua pau & kong bak pau** The Teochew Ah Hia here has taken liberties with what we know as pau, and given it his own Teochew twist. The pau is tiny, with very thin skin. The kong bak pau, which I find tasty, though a bit dry, is the most popular, and you have to call up to reserve this pau or it will be sold by noon. The tua pau is good—not super juicy, but it has a very different and attractive flavour.

Toa Payoh West Market & Food Court • 127 Toa Payoh Lorong 1 #02-02 S310127 • Tuesdays to Saturdays: 6am to 2pm, Sundays: 6am to noon, closed on Mondays and alternate Tuesdays • 62542053, 66595786

TECK KEE TANGLIN PAU

4.0 This is one of the oldest pau stalls in Singapore, and probably the most well known brand. Although they still make their pau by hand, they have to make pau that appeals to the masses in terms of presentation. As a result, for the tua pau (big pau), the skin is slightly thicker and the pau is healthier (as the fat from the meat has been removed). The char siew pau is slightly better—the char siew has got that nice smoky flavour but has all the nice charred bits removed, so it has lost its rustic edge.

83 Killiney Road S239531 • 9am to 10.30pm, closed on Mondays • www.teckkeepau.com

ENG CHEONG PAU

4.0 Eng Cheong Pau supplies handmade pau to coffeeshops around the island, and sells its products at its own little stall along Upper Paya Lebar Road. The story goes that they used to be owned by the folks from Tanjong Rhu Pau, who sold the business to the current owner with the assurance that the prized recipe would be passed on as well. As a result, the meat filling is quite similar to Tanjong Rhu Pau's. The next time you're in a coffeeshop and craving a pau, be sure to look for the Eng Cheong label.

416 Upper Paya Lebar Road S534995 • 7am to 7pm, open everyday • 68583652

DID YOU KNOW?

The best pau makers, like D'Bun, use a yeast starter that has never been discarded but has been kept alive for each new batch of dough. Like wine, yeast starters improve with age!

POPIAH

GOOD POPIAH MUST HAVE NICE, SOFT, CHEWY SKIN THAT LEAVES A SWEET carbo aftertaste. I especially love it when the hawker makes his own popiah skin, though this is quite rare these days. Good popiah must be packed with a generous amount of ingredients—sweet and savoury turnip filling and let's not forget those unidentified heavenly crunchy bits: I love my popiah loaded with crunchy bits, and folded tightly, looking like it's going to burst at the seams. When you put all the ingredients of popiah together, you get a wonderful matrix of flavours and textures. Chewy (skin), crunchy (crispy bits), juicy (turnips), crispy (lettuce and beansprouts), sweet (sauce) and spicy (chilli), and the contrast between the warm filling and cool vegetables. This is the beauty of an expertly rolled, fully packed and turgid popiah.

LESLIE'S PICK ✓

KWAY GUAN HUAT JOO CHIAT ORIGINAL POPIAH AND KUEH PIE TEE

4.6 If you are a popiah lover, you must visit this stall. The popiah here is quite simply shiok. The skin is translucent, yet holds a chock full of filling without breaking or allowing the sauce to ooze out. The texture is chewy and leaves a wonderful sweet carbo aftertaste. The savoury sweet turnip filling has that wonderful umami oomph, and contains crab meat, de-shelled from Sri Lankan crabs. Finally, the homemade crispy bits add a wonderfully sweet crunch. This stall started in 1938 when it sold popiah from a pushcart. It sells popiah on the weekends and by special order, but its popiah skin is on sale throughout the week.

95 Joo Chiat Road S427389 • 10am to 8pm, closed on Mondays (takeaway available on Mondays) • 63442875, 96773441

QI JI POH PIAH

4.5 The strength of the popiah here lies in the skin. Although it is super thin, it is amazingly resilient. Even when you tar pau (takeaway), it doesn't get soggy, but retains its chewy, slightly gummy texture. The filling is marvellous—the layer of crunchy stuff gives a good bite while the turnips are moist and sweet.

Funan DigitalLife Mall • 109 North Bridge Road #01-17 S179097 • 9am to 8.30pm, open everyday • www.qiji.com.sg

OLD LONG HOUSE POPIAH

4.25 The popiah here is almost legendary. The skin is homemade, so it is nice and chewy. The ingredients are fresh and the crispy bits are really crispy.

Kim Keat Palm Market & Food Centre • 22 Toa Payoh Lorong 7 #01-03 S310022 • 6am to 4pm, closed on Mondays • 91717157

MIOW SIN POPIAH AND CARROT CAKE

4.0 The popiah is not too bad, but not exceptional either. I was horrified when I realised that the skin was the factory made type and looked really synthetic, almost as if it had the words "Made in Kaki Bukit" printed on it! Alas, it seems the convenience of synthetic popiah skin has lured this stall over to the dark side!

Lavender Food Square • 380 Jalan Besar #01-04 S209000 • 9am to midnight,

KWAY GUAN HUAT JOO CHIAT ORIGINAL POPIAH AND KUEH PIE TEE

closed on alternate Wednesdays •
62928764

GLORY CATERING

4.0 They sell Nonya style popiah here, which uses egg skin, unlike the Hokkien style popiah skin, which is egg-less. You might not really take to this, because it is different from what you are used to. The texture is more tender, like the skin of kueh dah dah, and less dry than the common popiah. Try it soon though, because apparently, this is an old school popiah skin that is all but disappearing.

139 East Coast Road S428829 • 8.30am to 8.30pm, closed on Mondays except public holidays • 63441749

DID YOU KNOW?

Popiah was invented by the wife of Cai Fu Yi, a magistrate during the Ming Dynasty, who had no time to eat as his enemies instigated the Emperor to make him copy nine big boxes of ancient records on Chinese history. His wife wrapped his food in a skin made from ground rice and so invented the Chinese equivalent of burrito. It is purported that till today, the descendants of Cai Fu Yi are still selling rice wraps in China's Hokkien province.

PORRIDGE MAY NOT BE THE SORT OF DISH YOU SPECIALLY ARRANGE WITH friends to go out and eat, but it is the first dish I turn to on a cold night, when I am in need of some comfort. We are lucky to have several varieties of porridge in Singapore to satiate our cravings: while Teochew porridge is watery, Hainanese and Cantonese porridges are thick and pastey. Hainanese jook (porridge) is where rice is boiled till it is broken but still retains a grainy texture. It is cooked by the hawker only when you order. Cantonese congee, also called jook sometimes, is where rice is boiled to a smooth paste. A good bowl of porridge will be topped with only the freshest of ingredients. I prefer my porridge laced with fragrant sesame oil and accompanied by you char kway (fried dough fritter).

LESLIE'S PICK ✓

GEN SHU MEI SHI SHI JIA

4.5 Run by Uncle Gen, who used to be head chef of a major chain of Cantonese restaurants, Gen Shu stall serves up terrific congee because of Uncle Gen's exacting requirements. For him, the texture and smoothness of the porridge is paramount. That is why he combines two different types of rice to make the congee. The amazing smoothness is also the result of adding fragrant oil into the congee during the cooking process so that it becomes emulsified into the porridge. Try the fried fish porridge and sampan porridge here. Also recommended: lo mai kai.

Blk 74 Food Centre • Toa Payoh Lor 4 #01-03 S310074 • 6am till sold out around lunch time, closed on Mondays

HOE KEE

4.5 for century egg porridge A shiokalicious century egg porridge—with generous amounts of century egg and at such a value-for-money price! I loved the tasty, super smooth porridge. Seriously, I don't know how much better century egg porridge can get! Also recommended: homemade tofu.

Maxwell Road Food Centre • 1 Kadayanallur St #01-45 S069184 • Mondays to Thursdays: 6.30am to 2.30am, Fridays to Sundays: 6.30am to 4am

AH CHIANG'S PORRIDGE

4.25 A good place for congee and this place offers a wide variety of toppings, so you'll be spoilt for choice. It is wonderful to be able to order extra you char kway (fried dough fritter) for your porridge, as well as side dishes like raw fish and extra century eggs. The original stall at Tiong Poh Road has been around since 1971, but there is also a branch at Toa Payoh.

Blk 65 Tiong Poh Road #01-38 S160065 • 7am to 2pm and 6pm to midnight, closed on alternate Mondays • 65570084

Blk 190 Lor 6 Toa Payoh #01-526 S310190 • 7am to 9.30pm, open everyday • 63566009

SOON LEE

4.25 This stall is manned by a second generation hawker who proudly serves Hainanese porridge in the most traditional style. If you are hankering after a bowl of warm comfort food, then here is one stall to satisfy your craving. The porridge is thick and warm, the pork is fresh and savoury, and the hawker gives you a generous amount.

Blk 448 Clementi Ave 3 #01-50 S120448 • Mondays to Fridays: 6am to 9pm, Saturdays: 6am to 5pm, closed on Sundays

CHAI CHEE PORK PORRIDGE

4.25 The porridge at this stall hits all the right buttons. It is nicely flavoured, due to the long hours of cooking with the best pork bones Auntie can buy. And the minced pork is nice and savoury. Just right to warm the tummy on a cool night. So the porridge here certainly hit the right buttons in my book. The porridge was nicely flavoured which, according to Auntie is attributed to the long hours of cooking with the best pork bones a hawker can buy.

Fengshan Food Centre • 85 Bedok North St 4 Stall 210 & 250 S460085

Stall 210 • 5.30am to 3pm, open everyday

Stall 250 • 5.30pm to 2am, open everyday • 98343113

ZHEN ZHEN

4.0 This is a very famous stall, and its distinctive feature is that the grains have been cooked until they have all but dissolved. Although many people rave about the porridge here, I felt like I was eating a bowl of thickened cream soup. It was almost like eating pure starch! Still, the porridge here is value for money, since you get a chockful of ingredients and the fish is very fresh. Overall, a very unique bowl of porridge which is well worth a try.

Maxwell Road Food Centre • 1 Kadayanallur St #01-54 S069184 • 5.30am to 2.30pm, closed on Tuesdays

JOHORE ROAD BOON KEE PORK PORRIDGE

4.0 This 30-year-old porridge stall in Jalan Besar serves up Hainanese porridge. The flavour is robust and it is certainly value for money, given the generous amount of ingredients in each bowl.

Blk 638 Veerasamy Road #01-101 S200608 • Tuesdays to Sundays: 7am to 3.30pm, closed on Mondays • 62969100

DID YOU KNOW?

Sampan porridge is a traditional type of Cantonese congee served with pig skin, cuttlefish, sliced pork, peanuts and fish cake. Tradition has it that sampan porridge was served aboard sampans that plied Liwan Lake on the western outskirts of Guangzhou. It is popular for its fresh and sweet taste.

AH PRATA, ONE OF MY ALL TIME FAVOURITE BREAKFAST FOODS. MY PA USED to bring me to the coffeeshop at Toa Payoh Lorong 8 to eat prata. $1 used to buy me 10 pratas and I could bring an egg and ask the prata man to add it in for me.

These days, there are many types of prata in Singapore—from the soft chewy type to the super crispy type. My ultimate prata has to be big, thick and crispy on the outside, but fluffy and chewy on the inside. Unfortunately, with the proliferation of 24-hour prata joints, the standard of prata in Singapore has been waning, and in some places, it is just plain bad. In the past, men from India came to Singapore to etch out a living for themselves and through sheer hard work, made a name for themselves. These days, the guys flipping the prata are all hired hands from India and Malaysia. Unless the boss correctly incentivises them, it is difficult to ensure quality.

LESLIE'S PICK ✓

MR AND MRS MOHGAN'S SUPER CRISPY ROTI PRATA

4.75 **The pratas here are small, fresh and super crispy, and when eaten with the curry, they are like manna from heaven. The Mohgans prepare three different types of curry—viz dhal, mutton and fish. I find the fish curry the best, for the slight tang helps to cut through the fat and balance out the flavours. Add a bit of sambal ikan bilis for sweetness and you have the perfect Sunday breakfast!**

Poh Ho Restaurant • 7 Crane Road S429356 • 6.30am to 1.30pm, closed Tuesdays and Wednesdays on the third week of the month • 97943124

SIN MING ROTI PRATA

4.75 This is how prata should be. It is shatteringly crisp on the outside, but chewy and fluffy on the inside, leaving a buttery sweet taste at the back of the palate after you work through the satisfying chew. You get a selection of curries to go with your prata, all of which are on the spicy side, which, I am sure, will please a lot of prata fans out there.

24 Sin Ming Road #01-51 S570024 • 6am to 7pm, open everyday • 64533893

RIYADH MUSLIM FOOD

4.6 The pratas here are hard to beat. Though they are small, they are also crispy, flaky and very flavourful. This is probably one of the best versions of prata around, and the best thing is that the owner insists on making the prata only when you order, so you are assured of fresh prata all the time.

Soon Soon Lai Eating House • 32 Defu Lane 10 Stall 12 S539213 • 6.30am to 7pm, closed every last Wednesday of the month

SINGAPORE ZAM ZAM RESTAURANT

4.5/4.0 chicken murtabak/ mutton murtabak
While I really liked the crispy savoury topping of the mutton on the mutton murtabak, I felt it could have been more tasty. I had no complaints about the texture—crispy on the outside and chewy on the inside. On the other hand, the chicken murtabak was to die for—shiokalicious!

697 North Bridge Road S198675 • 8am to 11pm, open everyday • 62987011

THE PRATA PLACE

4.5 The prata here is excellent, and they offer a wide range

5 TIPS TO ENSURING A GOOD PRATA

\# 1: The stall needs to make its own dough. There is something about dough that is mixed and kneaded by hand that gives it a special texture and taste.

\# 2: Ask for two doughs and specify that you want your prata thick and fluffy.

\# 3: Check if the stall is frying your prata in ghee (QBB brand). That is the best!

\# 4: Stick around when the person starts flipping and specify you want them to flip the prata as big as possible, and then fold into many layers.

\# 5: Finally, eat the prata hot, or as soon as it hits your plate!

of curries to go with your prata. As it is air-conditioned, this is one of the most comfortable places to get a nice prata with a cup of teh tarik. The prata is crispy on the outside and fluffy on the inside, just the way I like it. The red bean prata here deserves special mention. Make sure you leave space for dessert!

1 Thong Soon Ave (Springleaf Estate) S787431 • 7.30am to midnight, open everyday

CASUARINA CURRY RESTAURANT

4.5 Casuarina Curry Restaurant is one of the best known places for prata. Even though it has expanded to many branches, it still manages to churn out prata that is crispy and quite shiok.

136 Casuarina Road (off Upper Thomson) S579514 • weekdays: 7am to 11.30pm, weekends and eve of public holidays: 7am to midnight • www.casuarinacurry.com

THE ROTI PRATA HOUSE

4.25 This prata is of the super crispy variety—when you bite into its crisp texture, it just dissolves in your mouth. It is heavenly together with the curry

DID YOU KNOW?

Thasevi at Jalan Kayu made famous the small, round crispy type of prata, and now, "Jalan Kayu" has become synonymous with prata and is used to describe that style of prata.

THE MIGHTY MURTABAK

The Singapore Zam Zam Restaurant is probably the most well-known murtabak stall in Singapore. It is certainly one of the oldest I know that is still in the same spot, since its inception in 1908.

When I walked in, the chef was flipping the most gigantic and awesome murtabaks I had ever seen! The way they make murtabak is a bit different from other places. In addition to an extra layer of pre-fried prata kosong, which they put at the base of the murtabak, they also add an extra egg on top of the folded murtabak and sprinkle some minced mutton before frying. The result—a massive murtabak with crispy fried mince topping!

they provide. The butter flavoured vegetable oil does make it very tasty, but oh so sinful.

246 Upper Thomson Road S574370 • open 24 hours daily • 64595260

SYED RESTAURANT

4.25 Be still my trembling tastebuds! Crispy on the outside, light and fluffy with micro-thin layers of dough on the inside, this is probably the best prata I have had in terms of texture. Unfortunately, the taste of cheap margarine was predominant, probably a result of using commercial dough instead of making it in-house.

326 Bedok Road S469496 • open 24 hours daily • 62425412

DID YOU KNOW?

Roti prata originated in a small part of southern India, predominantly in Chennai. Over there, the dish is simply called paratha or prata. Indian migrants brought this dish to Singapore, where it became known as roti prata. The Malaysians, however, named this dish roti canai. While some believe "canai" refers to "Chennai", others say "canai" is derived from the Malay word for the process of kneading and shaping the dough.

PRAWN MEE

A FULL BODIED ROBUST SOUP WITH A POWERFUL PRAWN FLAVOUR. THAT'S what I look for when it comes to prawn mee. The soup should be savoury and have oomph, without being overly salty. The stock should be made from prawns, though some places add secret ingredients such as dried scallops, crabs and other goodies. It really does make a difference to add sua lor, wild prawns that are harvested from the sea. Unlike farmed tiger prawns, the wild prawns have a special sweetness and texture that is hard to beat.

The success of prawn mee rises and falls with the quality of the soup. And the standard of the soup varies throughout the day; depending on when the hawker refills the soup with fresh stock. Topped with fresh shallots and freshly fried pork lard, there isn't another bowl of soup noodles that can satisfy that umami crave.

LESLIE'S PICK ★✓

WAH KEE PRAWN NOODLES

4.8 Wah Kee's prawn noodles are really a cut above the rest. Uncle uses six seafood ingredients to make the sweet broth, and the prawns here are some of the biggest I have ever seen—so sweet and juicy! The noodles are also excellent—the texture and taste are both spectacular.

Pek Kio Market and Food Centre • 41A Cambridge Road #01-15 S211041 • 7.30am to 2pm, closed on Mondays • 96883633

JOO CHIAT PRAWN NOODLE

4.5 The owners here are part of the family responsible for the famous Blanco Court Prawn Noodles (just like the owners of Beach Road Prawn Noodle House, Jalan Sultan Prawn Mee and Blanco Prawn Noodle House). The best stuff is the pork ribs—they are tender enough to bite and not too soft, and the meat is really pang (savoury). The soup is marvellous, though to be fair, I ate half an hour before closing time so the soup was really concentrated. My only complaint is that they don't serve nice long prime ribs and their prawns are only medium-sized.

Xin Hua Ji Food House • 15 Crane Road S429812 • 7am to 3pm, closed on Tuesdays

BEACH ROAD PRAWN NOODLE HOUSE

4.5 tiger prawn special This stall is helmed by the children of the famous Blanco Court hawker (just like the owners of Joo Chiat Prawn Noodle, Jalan Sultan Prawn Mee and Blanco Prawn Noodle House). If you order the wild tiger prawn special, you will get a soup that is very concentrated, with a wonderful umami kick. The regular bowl, on the other hand, is less impressive, as the soup tastes like it lacks a few ingredients. Here's a tip from the boss himself: order your prawn mee without beansprouts as they dilute the taste of the soup!

370 East Coast Road S428981 • 8am to 4pm, closed on Tuesdays • 63457196

JALAN SULTAN PRAWN MEE

4.5 This stall is another descendant of Blanco Court Prawn Noodles (just like Joo Chiat Prawn Noodle, Beach Road Prawn Noodle House and Blanco Prawn Noodle House). The soup version is better than the dry, as it has that wonderful oomph. This stall gives you the option of ordering jumbo king prawns in order to satisfy your prawn craving. The pork ribs here are big, tender and very shiok.

2 Jalan Ayer S347859 • 8am to 3.30pm, closed on Tuesdays

RIVER SOUTH (HOE NAM) PRAWN NOODLES EATING HOUSE

4.5 There is a simple reason why the prawn mee here is very tasty—the owner says it is because they sell many bowls of noodles a day, so they have to boil more prawns in the stock. More prawns, more taste!

31 Tai Thong Crescent (facing Jackson Centre) S347859 • 6.30am to 4.30pm, closed once a month on Mondays • 62819293

PENANG ROAD CAFE

4.5 This restaurant is run by a Singaporean man and his Penang wife, and they do a pretty mean prawn noodle soup. Guaranteed to hit all those umami receptors on your tongue. It hasn't hit the same level as the best ones in Penang, but it can definitely hold its own among the best versions of prawn mee here.

Novena Ville • 275 Thomson Road #01-08 S307645 • 11.30am to 2.30pm and 5.45pm to 9.15pm, closed on Mondays • 62563218, 97862079

NOO CHENG ADAM ROAD PRAWN MEE (ZION ROAD)

4.5 The soup version over at the Adam Road branch really lacks oomph, but this one is so much better! Anyone looking for an umami kick would be very pleased.

Zion Riverside Food Centre • 70 Zion Road
Stall 4 S247792 • noon to 3pm and 6pm
to 11.30pm, closed on Mondays

NOO CHENG ADAM ROAD PRAWN NOODLE (ADAM ROAD)

4.25 Noo Cheng serves sua
lor (wild prawns) that are
really tender and sweet! While their
soup version lacks oomph, the dry
version is super shiok! The chilli is
more savoury than spicy. Here's a
tip: if you have a bit of spare cash,
try their special giant prawn noodles,
where you get foot long Goliath
prawns at $25 a bowl!

Adam Road Food Centre • 2 Adam Road
#01-27 S289876 • 9.15am to 4pm and
6.30pm to 2am, open everyday

OLD STALL HOKKIEN STREET FAMOUS HOKKIEN MEE

4.25 The soup served by
this stall is good, but I
expected more—it does have kick,
but it did not hit the threshold for
the "Shiok!" reaction. The thing that
does have the oomph factor though is
the specially prepared chilli powder
that is fried with hae bee (dried
shrimp). The taste is very distinctive.
The chilli powder is so popular that
Uncle sells it in bottles.

Hong Lim Food Centre • 531A Upper Cross
St #02-67 S051531 • 9.30am to 4pm,
closed on Thursdays • 98539630

BLANCO COURT PRAWN NOODLES

4.25 The good thing here is that
you can order the jumbo
version that comes with luscious ang
kar prawns (if they are in season) and
wonderfully tender pork ribs. The soup
base reminds me of what prawn mee
used to be like when I was a kid—
dark, savoury and sweet, though you
don't get the same "prawny" oomph,
like in the Penang version of the
dish. This is the granddaddy of prawn
noodles, which gave rise to the other
famous prawn noodle stalls listed here
in this guide—Joo Chiat Prawn Noodle,
Beach Road Prawn Noodle House,
Jalan Sultan Prawn Mee and Blanco
Prawn Noodle House. (This stall is also
recommended for its ngoh hiang.)

243/245 Beach Road #01-01 S189754
• 7.15am to 4pm, closed on Tuesdays •
63968464

BLANCO PRAWN NOODLE HOUSE

4.25 The prawn mee here really
tastes like the prawn mee
I grew up eating, except that the
oiliness and saltiness have been toned
down to suit a more health conscious
generation. One of the daughters of
the famous Blanco Court hawker runs
this shop as a second career after her
children have grown up.

235 Jalan Kayu S799459 • 7am to
4.30pm, closed on Tuesdays • 68534426,
96343456

ROASTED MEATS

SHIOKALICOUS CHAR SIEW SHOULD BE THICKLY CUT, TENDER, MARBLED and juicy, with nicely charred and caramelised bits of fat on the outside and a melt-in-your-mouth texture. With each bite, you should be able to appreciate the smell of smoky charcoal. As for sio bak, even though the ingredients are simple, you need a lot of skill to cook it just right so that the rind is crisp while the meat is just cooked so that it is bouncy and juicy. The beauty of good sio bak is that with one bite, you can taste the nutty flavours of the meat combined with the crispy texture of the rind melded with the pork fat. It only takes the warmth of your mouth and a few chews to create the perfect porcine pleasure for your palate. Ahh... why does something so good have to be soooo bad for you?

LESLIE'S PICK ✓

FATTY CHEONG

4.75 **The char siew here is easily the best in Singapore, and very reasonably priced. Fatty Cheong's charcoal oven ensures that the pork gets that characteristic smoky flavour, and the char siew is always tender and juicy. The sio bak and roast duck here are both very good, but it is the char siew that has that extra oomph that gets you salivating when you think of it.**

ABC Brickworks Food Centre • 6 Jalan Bukit Merah #01-120 S150006 • 11am to 8.30pm, closed on Thursdays • 98824849, 94281983

FOONG KEE

4.6/4.5 sio bak/char siew Although more famous for wanton mee, I highly recommend this stall's char siew and sio bak as well. The char siew has a wonderful, bouncy texture and is well caramelised on the outside with that smokiness we all love about roasted meats. The sio bak is comparable to char siew sold at Crystal Jade but costs just a fraction of the price. The rind is thin and crisp, and the meat is seasoned all the way through, leaving a satisfying nutty, porky taste that lingers at the back of your throat. All you need to do is bring along your own French mustard and you'll be in pork heaven! (This stall is also recommended for its wanton mee.)

6 Keong Saik Road S089114 • 11am to 8pm, closed on Sundays and public holidays • 96953632

FU SHI TRADITIONAL ROASTED

4.6/4.25 char siew/sio bak & roast duck A lot of the sio bak you find nowadays lacks soul, but the juicy, tender, melt-in-your-mouth sio bak at Fu Shi will make you shout hallelujah like you are in a gospel choir in America's deep South! It is really good to see that there is a new generation of hawkers rising up to the challenge of serving hawker food with passion and quality! The char siew here is also excellent and can rival the best in Singapore.

Shunfu Hawker Centre • Blk 320 Shunfu Road #02-25 S570320 • 9am to 2pm, closed on Mondays and Tuesdays

KAY LEE ROAST MEAT JOINT

4.5/4.25 char siew & roast duck/sio bak Lao Ban Niang says that her sauce is one of a kind in Singapore, and she marinates her char siew with 11 kinds of yao chai (Chinese herbs). The char siew here is very shiok— wonderfully tender and chewy. I think that the duck is one of the best in Singapore. While it lacks that extra oomph, the skin is crispy, which sets it apart from a lot of other roast ducks in Singapore. One downside is that the meats tend to be on the pricey side. This stall is famous for putting its recipe and shophouse on the market for $3.5 million!

125 Upper Paya Lebar Road S534838 • 10am to 7pm, closed on Tuesdays • 67438778

LAU PHUA CHAY

4.5/4.0 char siew/sio bak & roast duck The Teochews are well-known for their braised duck, rather than roast duck. So when the Teochew Ah Hia at Lau Phua Chay told me that his char siew and roast duck are Teochew-style, it took me by surprise. He explained that Teochews have a sweet tooth, so he prepares his char siew much sweeter than usual, using bean paste and malt in the marinade. The sweet, lumpy

sauce he pours liberally over the rice is unique and suited my palate very well. Leaner cuts are available, but ask the stall owner which bits are the best and he will joyfully serve you the juiciest, fattiest bits.

Alexandra Village Food Centre • 120 Bukit Merah Lane 1 #01-20 S150125 • 11.30am to 3.30pm, closed on Saturdays • 96636862

NEW RONG LIANG GE HONG KONG ROAST

4.5/4.0 roast duck/char siew & sio bak When you see a stall with a long queue in Singapore, it is usually either because the food is very good, or it is just good and cheap. This stall falls into the latter category, for while the char siew and sio bak are good, they are not good enough to generate a long queue, except that they are very reasonably priced. The roast duck, however, is exceptionally good—the meat is fragrant, not gamey and very tender.

QS269 Food House • Blk 269B Queen St #01-235 S182269 • 9am to 8pm, closed on the first Wednesday of every month

---

DID YOU KNOW?

Conventional wisdom dictates that char siew is made by marinating pork with just fish sauce, sugar, white pepper and red colouring. But in reality, most hawkers add other ingredients, including tau cheo (salted bean paste), malt, oyster sauce, caramelised sugar and some even use yao chai (Chinese herbs) in the marinade!

TOH KEE

4.5/4.0 roast duck/sio bak
The Dark Lord of roast ducks, almost half black rather than the usual burnt sienna colour! Underneath the crispy dark skin is a very tender and highly agreeable duck meat. The next best thing is the sio bak. It has very crispy skin, and tender, fragrant flesh. I was underwhelmed by the char siew though, which while tasty, was a little dry.

People's Park Cooked Food Centre • 32 New Market Road #01-1014 S050032 • noon to 7.30pm, closed on Mondays • 63233368

YEE KEE SPECIALIST ROASTED DUCK

4.5/4.0 sio bak/char siew
This is a great place for old school roasted meats, especially sio bak. After many years of experience, this uncle's sio bak has crispy rind and juicy, tender meat that still retains that springy chew. The char siew is roasted perfectly, though I prefer it sweeter and stickier. Though the stall claims to specialise in roast duck, I find it quite unremarkable.

Blk 148 Silat Ave #01-14 S160148 • 11am to 4pm, closed on Sundays • 96977083

ALEX EATING HOUSE

4.25/4.0 char siew/sio bak
Alex Eating House has always been well known for its char siew. It is quite good, though I find it a bit dry. The sauce is very good, and definitely one of the better ones around. The sio bak was okay, but the skin was not as crispy, though the meat was still quite flavourful.

Chye Sing Building • 87 Beach Road #01-01 S189695 • 9am to 6pm, open everyday • 63340268

JIU JIANG SHAO LA

4.25/4.0 char siew/sio bak & roast duck
My plate of sio bak, char siew and roast duck was anything but stellar, contrary to my high expectations. While the marinade was very good, the meat was a tad dry, especially the char siew. However they managed to redeem themselves when I ordered another portion of char siew and got some juicy bu jian tian (pig's armpit) with enjoyable bits of caramelised charred fat.

Ghim Moh Market & Food Centre • 20 Ghim Moh Road #01-45 S270020 • 11am to 7.30pm, closed on Wednesdays

HUA FONG KEE ROAST DUCK

4.25 char siew & roast duck
The roast duck at Hua Fong Kee is set apart from the rest by its sauce, which is quite shiok. The sesame seeds add more savoury goodness to the flavour. The char siew was just above average the first time I tried it, but has improved to be juicy, tender and well caramelised. However, the sio bak lacks juiciness and umami kick, despite having a crispy skin.

FATTY CHEONG

The char siew at Fatty Cheong is easily one of the best versions of char siew in Singapore, and very reasonably priced. He offers a choice of both lean and marbled versions of char siew although connoisseurs would just go for the marbled version. His char siew is dipped intermittently during the roasting process in a marinade of soya sauce, sugar, oyster sauce and tau cheo (salted bean paste) to ensure that a thick, translucent and caramelised layer coats the char siew, and his charcoal oven ensures the pork gets that characteristic smoky flavour. Fatty Cheong's char siew is always tender and juicy. The sio bak and roast duck here are both very good, but it is his char siew that has that extra oomph to keep you salivating when you think of it.

Why is the shop called Fatty Cheong? Well, it turns out that it may be a case of self-fulfilling prophecy. When Mr Cheong started his shop 14 years ago, he was a slim young man. I think he must have chosen the name Fatty because he used to be an apprentice at Fatty Ox, a famous roast duck stall that has closed down. Since then, he has tweaked his char siew recipe to suit local tastes.

Blk 116 Toa Payoh Lorong 2 #01-140 S310116 • 8am to 8pm, open everyday • 96658595

Blk 128 Toa Payoh Lorong 1 #01-811 S310128 • 8am to 8pm, closed on Thursdays

LEE KHEONG ROASTED DELICACY

4.25 The char siew here is good, but it used to be better. Unfortunately, when Lee Kheong moved from People's Park to Hong Lim, standards dropped a bit. Still, worth a try if you have a char siew craving!

Hong Lim Food Centre • 531A Upper Cross St #02-15 S051531 • 10am to 6pm, closed on Sundays • 93804854

DID YOU KNOW?

For char siew, hawkers often use pork shoulder, known as wu hua rou, meaning "five flower pattern pork". But an even more prized part, according to Fatty Cheong, is the pig's armpit, known as bu jian tian, meaning "never see the sky".

SATAY

I LOVE SATAY THAT IS JUICY AFTER GRILLING, AND MADE FROM CHUNKY PIECES of meat. I prefer the meat to be sweet, with the fragrance of the marinade, made from a combination of spices, including lemongrass, generously assaulting my olfactory nerves as I survey my meal. The peanut sauce has to be thick, with a generous amount of coarsely ground peanuts. Of course, satay and sauce made at the stall are usually better than those bought from suppliers.

There are two types of satay in Singapore: one made by the Chinese and the other by the Malays. The Chinese style satay features a zebra crossing pattern of lean meat and fat. The marinade for Chinese style satay, or more accurately, Hainanese style, usually has Chinese five spice in it. These spices make it distinct from the Malay style. You can also find pineapple puree in the dipping sauce.

LESLIE'S PICK

CHUAN KEE SATAY

4.75 This is traditional Hainanese style satay—pork satay served with peanut gravy that comes with pineapple slush. The flowery bouquet from the freshly grilled skewers is too much of an unbearable tease, and the first bite is like being infatuated all over again. The meat is really tender and coated with spicy golden syrup that hints strongly of lemongrass and coriander. Fantastic!

Old Airport Road Food Centre • 51 Old Airport Road #01-85 S390051 • Tuesdays, Wednesdays, Fridays and Saturdays: 6pm till sold out, Sundays: 1pm till sold out

KWONG SATAY

4.75/4.5 kushiyaki style pork belly satay/ pork satay One of the secrets is that the hawker insists on using saffron in the marinade, which makes the satay very aromatic. The peanut sauce comes with crushed pineapple which would please most foodies, though it would have been more shiok if it were more "peanuty". They also serve an *ieat* creation, the Kushiyaki style pork belly satay, which is almost 2½ times the size of normal satay!

Sing Lian Eating House • 549 Geylang Lorong 29 S389504 • 5pm to 11pm, closed on alternate Wednesdays • 65650002

ROSRAIHANNA SOTO AND SATAY

4.5 Some might find the satay a bit on the sweet side, but I enjoyed the fragrance of the lemongrass, and the tender, juicy pieces of chicken thigh meat. They have one of the best sauces around—you know you are eating something made with passion when you see the pieces of uneven peanuts in the gravy that were pounded by hand!

Golden Mile Food Centre • 505 Beach Road #B1-19 S199583 • noon to 10pm, closed on Sundays

WARONG SUDI MAMPIR

4.5/4.0 beef tripe satay/ mutton satay Try the beef tripe satay, which absorbs the marinade very well, so that you can taste the zesty lemongrass and other spices! However, I dislike how they use chicken breast meat for the chicken satay. The mutton is a little on the tough side, though very yummy. The satay sauce was very commendable—lots of chunky peanuts and very sedap!

Haig Road Food Centre • 14 Haig Road #01-19 S430014 • weekdays: 10.30am to 7pm, weekends: 10.30am to 5pm, closed on Wednesdays and Thursdays • 64440167

POH KEE SATAY

4.25 The satay here will bring you back to the good old days. The satay is very good but it is the sauce that really blows me away. Embellished with pineapple, as any self-respecting Hainanese satay sauce should be, it has a wonderfully addictive rich peanut fragrance. I found myself wanting to order more ketupat just to mop up every last peanut!

212 Hougang St 21 #01-1349 S530212 • weekdays: 7pm to 1am, weekends: 5pm to 1am, closed on Thursdays • 94834868

FATMAN SATAY

4.0 Fatman Satay is an institution that has been around since 1948 and has had a loyal following since its days at the Satay Club. There are two big reasons to eat here. Firstly, for the sake of nostalgia, and secondly, for

its minced meat version of satay. The sauce is commendable but the satay could be a bit more juicy.

Lau Pa Sat Festival Market • 18 Raffles Quay Stall #1 S048582 • 5.30pm to 12.30am, open everyday

Old Airport Road Food Centre • 51 Old Airport Road #01-45 S390051 • 7pm to 11pm, closed on Tuesdays

HARON 30 SATAY

4.0 Haron 30 Satay is noteworthy for its substantial portions and the use of chicken pieces instead of mince in their satay. The satay is quite tasty and the homemade peanut sauce is memorable, generously sprinkled with peanuts. If the peanuts were ground a little coarser, that would be perfect. This is usually the first stall to close for the night—I guess that says something about the quality and popularity of their food.

East Coast Lagoon Food Village • 1220 East Coast Parkway Stall 55 S468960 • 2pm to 11pm, closed on Mondays • 64410495

DID YOU KNOW?

Kwong Satay's kushiyaki style pork belly is an *ieat* creation, meaning it was developed based on a suggestion I gave to the owners of Kwong Satay after I blogged about them a few years ago.

GOOD SATAY, WHERE HAVE YOU GONE?

Go to Lau Pa Sat or East Coast Lagoon Food Village, and you will be spoilt for choice by the large number of stalls offering satay. Unfortunately, the choice is between the bad and the so-so. I can't even name one great satay stall at these two so-called Satay Clubs. Gone indeed are the days when the word "Esplanade" meant shiokalicious and piping hot satay by the sea, rather than two big inedible durians. People fondly remember from those days the good old Satay Club, where names like Fatman Satay reigned supreme.

Perhaps the problem with these Satay Clubs is that business is good and the stalls do well enough by enticing customers with a perfunctory, "Satay, sir?" In other words, they don't see the need to maintain standards or improve their satay. Complacency mixed with contentment is a lethal concoction which results in blah food. Then, there is another problem: most Singaporeans do not want chicken skin in their satay. I am not saying that eating chicken skin is good for you. What I am saying is that the same people who frown upon eating chicken skin in satay also happily wolf down BBQ chicken wings, chicken rice and wagyu beef. This is clearly a form of gastronomic hypocrisy.

DID YOU KNOW?

Some people say that the word "satay" is derived from the Hokkien term "sar teh" which means "three pieces". This is not true. The term "satay" is derived from the Tamil word "sathai" which means "flesh".

SOYA SAUCE
CHICKEN

SOMETIMES YOU'RE JUST IN THE MOOD FOR SOMETHING DARK AND mysterious, so when light-skinned poultry just won't do, I reach for soya sauce chicken for that umami kick that I just can't get from my fair-skinned friends. Soya sauce chicken is cooked in a braising sauce of dark soya sauce, rock sugar and rose wine. The resulting dark brown, sweet and slightly sticky skin should be wonderfully fragrant, yet tender to the bite. It certainly takes a bit of skill to get the skin caramelised and fully infused with the sauce while making sure the meat does not overcook.

DID YOU KNOW?

Chickens used to make soya sauce chicken are smaller than those used for chicken rice, even though bigger chickens, above 1.8kg, have better flavour. This is because a large part of the flavour comes from the soya sauce, so a smaller chicken is acceptable.

LESLIE'S PICK ✓

MA LI YA VIRGIN CHICKEN

4.5 The chicken skin is heavenly and a joy to eat! Having soaked up the sauce, it is as good as I can imagine chicken skin can get. The meat is cooked to perfection—the marrow is still pink while the flesh is cooked all the way through, which means that it is not overcooked and the breast remains juicy and tender! There was something very irresistible about the sauce. The most noticeable difference was the addition of fried soya beans, something I used to see as a kid, but which has since gone out of fashion. The fried soya beans and sesame oil gave the sauce an ethereal fragrance that was dangerously close to being hypnotic!

Chinatown Complex Food Centre • 335 Smith St #02-176 S050335 • 7am to 4pm, closed on Mondays • 81637726

HONG KONG SOY SAUCE CHICKEN

4.5 The soya sauce chicken is really good! The sauce flavour on the skin is shiokalicious and is something I keep thinking of eating again and again. It is sweet and sticky—perfectly balanced with not too much of an herbal overtone. The real icing on the cake was that this stall's chicken is excellent value for money, which explains the perpetual queue. The chef is from Ipoh, Malaysia.

Chinatown Complex Food Centre • 335 Smith St #02-127 S050335 • 10am to 8pm, closed on Wednesdays

FRAGRANT SAUCE CHICKEN

4.25 The beauty of this soya sauce chicken lies in its sweet caramelised sauce-infused skin, and tender meat. Randy Tse, the owner, was from Hong Kong and his chicken is somewhere in between the local and Hong Kong versions, so the five spice flavour is significant but not overpowering. (This stall is also recommended for chicken rice.)

QS269 Food House • Blk 269B Queen St #01-236 S182269 • 10.30am to 8pm, closed on Thursdays • 98522245

CHEW KEE EATING HOUSE

4.0 Once upon a time, there was a happy family operating a coffeeshop along Upper Cross Street. One sibling sold soya sauce chicken rice and the other sold soya sauce

MA LI YA VIRGIN CHICKEN

chicken noodles. One day they decided to go their separate ways. Big Sis won the tender to the original stall and stayed put. Little Bro rented a place a few shophouses down the same street. The soya sauce chicken at Big Sis' stall, Chew Kee Eating House, tastes very homecooked: the flavour is dominated by dark sauce and the chicken flesh is firm to the bite, almost chewy. If you are adventurous, order some bishop's nose—chicken backside—to complement your rice.

8 Upper Cross St S048424 • 8am to 6.30pm, closed on Fridays • 62220507

CHIEW KEE CHICKEN NOODLE HOUSE

4.0 In comparison to the chicken skin at the sister's stall at

8 Upper Cross Street (see review above), the chicken skin at this stall is a lighter brown. The soya sauce chicken here is tender and succulent, and the sauce is lighter and slightly sweeter. The noodles are thinner, more yellow and a little softer to the bite, though still QQ (al dente). While it is better than the sister stall, it's not really one to rave about.

32 Upper Cross St S058339 • 8am to 7pm, closed on alternate Wednesdays • 62213531

SUP TULANG

IF YOU NEED AN EXCUSE TO EAT BONE MARROW, HERE'S ONE: IT IS nutritious. Even though it is made up of fat, it is the good sort of primordial unsaturated fat packed full of vitamins and substances which has been shown to have anti-cancer properties.

Sup tulang is the kind of dish that you always bring friends from overseas to try because of the novelty. Get your cameras ready when you hand them a bone and ask them to suck out the marrow. Then watch them desperately try to get the red colouring off their fingers after they are done. Priceless!

DID YOU KNOW?

Good marrow may look slug-like, but it has a melt-in-you-mouth texture. Marrow is very delicious and some animals kill their prey just to suck out its marrow, leaving the rest of the carcass untouched.

LESLIE'S PICK ★✓

AL MAHBOOB INDIAN ROJAK

4.5 I must admit that I haven't really eaten enough sup tulang and I did not really like eating sup tulang until I had it here. The sauce for the sup tulang is just right. Although there is a strong mutton flavour, it is nicely balanced by the fragrance of the spices and the sweetness of the sauce. Just a word of advice: if you don't want your fingers to have an orangey hue for the next two days, remember to bring some gloves! (This stall is also recommended for its Indian rojak.)

S11 Food Court • Blk 506 Tampines Ave 4 S520506 • 12.30pm to 9pm, closed on alternate Wednesdays • 67882257, 91322080

A RASHID KHAN

4.25 I highly recommend this sup tulang. The tendons are cooked till they turn to jelly and you will really enjoy gnawing at the bones and picking out the marrow. The soup has good flavour and is not too heavy, but could do with a bit more punch. It would still satisfy any sup tulang craving though.

Ayer Rajah Food Centre • Blk 503 West Coast Dr Stall 58 S120503 • 8.30am to 1am, closed on alternate Tuesdays • 84549321

HAJI KADIR

4.0 Haji Kadir is a popular spot for tourists to be introduced to the dish. As such, there are several stalls at the same food centre, all vying for your attention. However, this is the stall you'll want to try. You can tell your guests that this was where Anthony Bourdain and Bobby Chinn had their encounters with this devilish dish!

Golden Mile Food Centre • 505 Beach Road #B1-13/15 S199583 • 12.30pm to 1.30am, open everyday • 62940750

LESLIE'S TIP

To extract the marrow, try sucking it out by placing your mouth at the entrance of the bone. Or, tap the bone and if you're lucky, the marrow will slip out unbroken. Some stalls provide a straw together with the dish to help you with this!

Ar-Rahman
01-247

TEH TARIK

I LOVE THE SMOOTH TASTE OF TEH TARIK BUT SOMETIMES WHEN I NEED A bit more kick, I opt for teh halia (ginger tea). Take a sip and let the sweet aroma of comfort flow down your throat. Gulp, smack, ahhh! Ain't nothing like a good teh tarik. I think a good cup of teh tarik should be strong, brisk and creamy. When you drink it, your whole mouth should register a full bodied, creamy mouth feel with a floral fragrance wafting out of your nose. A bit of astringency would add to the briskness and give you that oomph at the end.

DID YOU KNOW?

Teh halia (ginger tea) is perfect after an oily meal. The tannin in the tea acts as an astringent to wash down the flavours, the fat in the milk binds with capsaicin and eases the heat, the sugar triggers the release of substances from the tongue that also eases burning sensation, and the ginger helps to relieve bloatedness.

LESLIE'S PICK ✓

HILMI SARABAT STALL

4.6 Want to feel like the president? Come down to this stall at Marine Parade and ask for the Presidential teh tarik! The one made by "Michael Bolton", a code name to protect the man's real identity, is full-bodied and fragrant, with an excellent post-gustatory punch. The teh halia tarik is just as good as well—strong, creamy and smooth, with enough punch from the ginger!

Marine Parade Central Market & Food Centre • 84 Marine Parade Central #01-146 S440084 • 5.30am to 11pm (Presidential teh tarik only available till 12.30pm)

RUMAH MAKAN MINANG

4.5 Don't hesitate to order a cup of teh tarik to accompany your Malay feast here. The father of the owner, Hazmi, has represented Singapore overseas as a teh tarik ambassador on several occasions and indeed, the teh tarik is very good. They use a very special blend of tea, custom made just for the restaurant. It has hints of rose and vanilla flavours, while the astringency is nicely balanced with the condensed milk, so that it is smooth and brisk. (This stall is also recommended for nasi padang.)

18 Kandahar St S198884 • 8am to 6pm, open everyday • 62944805

MR TEH TARIK CARTEL

4.5 The teh tarik here is smooth and creamy, the taste of the tea is strong enough, and it flows down the throat so smoothly! It's no wonder that there is a perpetual queue outside the stall.

Far East Square • 135 Amoy St #01-01 S049964 • 7am to 9.30pm, open everyday • www.mrtehtarik.com.sg

SRI VIJAYA RESTAURANT

4.5 There aren't many places in Singapore where people still boil their water in an aluminium pot over a gas fire. So if you want to drink a teh tarik that is both robust and rustic, this is one of the places to find it.

229 Selegie Road S188344 • 6am to 10pm, open everyday • 63361748

AR RAHMAN CAFE & ROYAL PRATA

4.25 The owner tells me that they order only the best grade ginger to make the concentrate.

TEH TARIK ◈ **215**

The ginger concentrate is then added to top grade Ceylon tea. This results in the tea having a good creamy mouth-feel balanced with just the right amount of astringency and spiciness from the ginger to give it that uplifting kick! Great to go with any of the India food stalls nearby!

Tekka Market & Food Centre • 665 Buffalo Road #01-247/248 S210665 • 7am to 10pm, open everyday • 91899420, 98554210

RAFEE'S CORNER

4.25 If you are after a teh tarik with a more local flavour, this popular mamak stall might be what you are looking for. They are popular for their teh halia tarik, but on the day that I tried it, the teh halia did not really hit the mark for me. However, the teh tarik is still good—smooth and creamy, and the tea flavour is robust without being too "waxy".

Amoy Street Food Centre • 7 Maxwell Road #02-85 S069111 • Mondays to Fridays: 6.30am to 6pm, Saturdays to Sundays: 6.30am to 2pm • 62214978, 90275153

TAJ MAHAL

4.25 The teh halia here is surprisingly refreshing. Unlike other teh halia I have tasted, this one is not overly milky, and has a good balance of ginger and tea flavours. It is perfect for washing down all the oil and spices after a meal!

Adam Road Food Centre • 2 Adam Road #01-15 S289876 • open 24 hours daily

NO NAME SARABAT STALL

4.25 This little hole in the wall is a great place to stop for a good (and affordable) teh tarik in Kampung Glam. The ambience of this unassuming, quaint little shop, manned by two elderly men with distinguished beards, really adds to the whole teh tarik experience.

21 Baghdad St S199660 • 6.30am to midnight, open everyday

DID YOU KNOW?

The Malaysians have set up Institut Teh Tarik, which confers its Standard of Quality to Malaysian stalls that serve teh tarik that fulfils its criteria for good teh tarik. Should Singapore do the same?

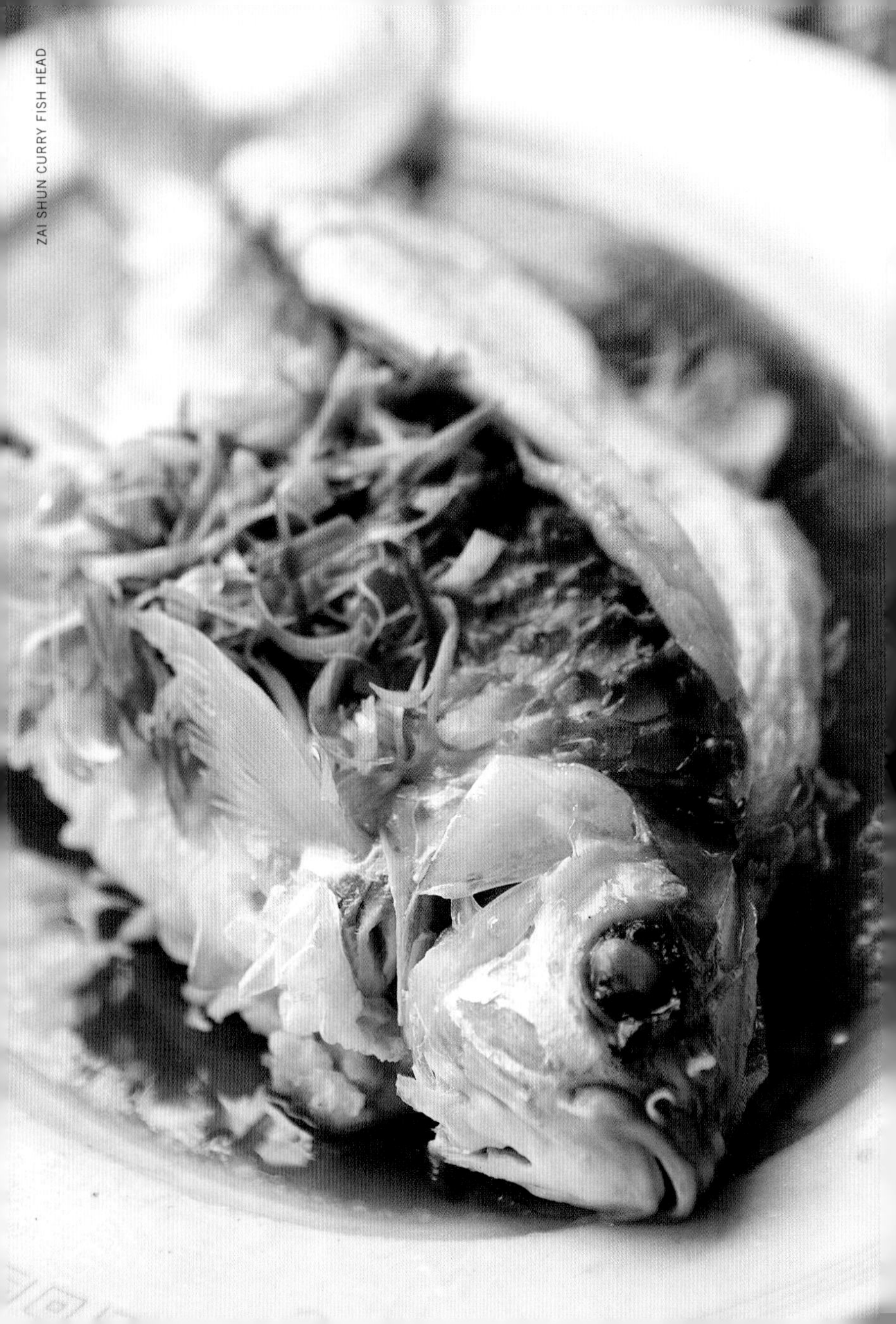

ZAI SHUN CURRY FISH HEAD

TEOCHEW PORRIDGE

THE ENJOYMENT OF TEOCHEW PORRIDGE, ALSO KNOWN AS TEOCHEW MUAY, comes from gulping down the plain, hot watery porridge after you have taken a mouthful of the often salty accompanying dishes. The experience of the warm porridge sliding down your gullet—shiok! Teochew porridge is quintessential comfort food! Teochew porridge should be accompanied by dishes like chye poh (preserved radish) omelette, braised pork belly, sliced lup cheong (waxed Chinese sausages) and braised peanuts.

Other must-order dishes include steamed peh dou her (rabbit fish), steamed mullet, and steamed squid in tau cheo (fermented bean sauce) and chilli. And if you need to impress a potential future mother-in-law who happens to be Teochew, ordering a steamed Chinese silver pomfret will put you well ahead of the competition!

LESLIE'S PICK ★✓

XU JUN SHENG TEOCHEW CUISINE

4.75/4.5 prawn rolls/ lor bak & fish cake Xu Jun Sheng is the Gold Standard for Teochew muay. I would bring anyone who wants to eat Teochew muay here. This is one of the very few places where you can select from a wide array of readily prepared dishes and also order a la carte dishes. The taste of the white pomfret is as good as it gets, and the lor bak (braised pork belly) has a very balanced flavour, with one of the best lor (braising sauce) I have come across. Even the simple braised cabbage is a cut above the rest!

121 Joo Chiat Road S427410 • Mondays to Saturdays: 11am to 3.30pm and 5.30pm to 9pm, Sundays: 10.30am to 3.30pm, closed on Wednesdays • 98472946, 90308600

ZAI SHUN CURRY FISH HEAD

4.6/4.5 thai silver barb fish/ bittergourd fried eggs If you love to eat fish, this is the place for really fresh, exotic steamed fish at a really good price! Fish fanatics will love that ikan kelawat (also known as Sultan fish), mouse grouper and soo mei (napoleon wrasse) are available. Also recommended: hae bee hiam and braised pig's trotters.

Blk 253 Jurong East St 24 #01-205 S600253 • 7am to 3pm, closed on Wednesdays • 65608594

SOON KEE TEOCHEW MUAY

4.5/4.25 steamed fish & mei cai/braised pork This Teochew porridge stall in quiet Sembawang has a certain rustic charm. You will see crowds of people seated along the sidewalk, contentedly slurping their hot porridge. The food is equally old-fashioned, oily, tasty and cheap. The steamed fish is close to perfection—tender and moist—and the steaming sauce, delicious. The equally delicious mei cai goes especially well with the braised pork which isn't prepared in the conventional Teochew style: it is doused in a thick gravy rather than the watery version. Given the quality of food here, it's not surprising they often sell out by 1pm, so go early to avoid disappointment.

33 Sembawang Eating House • 33 Sembawang Road #01-04/07 S779084 • 6am to 2pm, closed on Sundays • 98329787

CHOON SENG TEOCHEW PORRIDGE

4.5 steamed fish & sambal minced pork This is another good place for steamed fish, but come early for their prawn omelettes, made with sua lor (wild prawns). They are an umami bomb.

Blk 43 Cambridge Road #01-09 S210043 • 11am to 2.30pm, closed on Sundays and public holidays • 62930706, 96788458

LIM JOO HIN EATING HOUSE

4.5/4.25 peanuts with ikan bilis/lor bak Surprisingly, their most outstanding dish is the simple dish of peanuts and ikan bilis that comes with some really addictive crunchy bits that I later found out was a mixture of chilli with sugar. The other dishes are generally quite good. I would recommend the hae bee hiam, gu lou yoke and lor bak (braised pork belly), though not their braised peanuts. Their porridge could have been hotter, though this is still one of the better ones I have come across. This is one of the haunts of Hong Kong actor Chow Yun Fatt, whose photo from the 1980s adorns the wall of the stall.

715/717 Havelock Road S169643 • 11am to 5am, open everyday • 62729871

SOON SOON TEOCHEW PORRIDGE

4.5/4.25 minced pork/ braised pork & steamed fish One of the cornerstones of Teochew muay is braised porcine anatomy in a good braising sauce. The sauce here is powerfully good—dark and caramel sweet. My other "must order" dish is the minced pork, which has a good bite and is packed with salty umami goodness! Also recommended: fried leatherjacket in black bean sauce and fish cakes.

13 Simon Road S545897 • 11am to 10pm, closed on Tuesdays

TEOCHEW PORRIDGE (MACPHERSON ROAD)

4.25/4.0 steamed sea bass & steamed mackerel/ minced pork Steamed fish is one of the signature dishes at this stall. The freshly steamed giant sea bass has wonderfully tender flesh and the steaming sauce has a light touch, allowing you to appreciate the fish's

DID YOU KNOW?

The secret to a good minced pork dish is the addition of dang chye (brown pickled cabbage). Chinese cabbage is full of tasty glutamates especially when pickled. Pork, on the other hand, contains inosinate, another flavour compound. Glutamates and inosinates work synergistically to boost umami levels!

delicate flavour. Or if you prefer something stronger, try the mackerel, which has a wonderful umami flavour that complements the hot, watery porridge well. The finely minced pork is also worth trying, though it is a bit too mushy for my liking.

554 MacPherson Road S368230 • 11am to 3.30pm and 5pm to 9pm, closed on Sundays • 92280828

ECONOMIC MIXED VEGETABLE RICE

4.25 minced pork with fermented soya beans People start queuing up by 5pm for their opening at 6.45pm! Yet, I went away wondering why the queue was so long. The duck was a little dry and tough, and while the pomfret was good, it wasn't really a class above other stalls. The one dish that I was

---

LESLIE'S TIP

A good bowl of Teochew porridge has to have the right proportion of water and rice. Firstly, look for the "swa ga hai" (mountain and sea), which shows that the porridge has the right proportion of rice to water and reminds Teochews of Swatow, where the mountain meets the sea. Secondly, the rice must be unbroken. The best Teochew muay places discard the porridge when the rice grains are broken.

---

impressed with was the minced pork, which was bold and salty.

Teck Ghee Court • Blk 341 Ang Mo Kio Ave 1 Stall 13 S560341 • 11.30am to 2pm and 6.45pm to 10pm, closed on Mondays

TEO HENG PORRIDGE STALL

4.25 seasoned eggs & braising sauce You cannot discuss Teochew porridge if you have not eaten the porridge here! Mr Liew has been dishing out hawker food for 60 years—and he's still remarkably fit and has a keen mind. He serves up a perfectly balanced and fragrant braising sauce with various porcine parts stewing in its goodness. Unfortunately, their steamed fish dishes had sold out when I got there after 1pm. Look out for their braised eggs which have runny yolks, like those served at ramen stalls!

Hong Lim Food Centre • 531A Upper Cross St #01-125 S051531 • 8am to 1.30pm, closed on Saturdays, Sundays and public holidays

XIN JIA PO HE PAN
TEOCHEW RICE AND PORRIDGE

4.25 The steamed squid, homemade fish cake and braised pork belly are all very good, but the one that caught my attention was the sambal shark's meat! It is the kind of dish that goes really well with plain porridge because it coats the mouth with all the tasty goodness that just begs to be washed down with piping hot porridge.

BLACK, WHITE OR SILVER?

There is a world of difference between a white pomfret (pampus agenteus) and a black pomfret (parastromateus niger). While white pomfret is a welcome dish to be paired with Teochew porridge, no self-respecting Teochew would ever serve black pomfret to an honoured guest. (Of course, if you feel the guest has overstayed his welcome, then an oversteamed black pomfret might be just the thing to serve!)

For those who are really in the know, there is one type of pomfret that is even more prized than the white pomfret—it is what we call dao chior, or Chinese silver pomfret (pampus chinensis). This pomfret is the type of pomfret you should serve if you are trying to impress someone who happens to be Teochew. The Chinese silver pomfret is more expensive and also less readily available than the white pomfret. The flesh is even more delicate compared to the white pomfret.

Maxwell Road Food Centre • 1 Kadayanallur St #01-98 S069184 • 10.30am to 8.30pm, open everyday

AH SEAH EATING HOUSE

4.0 homemade fish cakes & chye bueh Hougang is one of the Teochew enclaves in Singapore and it is here that you will find Ah Seah Eating House, renowned for its Teochew porridge. This establishment has been around for a long time and is synonymous with the neighbourhood. The best time to eat the porridge is in the evening when the steamed fish is ready. The porridge is also well complemented by soft, flavourful braised peanuts and chye bueh. I especially recommend the homemade fish cakes and meatballs. The latter is essentially fish cake with minced pork, a departure from the usual steamed minced pork with salted eggs. The texture of the fish cakes and the contrast between their coolness and the hot porridge is excellent.

31/33 Teck Chye Terrace • S545731 • 11am to midnight, closed on alternate Mondays • 62837409

WANTON MEE

WANTON MEE IS QUINTESSENTIAL STREET FOOD, YET I HAVE HAD MUCH difficulty finding one that I can truly call "the best". I really cannot understand why it is so difficult to make a great wanton mee. You just need (1) great noodles, QQ (al dente) with a lovely bite and springy texture, (2) an addictive sauce, (3) juicy, succulent char siew and (4) large wantons swollen with juicy meat filling. Is that so difficult? Yet no one seems to be able to get everything right! The dry version of wanton mee, with char siew added, is something that evolved in Malaysia and Singapore. The Hong Kong and Canton versions of wanton mee do not have char siew! Similarly, the addition of tomato and chilli sauces to dry wanton mee is also unique to Singapore.

LESLIE'S PICK ★✓

ENG'S NOODLES HOUSE

4.5 Probably the oldest wanton mee joint in Joo Chiat, Eng's has graduated from being a stall in Dunman Food Centre to having its own shophouse. The distinctive feature of the wanton mee here is the super hot, sweat inducing chilli sauce that sets your palate ablaze like a one ton (read: wanton) napalm bomb. But even if you eschew spice, you'll love the slippery and tender wantons and the custom made egg noodles that are tender and springy, with a nice eggy fragrance. For non-chilli eaters, Eng's non-spicy wanton mee does not contain tomato sauce, but comes with a secret sauce made from pork bones and lard. The 60-year-old recipes from this stall, helmed by second generation owner, Mr Ng, are all round shiokalicious!

287 Tanjong Katong Road S437070 • 11am to 9pm, open everyday • 86882727

NAM SENG WANTON MEE

4.5 Senior Minister Goh Chok Tong recounted eating these noodles during his early dating days at the National Library. The noodles take centrestage here, and come with a secret sauce that will make you stop and wonder. While the char siew is not the juicy charred type that I like, the wantons are very good, though not the best that I have tasted. (This stall is also recommended for hor fun.)

Far East Square • 25 China St #01-01 S049567 • 8am to 8pm, closed on Sundays

WANTON NOODLE

4.5 Both the sauce and noodles are good here, but they are backup singers for the char siew, which is perfectly caramelised with the fat waiting to dissolve as it meets your tongue. Just be forewarned that the pig's armpit cut, the best cut of char siew, sells out earlier than the normal cuts, so you want to get there early.

Tiong Bahru Market & Food Centre • 30 Seng Poh Road #02-30 S168898 • 10.30am to 3pm, closed on Fridays

DA JIE FAMOUS WANTON MEE

4.25 The noodles and sauce from this stall really hit the U-spot (umami spot). The texture of the noodles is perfect, coming alive when you slurp and chew on them. Now, if this wanton mee had big, juicy wantons and char siew that had a little more fatty burnt bits, then I would have found perfection.

209 Jalan Besar S208895 • 7am to 2pm, closed on Sundays and public holidays

FOONG KEE COFFEE SHOP

4.25 The strength of this stall lies in the fact that they roast their own char siew and use a very good cut of pork. The char siew quality is good, tender and juicy. The noodles have a quality taste and texture to them, and while the sauce is good, it is a little too bland for me. The wantons and shui gao are also good, though not outstanding. (This stall is also recommended for char siew.)

6 Keong Saik Road S089114 • 11am to 8pm, closed on Sundays and public holidays

YI SHI JIA WANTON MEE

4.25 The wanton mee here is still very old school. You get a generous helping of crispy pork lard as well as the traditionally thin slivers of tasty char siew. While the noodles are of good quality, it is the wantons that are the star of the show—they are very tasty and some of the best I have ever tasted.

Kovan Food Centre • 209 Hougang St 21 Stall 57 S530209 • 7.30am to 8pm, closed on Sundays • 92957134

HONG MAO WANTON MEE

4.0 This stall was bought over by a long-time customer who was an executive chef at Park Royal. While this wanton mee is very good, I do not think that it is exceptional. The char siew is the stumbling block, for while the texture and taste of the noodles are nice, as are the wantons, the char siew just "cannot make it".

182 Joo Chiat Road S427453 • 7am to 8pm, closed on Mondays • 98759659

HONG JI MIAN SHI JIA

4.0 What makes its wanton mee special are the noodles. They are really thin, translucent and flat, giving them a lively bite and more curl. The wantons are disappointing though—they are full of wanton skin with very little meat. However, the

---

DID YOU KNOW?

The father of the current owner of Eng's Noodles House developed an extra hot chilli sauce to cater to the palates of Joo Chiat residents, who were mostly Peranakans. This chilli sauce is still made from the same blend of eight different dried chillies from India, balanced with salt, sugar and vinegar.

char siew is sweet and succulent, with just enough crunchy burnt bits.

Telok Blangah Drive Food Centre • 79 Telok Blangah Dr #01-05 S100079 • 7am to 7pm, closed on Fridays

KOK KEE WANTON MEE

4.0 Another famous wanton mee stall that has frequent long queues and long waits. I liked the noodles but the real winner was the sauce—it is the stall's boiling cauldron of secret elixir that keeps customers addicted and coming back for more.

Lavender Food Square • 380 Jalan Besar #01-06 S209000 • noon to 2am, closed every 3 weeks on Wednesdays and Thursdays

SOON HENG NOODLE

4.0 The wanton mee here is not bad—the noodles are eggy and QQ (al dente), and very nice with a splash of thick soya sauce a la Malaysian style. Unfortunately, the

> **DID YOU KNOW?**
>
> One of the stumbling blocks for most wanton mee sellers is the char siew. Unless you are able to chargrill your own, it is difficult and expensive to get good char siew. Most wanton mee hawkers end up serving dry, thin slivers of excuses for char siew.

char siew was a little dry, and the wantons were not great.

114 Pasir Panjang Road • 5.30am to 2.45pm, closed Sundays and public holidays

HWA KEE HOUGANG FAMOUS WANTON MEE

4.0 This stall, started by the current owner's father, has been around for more than 40 years. They used to hand make their noodles but now have it made by a factory, though to their own specifications. The sauce is special: the non-chilli version is made from four different unmarked bottles of sauces. A veil of secrecy hangs over the whole stall, which is almost fully covered. You only get to peer in from a narrow doorway! Thankfully, the noodles, with their QQ (al dente) texture, do taste really good, as do the char siew and wantons.

Old Airport Road Food Centre • 51 Old Airport Road #01-02 S390019 • 11am to 10.50pm, closed on Mondays • 96201543

KALLANG WANTON NOODLE

4.0 The owner is very modest about her noodles. The char siew is procured from other sources and is good though not remarkable. Her noodles are also of good quality, with a pleasing texture. But what I especially like is the sauce. It is a little bit sweeter than usual, which agrees with my taste buds.

HWA KEE BBQ PORK NOODLES

Old Airport Road Food Centre • 51 Old
Airport Road #01-61 S390019 • 10am to
11.30pm, closed on Tuesdays

HWA KEE BBQ PORK NOODLES

4.0 This stall is famous for
dousing its noodles with
sweet char siew sauce. While it is
nice, I am not crazy about it. The
char siew is good though not stellar,
despite being charcoal roasted on the
premises. The wantons are also good
but not remarkable.

East Coast Lagoon Food Village • 1220
East Coast Parkway Stall 45 S468960 •
7.30pm to 12.30pm, closed on Wednesdays
• 64453372

SHAN ZAI DING JI JI WANTON NOODLE SPECIALIST

4.0 This stall has been around
for over 40 years and serves
Hong Kong-style wanton mee:
noodles in a dark soya sauce-based
gravy. Their noodles are especially
noteworthy, lively and springy to the

DID YOU KNOW?

There are two types of sauces for
wanton mee—the Hong Kong style
soya sauce and the Singapore style
chilli and tomato sauce combination,
which though simple, has a fierce
loyal following.

MOVING ON UP!

Eng's Noodles House joins the rank of wanton mee stalls that have progressed from a hawker stall to owning a shophouse, just like Fei Fei and Hong Mao Wanton Mee. Stalls serving dishes like chicken rice, prawn mee, bak kut teh, laksa, beef kway teow, nasi lemak and bak chor mee have made similar progression from pushcart hawker to a stall in hawker centre/coffeeshop to standalone eateries.

The way I see it, this trend will invariably continue as the next generation of Singaporeans takes over their parents' businesses and develops boutique eateries or chains, with the potential for expansion. Unfortunately, this trend of progress seems to be happening with only certain dishes, namely hawker foods that can be cooked in a central kitchen. Other dishes like char kway teow and carrot cake, which depend on the frying skills of the hawker, do not seem to making a similar jump into becoming standalone eateries. Wouldn't it be a great day for hawker food if someone opened Singapore's first specialty char kway teow shop!

bite. The homemade char siew is properly grilled, tender and juicy. The sauce and wantons do not disappoint either, making this a fairly satisfying plate of wanton mee. Little surprise then that they count among their customers a good number of regulars.

Hong Lim Food Centre • Blk 531A Upper Cross St #02-49 S051531 • 10.30am to 8pm, open everyday • 65322886

KOUNG'S WANTON MEE

4.0 Noodle lovers will love the simple, delicious noodles at this place. I loved the liberal use of crispy pork lard and the char siew and chilli sauce were nice too.

205 Sims Ave Geylang Lor 21A S387506 • 7.30am to 8.30pm, open everyday • 67480305

YONG TAU FOO

I EAT YONG TAU FOO WHEN I WANT SOMETHING REASONABLY TASTY YET healthy, with less cholesterol. Although I like yong tau foo, I used to find it hard to rave about something as simple as beancurd with fish paste. This was until I tried it the way it should be served. The way to really appreciate yong tau foo is to have it piping hot, with a drizzle of fragrant oil. The ingredients in yong tau foo must be fresh, and it is the quality of the sweet sauce and the fish/meat paste that will distinguish a great yong tau foo from a so-so version.

In Singapore there are three different styles of yong tau foo. The most popular style and subsequently the style found in most food courts is the yong tau foo with fish paste filling. Then there is Hakka yong tau foo, which contains a mix of pork and fish filling. Finally, there is a sprinkling of shops selling Ampang yong tau foo, which is deep fried and served in a platter with light brown gravy.

LESLIE'S PICK

XI XIANG FENG YONG TAU FOO

4.5 **Lao Ban Niang tells me that this stall has been here since it first opened over 30 years ago! The two things that are really outstanding here are the beehoon and the sweet sauce, as they are both very different from the ones you get at your run-of-the-mill yong tau foo stalls. The fresh beehoon has a wonderfully chewy texture and an excellent fragrance, while the sweet sauce is spiked with lots of sesame seeds and is very addictive.**

Ang Mo Kio Central Food Centre • 724 Ang Mo Kio Ave 6 #01-23 S560724 • 7am to 7pm, closed on Sundays • 90932009

HONG HAKKA YONG TAU FOO

4.6 You will be spoilt for choice as this stall boasts 60 yong tau foo items, 16 of which are not found anywhere else in the world! If normal yong tau foo were a sightseeing tour, this stall would be an expedition! A definite must-try for yong tau foo lovers!

Tampines Round Market & Food Centre • 137 Tampines St 11 #01-01 S521137 • 7am to 1pm (when food is usually sold out), open everyday

FU LIN TOU FU YUEN

4.5 If you are craving something healthy, this is not the place to go, for they actually deep-fry everything before serving it in a soya-based minced pork sauce. But that is what makes this yong tau foo so shiok! Another unique thing about this yong tau foo is that it is served with thick beehoon in a meat sauce made from minced chicken, a style of yong tau foo that the owner claims to have started over a decade ago.

721 East Coast Road S459070 • 8.30am to 8.30pm, open everyday • 64462363

HUP CHONG HAKKA NIANG DOU FOO

4.5 The trays of deep-fried wantons, meatballs and ngoh hiang here are simply irresistible. The Hakka style minced meat stuffing used here is shiokalicious and very addictive. It is already great in the tofu, but when deep-fried as a meatball and dipped into the sweet sauce... Shiokalicious!

Blk 206 Toa Payoh North S310206 • 6.30am to 3pm and 5pm to 8.30pm, closed on Sundays

RONG XING YONG TAU FOO

4.25 both stalls This used to be one stall before the

sisters had a fall out. Now there are two. The yong tau foo at these stalls are almost the same. But the soup at the younger sister's stall has a wonderful umami kick that is lacking in the older sister's. On the other hand, the older sister's sweet sauce is much better.

Tanjong Pagar Market & Food Centre • Blk 6 Tanjong Pagar Plaza S081006

Older Sister Stall • #02-04 • 7am to 2.30pm, closed on Sundays and public holidays

Younger Sister Stall • #02-01 • 8.30am to 2.30pm, closed on Saturdays

SIMPANG YONG TAU FOO

4.25 This stall sells the Ampang yong tau foo where the items are first deep-fried then soaked in a sauce. The sauce here is quite unique—sweet, a little tangy, and mildly spicy—perhaps the right adjective is "piquant". It is quite shiok, and definitely unique!

301 Changi Road S419779 • 10am to 6.30pm, open everyday • 64449986

928 NGEE FOU RESTAURANT AMPANG YONG TAU HU

4.0 This stall was opened by a Malaysian boss who ran a successful Ampang yong tau foo stall in Kuala Lumpur. The braising sauce here is very good, and I'd even say it is better than the ones in Ampang! However, they have stopped using pork to fill the yong tau foo and use only fish paste. The other stark difference is the amount of filling in each item, for the ones here are emaciated and wrinkly such that you feel like you are eating mainly fried beancurd skin.

928 Upper Thomson Road S787121 • 10am to 8pm, open everyday • 64521801

GOLDHILL HAKKA RESTAURANT

4.0 The beancurd served here is excellent—the silken tofu is smooth as silk. Every day, fresh ikan parang (wolf herring) is cut into fillets and beaten to a paste by hand, which is then used to stuff chilli, bittergourd, tau pok (fried beancurd) and ngoh hiang. They also serve one of the best sweet sauces I have ever tasted! It is really thick, sweet and substantial.

DID YOU KNOW?

Over time, the Hakka practice of using pork stuffing was replaced by fish paste, perhaps because our ancestors wanted to make the dish suitable for Muslims. The stalls selling the version with meat stuffing, began to distinguish themselves by calling their dish Hakka yong tau foo.

299A Changi Road (after SPC Station)
S419777 • 11.30am to 4pm, open
everyday • 68424283

YONG XIANG XING YONG TAU FOO

4.0 This stall had the longest queue I'd ever seen! Here, everyone gets a standard bowl of yong tau foo, with no options for noodles or beehoon, no questions asked. The fresh beancurd roll with fish paste is definitely the star of the bowl—it is freshly fried and tastes better than anything I've tried from other yong tau foo stalls. It is no wonder since everything in the stall is handmade.

People's Park Cooked Food Centre • 32
New Market Road #01-1084A S050032
• 1pm till sold out (4pm latest), open
everyday

POY KEE YONG TAU FOO

4.0 If you don't feel like queueing up behind 30 people at Yong Xiang Xing, head over to the other end of People's Park Cooked Food Centre to this stall. The soup is very different from Yong Xiang Xing, but the tofu items and ngoh hiang are all pretty good and at least you get to choose what you want to include in your bowl!

People's Park Cooked Food Centre • 32
New Market Road #01-1066 S050032 •
11am to 7pm, open everyday

GOLDEN MILE SPECIAL YONG TAU FOO

4.0 So here's the secret of this shop's success: they make their own fish paste and insist on using the traditional hang zse her (yellowtail) fish. The fish paste is then used to fill capsicums, brinjal, tau pok (fried beancurd) and okra. The water that the fish paste is soaked in is used to make the soup which is delicious, and the fishballs are exceptional! They are not overly bouncy, but have that authentic bite and taste like unadulterated fish meat (which is what it really is). With 10 over handmade items, this stall is worth a try!

Golden Mile Food Centre • 505 Beach
Road #01-44 S199583 • 11am to 2.30pm,
closed on Sundays • 62985908

XIU JI IKAN BILIS YONG TAU FOO

4.0 This stall hand makes the fish paste that goes into its yong tau foo. The addition of ikan bilis (dried anchovies) gives an extra savoury taste to the soup. The other thing is that they serve the yong tau foo with only chilli sauce, with no option for sweet sauce. Make sure you visit them either very early or very late or you'll have to wait in line for your bowl of yong tau foo.

Chinatown Complex Food Centre • 335
Smith St # 02-88 S050335 • 6am to 3pm,
open everyday

MORE OF LESLIE'S PICKS

JUST WHEN YOU THINK YOU'RE AT THE END OF THE BOOK, WAIT!
There's more! There are a few more gems that I really need to tell
you about. They are just too good to leave out. If you have guests
in town, or if you are a serious foodie looking for seriously stunning local food, you will not regret travelling across the island to
try these personal favourites of mine. The list consists of the best
places that I have found so far for these gems. Enjoy!

APPAM

Visit Heaven's Indian Curry for a taste
of the past—appam, like putu mayam,
is in danger of extinction. Made from
rice flour, served with orange sugar
and coconut, it has crispy edges and a
slight tang that comes from fermented
milk. Try it once and it may become
one of your regular breakfast items!

Heaven's Indian Curry
4.5/5
Ghim Moh Market & Food Centre • 20
Ghim Moh Road #01-15 S270020 • 6am
to 1.45pm, open everyday • 94837241,
91652868

BEEF BRISKET NOODLES

I adore Tai Fatt Hau's beef brisket

noodles—the gravy is superb and the brisket has a wonderful beefy, five spice flavour. Owner Mr Wong has been running the stall for the last 30 years but has only focused on beef brisket noodles in the last six years or so. His boast that his recipe is worth $300,000 is not unfounded—he has apparently been approached by investors about franchise opportunities and that was the price being negotiated for his recipe! Lucky for us then, that we only have to pay about $5 to get a taste of his delicious dish.

Tai Fatt Hau Cuisine
4.5/5
Blk 127 Bukit Merah Lane 1 #01-230 S150127 • 7am to 4pm, closed on Sundays 96405171, 98812393

BUTTER PORK RIBS
Make a beeline for Two Chefs Eating Place for their signature dish, the sensationally tender pork chops that melt-in-your-mouth. These innovative, amazing porcine pleasures are covered with golden yellow butter powder and curry leaves, and fried to perfection. The butter powder got me so excited, I couldn't stop thinking about it for a long time.

Two Chefs Eating Place
4.5/5
Blk 116 Commonwealth Crescent #01-129 S140116 • 11.30am to 2.30pm, 5pm to 11.30pm, closed on Mondays during lunch • 64725361, 94379712

CLAYPOT RICE
A truly authentic claypot rice—Le Chasseur makes its claypot rice from scratch, cooking fragrant basmati rice in chicken stock over a smoky charcoal fire to achieve excellent texture, aroma and bite. Worth eating, over and over again.

Le Chasseur
4.5/5
31 New Bridge Road S059393 • 11am to 11pm, open everyday • 63377677, 91440322

KIAM CHYE ARH
Hawker legend Leng Heng serves up a superbly shiok kiam chye arh, the sort that might just clear your ailments and restore your health. Take time to savour this piping hot soup, with the salty tangy taste of the kiam chye and sour plums. Life restoring!

Leng Heng BBQ Seafood & Claypot Deluxe
4.5/5
East Coast Lagoon Food Village • 1220 East Coast Parkway Stall 51 S468960 • 3.30pm to 11pm, closed on Thursdays • 64450513

KUEH TUTU
Tan's Tu Tu Coconut Cakes makes kueh tutu the way it should be—not dry and floury, and made from commercially sourced rice flour, but made from pounded rice, with handmade peanut and coconut filling. The result? Moist, springy kueh tutu, a true labour of love by the descendants

of Tan Yong Fa, the inventor of kueh tutu!

Tan's Tu Tu Coconut Cakes
4.5/5

Blk 22B Food Centre • 22B Havelock Road #01-25 S162022 • 9am to 3pm, open everyday • 97372469

449 Clementi Ave 3 #01-211 S120449 • 3pm to 9.30pm, open everyday

MUAH CHEE

Hougang 6 Miles Famous Muah Chee is the last keeper of the muah chee tradition in Singapore. If you consider yourself a foodie, then a visit to this stall is a necessary pilgrimage! Made fresh everyday, the texture of the muah chee here is sublime, with an intense fragrance of the peanuts.

Hougang 6 Miles Famous Muah Chee
4.5/5

Blk 69 Bedok South Ave 3 #01-468 S460069 • noon to 10pm, open everyday • 98621501, 81206519, 97305513

PEANUT PANCAKE

Nostalgia doesn't get better than this. This is peanut pancake old style—no commercial yeast, with peanuts roasted and ground at the stall. I love the unique taste of the peanut pancake—it is slightly gummy while the outer crust is chewy. The best time to eat at this stall is on Saturdays, because it is closed on Fridays to roast and grind the peanuts.

Tanglin Halt Original Peanut Pancake
4.5/5

Tanglin Halt Market • 48A Tanglin Halt Road Stall #01-16 S148813 • 5am to 11am, closed on Mondays and Fridays • 97123653

PIG'S EARS BISCUITS & CUTTLEFISH

This stall is the reason why I find myself leaving the house for the sole purpose of buying pig's ears biscuits. They are unbelievably good, probably because Mr Tan Nor Chai has been making them since he was 15. When handmade, they are thinner, making them crunchier and tastier. Mr Tan also makes fresh cuttlefish, which is shatteringly crisp and so addictive!

Chai Wee Cuttlefish
4.5/5

Chinatown Complex Food Centre • 335 Smith St #02-59/65 S050335 • Sundays through Fridays: 10am to 3pm, 6pm to 8.30pm, closed on Mondays • 97511986

PUMPKIN PRAWNS

You will not regret ordering the pumpkin tempura prawns at Siang Hee Restaurant. The pumpkin butter cream sauce is so addictive, I could take it with just plain rice. Simple but satisfyingly shiok!

Siang Hee Restaurant
4.5/5

Serangoon Garden Market & Food Centre • 49A Serangoon Garden Way Stall 20 S555945 • 11am to 11.30pm, closed fortnightly on Mondays • 97364067

PUTU PIRING

Who can resist the finest grade gula melaka (from Malacca of course) oozing out of putu piring when it is piping hot? After 14 years of perfecting his craft, Uncle from Putu Piring stall is serving up putu piring paradise—try it before this near-to-extinct handmade snack goes the way of the dodo!

Putu Piring

4.75/5

Mr Teh Tarik Coffee Stall • 970 Geylang Road #01-02 S423492 • 11am to 10pm, open everyday

Haig Road Food Centre • 14 Haig Road #01-08 S430014 • open everyday

TOFU PRAWNS

This is the best version of tofu prawns I've ever had—the sauce has this wonderful umami flavour that has been extracted from the large ang kah prawns. It tasted like melted prawn crackers! An absolutely shiokalicious dish that everyone must try.

Sik Wai Sin

4.6/5

287 Geylang Road (between Lor 13 and 15) S389334 • 11.45am to 2.30pm, and 5.45pm to 9.30pm, open everyday • 67440129

WHITE BEEHOON

You Huak Restaurant is famous for its very unique white beehoon, which is simmered in a rich stock made from old mother hens. The dish as a whole is not heavy on the palate. It's very light and tasty, and while you are there, you must order their leatherjacket with fermented black beans! Absolutely shiokalicious!

You Huak Restaurant

4.5/5

22 Jalan Tampang S758966 • 11.30am to 10.30pm, closed on Wednesdays • 98434699

XIAO LONG BAO

The best xiao long bao I have had in my life is at Shanghai Renjia. The flavours are so balanced that you do not need to dip it in the ginger-vinegar sauce. Just enjoy the natural flavour of the pork!

Shanghai Renjia

4.5/5

Blk 151 Ang Mo Kio Ave 5 #01-3046 S560151 • 11am to 3pm, 6pm to 10pm, closed on Mondays • 63686927

DID YOU KNOW?

Kueh tu tu got its name from the sound the boiling steamers make when steaming this snack: tu tu tu tu…

THE *IEAT* FOOD TRAILS

THE NEIGHBOURHOODS OF CHINATOWN AND JOO CHIAT/KATONG ARE BURSTING with hawker food gems. With such a rich concentration of stellar hawkers, all within walking distance, these two neighbourhoods are great places for visitors, or even local foodies, to savour shiokalicious local hawker food.

So be adventurous—follow these trails and eat your way through classic and authentic Singapore hawker foods and, at the same time, experience Singapore's interesting and delightful local street culture.

1. CHINATOWN

❶ Good Morning Nanyang Café (p131)

❷ **Hong Lim Market & Food Centre**
Outram Park Fried Kway Teow Mee (p49) / Cantonese
Delights (p140, for laksa) / Ah Kow Mushroom Minced
Pork Mee (p7)

❸ FOOD VISIT Head over to Mosque Street to visit Pek Sin
Choon tea merchant to buy some teas (p17)

❹ **People's Park Cooked Food Centre**
Poy Kee Yong Tau Foo (p234) / Yong Xiang Xing Yong Tau
Foo (p234) / Toh Kee (p196, for roast duck and sio bak)

❺ **Chinatown Complex Food Centre**
Teochew Street Mushroom Minced Meat Noodles (p10) /
Xiu Ji Ikan Bilis Yong Tau Foo (p234) / Hong Kong Soy
Sauce Chicken (p206) / Ma Li Ya Virgin Chicken (p206, for
soya sauce chicken)

❻ Lee Tong Kee Ipoh Sar Hor Fun (p126)

❼ Tong Heng Confectionary (for egg tarts)

❽ **Maxwell Road Food Centre**
China Street Fritters (p160) / Tian Tian Hainanese Chicken
Rice (p54) / Zhen Zhen (p179) / Jing Hua Sliced Fish
Bee Hoon (p94)

2. JOO CHIAT/KATONG

❶ Geylang Serai Market
Hajjah Mona Nasi Padang (p154) / Sinar Pagi Nasi Padang
(p156) / Geylang (Hamid's) Briyani Stall (p32)

❷ Haig Road Market
Putu Piring (p242) / Warong Sudi Mampir (p200)

❸ Kway Guan Huat Joo Chiat Original Popiah & Kueh Pie Tee (p174)

❹ Xu Jun Sheng Teochew Cuisine (p218, for Teochew porridge)

❺ Mr and Mrs Mohgan's Super Crispy Roti Prata (p182)

❻ Joo Chiat Prawn Noodle (p188)

❼ Nam San Otah

❽ Lau Hock Guan Kee (p86, for fish head curry)

❾ **Dunman Food Centre** – Lau Hong Ser Rojak (p62)

❿ D'Bun (p168)

⓫ Sin Heng Claypot Bak Koot Teh (p15)

⓬ Tian Tian Hainanese Chicken Rice (p54)

⓭ Glory Catering (p175)

⓮ Astons Specialties (p108)

⓯ Boon Tong Kee (Katong) (p54)

⓰ Katong Durian (p269)

⓱ Chin Mee Chin Coffee Shop (p130)

⓲ Beach Road Prawn Noodle House (p188)

⓳ Geylang Lorong 29 Fried Hokkien Mee (p112)

⓴ 818 Durian and Pastries (p268)

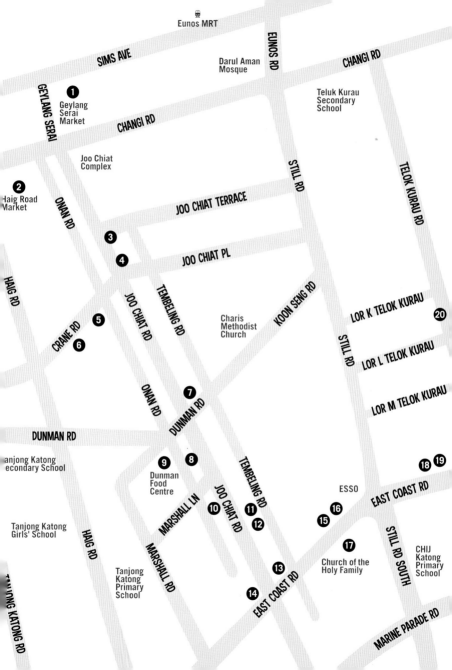

THE BEST IEAT GUIDE TO DURIANS EVER!

WHEN IT COMES TO DURIANS, SINGAPOREANS WILL THROW ALL MANNER OF of decorum out the window. Eating durian is one of the few times in life when it is socially acceptable to eat with your hands, get food all over your face, and talk with your mouth full. No one will bother that the table is not clean, and no one will blink an eye when you throw the durian seed back into the dirty plastic box, and stuff a whole durian segment in your mouth, while simultaneously using your hands to open the next durian!

These days, durians come with all sorts of fancy names and "D"s attached to them. Branded durians, like Mao Shan Wang, D24 and Ang Hei, are grown in many plantations in Malaysia. I don't remember eating such durians when I was growing up in the 1970s. Back in those days, I only remember people speaking of Segamat durians.

One of the main concerns when eating durians is how not to get cheated. According to a Harris Poll, the least trusted occupations in the U.S. are actors, lawyers and stockbrokers. In Singapore, I think durian sellers must be one of the top three. How many of us have been tricked by a durian seller before? Oh yes, I have heard of and experienced first hand how durian sellers switch durians, rig the scales, try selling you the one with the worms, and trick you into thinking that a Thai durian is a D24. Thankfully, there are some reliable durian sellers around, and if and when you find them, stick with them. If you are a serious durian lover, you need to have your own personal durian broker.

> You can't just rely on your durian seller. You yourself have to be able to tell a branded durian from a fake. And what's more, a real durian connoisseur will seek after the less well-known cultivars for their more subtle nuances in flavour and aroma.

However, if you want to call yourself a real durian connoisseur, you have to go one step further. You can't just rely on your durian seller. You yourself have to be able to tell a branded durian from a fake. And what's more, a real durian connoisseur will seek after the less well-known cultivars for their more subtle nuances in flavour and aroma. These lesser known cultivars are not "pop culture durians" that appeal to the masses, but have more complex characteristics that appeal only to the more discerning.

So how do you tell a branded durian from a fake? Or how do you spot the lesser known brands that are just as good as the famous ones, or even better? Just follow the *ieat* guide to durians, that's how!

MAO SHAN WANG/RAJAH KUNYIT (D197)

Mao Shan Wang is by far the most famous and sought after durian among durian lovers. Most of the seeds are what we Teochew call "zhu hook", meaning they are shrunken. You get lots of flesh and very little seed. Mao Shan Wang can be sweet, really creamy and have a bitterness that hits you at the back of your palate, leaving a nice "karm karm" (neutralised) aftertaste.

Mao Shan Wang durians are oval to ellipsoid shaped, light green in colour, with thick and short spines. The light green colour is sometimes difficult to spot because I have seen some that are more dusty brown in colour. The tell tale sign is the star-shaped pattern at the bottom of the durian. This is an area of brownish discolouration that looks like a starfish hanging onto the durian for dear life.

The flesh of the Mao Shan Wang is a very characteristic deep buttery (almost fluorescent) yellow colour. It should have a very rich, sweet and sometimes bitter taste.

The quality of Mao Shan Wang depends on which plantation it comes from and on the weather. In Singapore, Mao Shan Wang generally comes from two places: Johor Bahru and Pahang. The

BEWARE THE OFF SEASON IMPERSONATOR

In between Mao Shan Wang seasons, some sellers may sell a Thai breed called Chanee and pass it off as Mao Shan Wang. It is easy to tell the two apart as the Chanee does not have the star-shaped pattern of the Mao Shan Wang.

Mao Shan Wang: star-shaped pattern at the base

Mao Shan Wang: deep buttery flesh

Mao Shan Wang: shrunken seeds

ones coming from the Bentong region in Pahang are considered the best and among these, the cream of the crop are the ones growing on top of the hill!

Mao Shan Wang has its own specific seasons: around March to April, June to August, and October to November. In between these seasons, some suppliers bring in the Thai Chanee, whose flesh has a similar yellow hue but lacks the pungent odour of a real Mao Shan Wang.

Just because you have been sold a $25/kg Mao Shan Wang doesn't necessarily mean that it is the best. In fact, the best Mao Shan Wang you are going to eat would probably cost less because it would be sold at the peak of the season, when the prices drop due to the large number of fruits falling off the trees.

The fruit from young trees are easy to spot as they are not very fleshy and the seeds are not shrunken. The flesh also doesn't have the same sheen as a premium Mao Shan Wang and you should not be paying top dollar for such a fruit.

SIGNS OF GOOD MAO SHAN WANG

1. Shrunken seeds and lots of flesh.
2. Flesh should be buttery (almost fluorescent) yellow in colour.
3. Pungent, very creamy, sweet and bitter at the same time.
4. Flesh is easy to peel off the seed.
5. You can often see the seeds peering out of the flesh.
6. It should not have any fibres.

D24: base the size of 20 cents

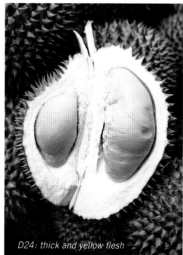
D24: thick and yellow flesh

D24

A very popular cultivar that has been nicknamed "Sultan" because it is so good, it is fit for royalty. D24 durians are small to medium sized, weighing between 1 to 2kg with thick, light green husks. One of the ways to tell a D24 is to look at the base that is devoid of spines. It is, on average, the size of a 20 cent coin. The flesh of a D24 durian is thick and yellow, very smooth and creamy, with a bit of fibre that develops more flavour as you chew.

GOLDEN PHOENIX

If Mao Shan Wang is the current King of Durians then many say that the Golden Phoenix is the Queen. It is a breed of durian that can be quite small, some being the size of my hand and weighing only 0.5kg. However the Golden Phoenix is very fleshy, the seeds are tiny, so you get quite a bit of flesh for such a small durian.

The fruit is often roundish and oval in shape and the spines are small and they converge, culminating in a distinctive tip at the base of the fruit. The colour can vary from light green to greyish brown if they are grown on the top of the mountain. The flesh is pale yellow in colour, dry but not overly pastey, and it has a floral aroma.

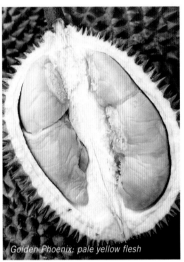

Golden Phoenix: pale yellow flesh

Golden Phoenix: spines converging in a tip

D24 VS GOLDEN PHOENIX

The flesh of a D24 may be generous, but you actually get more flesh from a Golden Phoenix than a D24. However, D24 lovers will tell you that D24 flesh is so satisfying that you only need a few seeds to be completely satisfied!

XO DURIAN

The other favourite of mine is the XO durian; so named because it tastes a bit like cognac. When taken very ripe, the watery greyish yellow flesh is distinctly bittersweet and has a nice alcoholic buzz. The fruit is usually smaller than others. The husk is thin, brownish green in colour, and has a star-shaped depression at the base. Served slightly runny so that it has some time to ferment, the flesh is not as creamy as other durians, but is very pungent.

XO: star-shaped depression at the base

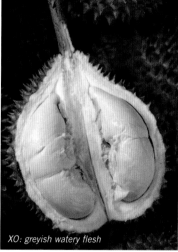
XO: greyish watery flesh

THE ONE TO SCARE FOREIGNERS

The XO durian might not be for everyone, but it's the one to choose if you wish to scare some unsuspecting foreigners!

DURIAN MAS (D101) & D13

There are two other cultivars that are available around the same time as the Mao Shan Wang. D101 and D13 are equally good and cost only around $6/kg. The flesh of D101 and D13 are sometimes passed off as Mao Shan Wang because they look similar. The best way to spot the difference is to look at the shape of the fruit.

The D101 is a large, ellipsoid shaped fruit with spines that are long and thin as opposed to the short, thick spines of the Mao Shan Wang. The flesh of D101 is thick, sweet, creamy and less pastey. The reddish orangey colour of the flesh is similar to another cultivar from Penang called the Ang Hei (D175), which is why D101 is sometimes erroneously called a Johor Ang Hei. D101 spoils rather quickly, so if you plan to buy it home, eat it quickly to avoid disappointment!

The shape of the D13, on the other hand, is typically sharp and pointed at the bottom end as opposed to the more rounded rectangular shape of the Mao Shan Wang, and the thorns are thicker. The D13 has a similar orangey coloured flesh but it has a thicker and heavier husk, so you end up paying a little more for a fruit of the same size as the D101.

D101 VS D13

Some people feel that the D13 is a better tasting fruit than the D101. However the seeds tend to be full sized so you don't get as much flesh. The D13 can sometimes be bitter while the D101 is always creamy, sweet and easy on the palate.

D101: large ellipsoid shape

D101: deep orangey flesh

D13: sharp and pointed tip

D13: deep orangey flesh

GREEN BAMBOO (D160) OR TEK KAH

Green Bamboo or Tek Kah (D160) is a breed of durian very sought after by durian devotees. This durian is very easy to recognise because of the yellowish hollow core which is colloquially known as the longgang (drain). The flesh is thick and creamy, which is similar to the D24, but it has a very unique flavour that harks back to the kampung durians of yesteryear, particularly the bitter and unique aftertaste.

Unfortunately, the yield for Green Bamboo is not very high and as a result, they are being replaced with more commercially viable cultivars like Mao Shan Wang. So, they are getting more difficult to come by.

Green Bamboo: short, thick spines

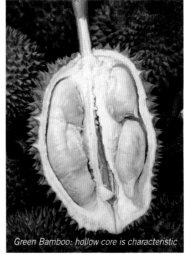
Green Bamboo: hollow core is characteristic

BLACK PEARL

The Black Pearl is easily recognised by its elongated rugby ball shape. The flesh is greyish white and most of these durians have little "pearls" of black in the flesh. The shape of the segments are elongated, looking very much like fried fish cakes. The texture is pastey and the aroma is only mildly pungent. However, it is distinctly sweet with a unique taste.

The small size of the segment is offset by the tiny shrivelled seeds, so you still get quite a nice mouthful of flesh. I am told that it is best to pop the whole segment into your mouth, spit the seed out and spend the next few minutes savouring the taste while swallowing a little at a time.

Black Pearl: greyish white flesh

Black Pearl: shrivelled seeds

GANG HAI

Gang Hai is a breed with cult status. Connoisseurs specially go for the ones grown in Segamat which have not been grafted, i.e., the trees were grown naturally from seeds. The flesh is drier, fibrous and pastey—it coats the mouth as one chews, something a true blue durian connoisseur goes for. The seeds are always shrunken and bell-shaped. Incidentally, Gang Hai is a good durian to introduce to someone who doesn't like the pungent smell of durian.

Gang Hai: pastey flesh

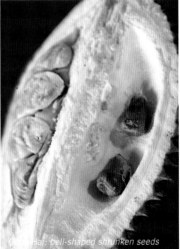
Gang Hai: bell-shaped shrunken seeds

SO RARE SO PRECIOUS

There are only four original plantations in Segamat that still produce Gang Hai. The trees are all very old, so the quality is very good. The season for Gang Hai is very short, lasting only three weeks in June and three weeks in July.

LAO TAI PO

Lao Tai Po (Grand Old Lady) durians are only grown in Yong Peng. The plantations have been around for a while so the durians come from very old trees. The fruit is mid to large size, elongated with a dark green husk and small spines. If you like Mao Shan Wang, you will probably like this durian because of the similar thick, yellow, smooth and creamy flesh, and small vestigial seeds, though the flavour is a little different. Overall, this is one of those durians that

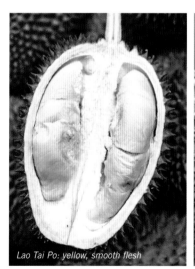

Lao Tai Po: yellow, smooth flesh

Lao Tai Po: star-shaped pattern at the base

LOOK AT THE CENTRE

The Lao Tai Po durian has a star shaped pattern at the base, like the Mao Shan Wang. But look carefully, the centre of the star is empty! This is the key to telling the two apart.

most people will like. The thin husk and small vestigial seeds also mean that you get quite a bit of satisfaction from each fruit.

ANG HEI (D175)

The Ang Hei, also known as D175, is a much coveted fruit, especially in Penang where it is said that it is even more popular than the Mao Shan Wang. I have yet to eat an Ang Hei durian from Penang since the journey is too long for the lorries to transport them to Singapore. Most of the Ang Hei here comes from Johor. And I am told by the durian experts that the Johor Ang Hei is nowhere near Penang's. I hope to experience the Penang Ang Hei one day.

...shaped like a light bulb

Ang Hei: pastel orange flesh

The Ang Hei is a fairly large fruit that can weigh between 1.5kg to 3kg. It is usually ellipsoid, elongated in shape and the thorns are brownish green colour. It looks like it's been covered with ash. The flesh itself is a pastel orange colour, dry and creamy with a very distinct flavour. The flesh is sweet but can be wonderfully bitter when you get the right fruit. I have tasted several Ang Hei this season but the ones at **717 Trading** (see listing) were the best so far.

D100

This is a new hybrid of durian that is just hitting the market. Durian lovers who like their durians to have a bitter bite will be very pleased when they see the slightly grey tones in the yellow flesh. Its flesh is thick, super creamy, with a slightly bitter taste that is darn shiok!

OTHER CULTIVARS

D2: Also known as Dato Nina, this durian is not too popular as it is not fleshy and difficult to open despite its thin husk. However, its flesh tastes like raisins soaked in cognac. Definitely worth a try!

D78: Medium to large sized, this cultivar is shaped like a rugby ball with thick thorns. It has a mild taste, not distinctive in any way, making it a good durian to eat at the beginning of your durian feast.

D88: Medium sized and pear-shaped, the flesh is stunning because

PULAU UBIN DURIANS

Did you know that durians litter the forests of Pulau Ubin around June each year? They are free for anyone to pick up. These are truly organic durians—nobody looks after them, and most of them come from very old trees that have been left undisturbed in the wild. These miscellaneous durian trees produce highly coveted fruits with distinct character, making them feel like vintage cars alongside the mass-produced Mercedes of Mao Shan Wangs.

Ah Di of Wan Li Xiang is the only durian seller I know that sells these old school kampung durians in Singapore. Now in his eighties, Ah Di has been in the durian business since the 1950s, and his Ubin durians command a faithful following of durian devotees. When he sets up shop, at the Fringe Car Park Lot 51/53 off Dempsey Road, you will see customers parking their BMWs and walking over to Ah Di, who will ask them a simple question, "You like sweet or bitter?" The experienced durian monger will then choose a durian for his customer, based on their preferences. The Ubin durian Ah Di chose for me had a wonderful bitter sweet taste, and a flavour which reminded me of the durians I used to eat as a kid! It might not have been as creamy as a Mao Shan Wang, or as bitter as an XO durian, but it was one of those durians which, without a doubt, tasted truly Singaporean!

of its pastel chrome yellow colour. It is not too sweet and has a very distinct bitterness.

D145 or Cheh Kak (Green Husk): With flesh that is predominantly sweet and not too pungent, this durian will appeal to those who eschew bitterness, though to me, this cultivar lacks character.

D163 or Hor Lor: This durian won awards in the 1987/1988 Penang Durian Competition. Its flesh is dry, sticky and bittersweet, good for those who enjoy the thick pastey type of flesh that coats the palate and the throat.

Kasap Merah: This is a boutique durian that does not have the mass appeal of a Mao Shan Wang. But it does have its own fans who specially seek it out for its dry, pastey and sticky flesh that is distinctly less sweet that other more popular cultivars.

Tai Yuan: This durian has a very unique taste—its flesh is greyish yellow in colour, often quite watery and bitter. It reminds me of the kampung durians I ate as a kid.

Tawa: An oblong-shaped durian with very pungent flesh, similar in flavour to the XO durian.

Ten Ten: If you like XO durians, you will like Ten Ten. These durians are small and easy to identify because of the light green husk, usually spotlighted with an area of light yellow. The bitterness of the flesh is very distinct and lingers at the back of your palate.

Tian Xiang: This very special D24 durian grows in a mountain top plantation in Pahang. It is sold only at **818 Durian and Pastries** (see listing). The husk has a slight purplish hue, the flesh is thick, bitter sweet and creamy, and the seeds are tiny. I highly recommend it though it is not always available.

LESLIE'S PICKS FOR DURIAN SELLERS

717 TRADING

717 stocks excellent quality durians. The prices are usually a little higher than other places, but as owner Goh Kwee Leng says, it is better to spend a little more on a good durian than to spend the same amount of money buying many durians of lesser quality. This is one of the few places where you can find D100 durians. There is a basement car park with ample lots, making it a very convenient place to park and eat your durians!

Highland Centre • 22 Yio Chu Kang Road #01-01 S545535 • 9am to 11pm every day • 96751821

818 DURIAN AND PASTRIES

Ah Chiang started selling durians at 13, his father being none other than Goh Kwee Leng of 717 Trading. 818 is a good place for fresh and excellent quality Mao Shan Wang. Although more expensive than other places, you are assured of quality, and the quiet neighbourhood means you can find parking easily and there are tables where you can eat your durians on the spot. There are not many types of durians for sale, as Ah Chiang specialises in Mao Shan Wang and Tian Xiang.

201 Telok Kurau Road #01-02 S423910 • durian season: 11am to 11pm, open everyday, non-durian season: 11am to 8pm, closed on Mondays • 96932727

AH SENG DURIAN

Ah Seng is very customer oriented and his policy is to make sure each customer leaves satisfied. His prices are very competitive and he carries a very good range of durians, including excellent Mao Shan Wang from Bentong in Pahang, Kasap Merah and Gang Hai. Ah Seng also does catering for company functions. The only problem is that there isn't a decent place to sit and eat durians.

Ghim Moh Market & Food Centre • 20 Ghim Moh Road #01-197 S270020 • 1.30pm to 8.30pm, open everyday • 94656160

COMBAT DURIAN

Combat Durian has a solid reputation and owner Mr Ang started selling durians in Balestier in 1957. He is one of Singapore's durian pioneers, being one of the first to give different durians catchy names, like "Sultan durian" for D24. If you are looking for the best of the best Mao Shan Wang, also known as King of Kings durian or Wang Zhong Wang, this is the place to get it!

Balestier Point • 279 Balestier Road S329727 • 3pm to midnight, open everyday • 92789928, 81430495

DEXTER FRUITS

Dexter Fruits specialises in Gang Hai from Segamat. Ah Kok also brings in good quality Mao Shan Wang from Bentong in Pahang, and Tai Yuan.

Blk 441A Pasir Ris Dr 6 #01-74 S511441
• 6am to 8pm, open only during durian season • 86222202

DURIAN SENG

Mr Yap is quite a gregarious character and is known to throw in free durians if you buy a certain quantity from him. I've been told he may even buy you beer or have durian giveaways, like he did on his birthday several times! This stall is known for its Lao Tai Po, Ten Ten and D2 durians. Prices are competitive, so check it out!

Sembawang Garden Arcade • 12 Jalan Tampang S758956 • 3pm to 11pm, open everyday during durian season • 93441512, 97598265

KATONG DURIAN

Previously known as Ah Loon and Ah Teck, Katong Durian is the stall you go to when you are looking for a variety of durians at reasonable prices. It is my go-to stall whenever I have a durian craving! Ah Loon has been selling durians for over 20 years but always from a makeshift stall outside a fruit shop. Now that he has his own stall, you can buy your durians and eat them along the five foot way by East Coast Road. His specialty is Black Pearl.

227 East Coast Road (opposite Jago Close) S428924 • 12.30pm to 10.30pm, open only during durian season • 97514828

KONG LEE HUP KEE TRADING

This stall is great if you are looking for a good variety of durians. Mr and Mrs Chia Boon Huat were the pioneer wholesalers who brought in Tiger Hill Durians. Being a neighbourhood stall, the prices are also very reasonable. I would recommend XO durians, D13 and mini Mao Shan Wang durians.

Blk 440 Pasir Ris Dr 6 #01-03 S510440 • 3pm to 8pm, open everyday during durian season • 98517753

WAN LI XIANG

The only place I know that sells Pulau Ubin durians. Though not the cheapest, Ah Di, one of the oldest durian sellers around, has a steady stream of customers who attest to the quality of his kampung durians. One of the best things about Ah Di is that he operates in an empty parking lot, so you can drive up, park, have your durian fix, then drive off again!

Holland Road • Fringe Car Park Lot 51/53 off Dempsey Road • 3pm till evening during durian season • 97562385, 90182853, 84843957

LESLIE'S TIP

If you get a sore throat after eating durian, try this: add one teaspoon of salt to a cup of warm water and gargle. I find gargling with ENO also helps. The medical community, however, is skeptical on whether "durian sore throat" really exists.

STALLS BY LOCATION

Defu Lane, Hougang, Jalan Kayu,
Kovan, Marsiling, Sembawang,
Serangoon, Upper Thomson,
Yio Chu Kang, Yishun

CASUARINA ROAD
Casuarina Curry (for prata)
136 Casuarina Rd
(off Upper Thomson) S579514
Mons to Fris: 7am to 11.30pm,
Sats, Suns and eve of pub hols:
7am to midnight
www.casuarinacurry.com
64559093

CHOMP CHOMP FOOD CENTRE
Ah Hock Fried Hokkien Noodles
20 Kensington Park Rd
Stall 27 S557269
5.30pm to 11pm, closed once
a fortnight

Carrot Cake
20 Kensington Park Rd
Stall 36 S557269
5.30pm to midnight, closed on
alt Tues

**Chia Keng (previously Che Jian)
Fried Hokkien Mee**
20 Kensington Park Rd
Stall 11 S557269
5.30pm to 1am, open everyday

DEFU LANE
Riyadh Muslim Food
(for prata)
Soon Soon Lai Eating House
32 Defu Lane 10
Stall 12 S539213
6.30am to 7pm, closed every
last Wed of the month
62812664

HOUGANG
Man Ji Handmade Pau
327 Hougang Ave 5 S530327
6am to 1pm, open everyday
98359221

Poh Kee Satay
212 Hougang St 21
#01-1349 S530212
w/days: 7pm to 1am, w/ends:
5pm to 1am, closed on Thurs
94834868

Punggol Noodles
(for bak chor mee)
Hainanese Village Centre
105 Hougang Ave 1
#02-24 S530105
7am to 2.30pm, closed on Suns
97225590/92955909

JALAN KAYU
Blanco Prawn Noodle House
235 Jalan Kayu S799459
7am to 4.30pm, closed on Tues
68534426/96343456 (Susan)

Thohirah Restaurant (for biryani)
258 Jalan Kayu S799487
Open 24 hours daily
64812009

KOVAN FOOD CENTRE
Yi Shi Jia Wanton Mee
209 Hougang St 21
Stall 57 S530209
7.30am to 8pm, closed on Suns
92957134

MARSILING LANE
Hong Ji Claypot Pork Rib Soup
Blk 19 Marsiling Lane
#01-329 S730019
8am to 9pm, open everyday

www.hongji-bkt.com
90901855 (Ah Lim)

SEMBAWANG
Chong Pang Nasi Lemak
447 Sembawang Rd S758458
5pm to 7am, open everyday
96551868 (Edmund Lee)

Durian Seng
Sembawang Garden Arcade
12 Jalan Tampang S758956
3pm to 11pm, open everyday
during durian season
93441512, 97598265

Soon Kee Teochew Muay
33 Sembawang Eating House
33 Sembawang Rd
#01-04/07 S779084
6am to 2pm, closed on Suns
98329787

You Huak Restaurant
(for white beehoon)
22 Jalan Tampang S758966
11.30am to 10.30pm, closed
on Weds
98434699

SERANGOON GARDEN MARKET
& FOOD CENTRE
Ah Seng Braised Duck Rice
49A Serangoon Garden Way
Stall 44 S555945
11am to 9pm, closed on Suns
62888880

**Blanco Court Garden Street
Kway Chap**
49A Serangoon Garden Way
Stall 21 S555945
8am to 3pm, closed on Mons
90017844

Rolina
(for curry puff)
49A Serangoon Garden Way
Stall 32 S555945
7.30am to 5pm, closed on Mons
92358093

**Seng Kee Mushroom
Minced Pork Noodles**
(for bak chor mee)
49A Serangoon Garden Way
Stall 4 S555945
7.30am to 3pm, closed on Mons
84390434

Siang Hee Restaurant
(for pumpkin prawns)
49A Serangoon Garden Way
Stall 20 S555945
11am to 11.30pm, closed
fortnightly on Mons
97364067

Tan Soon Mui Beancurd
49A Serangoon Garden Way
Stall 41 S555945
8am to 8pm, closed on Mons
97999568

SERANGOON ROAD
Macpherson Minced Meat Noodles
(for bak chor mee)
1381 Serangoon Rd
(Opal Crescent) S328254
6.30am to 2.30pm, open
everyday

**Original Serangoon Fried
Hokkien Mee**
556 Serangoon Rd S218175
4.30pm to 11.15pm, closed
on Mons

**Tian Wai Tian Fishhead
Steamboat**
1382 Serangoon Rd
(Opal Crescent) S328254
w/days: 5.30pm to 11pm,
w/ends: 5pm to 11pm
91722833

**Yeo Keng Nam (Traditional)
Hainanese Chicken Rice**
562 Serangoon Rd S218178
11.30am to 11pm, open
everyday
62991128, 62990218

TECK CHYE TERRACE
Ah Seah Eating House
(for Teochew porridge)
31/33 Teck Chye Terrace
S545731
11am to midnight, closed on
alt Mons
62837409

THONG SOON AVENUE
The Prata Place
1 Thong Soon Ave
(Springleaf Estate) S787431
7.30am to midnight, open
everyday
64595670

UPPER SERANGOON ROAD
**Hock Lam Street
Beef Kway Teow**
949 Upper Serangoon Rd
S534713
10am to 11pm, open everyday
62856119

Oyster Omelette Stall
965 Upper Serangoon Rd
S534721
6pm to 10pm, open everyday

Ponggol Nasi Lemak Centre
965 Upper Serangoon Rd
S534721
6pm to 5am, closed on Thurs
62810020, 97805597

Simon Road Fried Hokkien Mee
941 Upper Serangoon Rd
(corner of Simon Rd and Upper
Serangoon Rd) S534709
Noon to 11pm, closed on Mons
98202888

Soon Soon Teochew Porridge
13 Simon Rd S545897
11am to 10pm, closed on Tues
91128112

UPPER THOMSON ROAD
**928 Ngee Fou Restaurant
Ampang Yong Tau Hu**
928 Upper Thomson Rd
S787121
10am to 8pm, open everyday
64521801

Nasi Lemak Kukus
908 Upper Thomson Rd
S787111
6pm to 3am, closed on Mons
82229517 (Reni)

Shui Kway
(for chwee kueh)
Sembawang Hills Food Centre
590 Upper Thomson Rd
#01-16 S574419
Mons to Sats: 6am to 1.45pm,
Suns: 6am to 10am

The Roti Prata House
246 Upper Thomson Rd
S574370
Open 24 hours daily
64595260

YIO CHU KANG ROAD
717 Trading
(for durians)
Highland Centre
22 Yio Chu Kang Rd
#01-01 S545535
9am to 11pm, open everyday
96751821 (Mr Goh Kwee Leng)

YISHUN
928 Yishun Laksa
Blk 928 Yishun Central 1
S760928
10am to 7pm, open everyday
97319586

EAST

Aljunied, Bedok, Changi Road, Changi Village, East Coast Parkway, East Coast Road, Elias Road, Eunos, Geylang, Geylang Serai, Jalan Besar, Joo Chiat, Katong, Macpherson, Marine Parade, Old Airport Road, Paya Lebar, Siglap, Tampines, Telok Kurau

ALJUNIED MARKET & FOOD CENTRE
Citizoom Minced Fish Noodles
(for fishball noodles)
117 Aljunied Ave 2
#01-34 S380117
7am to 3pm, closed on alt Thurs
97420865

Ng Soon Kee Fish And Duck Porridge
(for fish soup)
117 Aljunied Ave 2
#01-11 S380117
Noon to 9pm, closed on Suns
67476014 (Ng Hoe Soon)

BEDOK
Hougang 6 Miles Famous Muah Chee
Bedok South Ave 3 Blk 69
#01-468 S460069
Noon to 10pm, open everyday
98621501, 81206519, 97305513 (Mr Teo)

Yue Lai Xiang Hot and Cold Cheng Tng
Bedok Corner Food Centre
1 Bedok Rd Stall 31 S469572
Noon to 8pm, closed on Mons

BEDOK INTERCHANGE FOOD CENTRE
(New Upper Changi Road Food Centre)
Bedok Chwee Kueh
207 New Upper Changi Rd
#01-53 S460207
7am to 11pm, open everyday

BEDOK MARKET PLACE
Simpang Yong Tau Foo
301 Changi Rd S419779
10am to 6.30pm, open everyday
64449986

BEDOK NORTH
Changi Lorong 108 Fei Lao Seafood
(for hor fun)
86 Bedok North St 4
#01-165 S460086
11am to 2pm and 5pm to 10pm, closed on Tues
63464116

Marine Parade Laksa
Blk 128 Bedok North St 2
#01-02 S460128
9.30am to 5pm, open everyday

Rui Xing Coffee
(for kopi and toast)
216 Bedok North St 1
#01-42 S460216
3am to 11am, closed on Mons

BEDOK ROAD (SIMPANG BEDOK)
Syed Restaurant
(for prata)
326 Bedok Rd S469496
Open 24 hours daily
62425412

BEDOK SOUTH
Hill Street Char Kway Teow
Bedok South Market & Food Centre
16 Bedok South Rd
#01-187 S460016
Noon to 4pm, and 6pm till Uncle runs out of food, closed on Mons
90421312 (Mr Ng)

No Name Cheng Tng
Blk 69 Bedok South Ave 3
S460069
Noon to 9pm, open everyday

CHANGI BUSINESS PARK
Song Fa Bak Kut Teh
UE BizHub East Unit
6 Changi Business Park Ave 1
#01-38 S486017
10.30am to 9.15pm, open everyday
66948098

CHANGI ROAD
Goldhill Hakka Restaurant
(for yong tau foo)
299A Changi Rd
(after SPC Station) S419777
11.30am to 4pm, open everyday
68424283

CHANGI VILLAGE MARKET & FOOD CENTRE
Guan Kee
(for carrot cake)
2 Changi Village Rd
#01-02 S500002
11am to 11pm, closed on Mons

Wing Kee Ipoh Hor Fun
2 Changi Village Rd
#01-04 S500002
Mons to Fris: 10.30am to 11pm
Sats and Suns: 8am to midnight
65456425

CIRCUIT ROAD FOOD CENTRE
Joo Huat Pau
79A Circuit Rd
#01-62 S371079
Noon to 11pm, closed on Mons and Tues
97558688

Yong Lai Fa Ji Cooked Food
(for fish soup)
79A Circuit Rd
#01-648 S371079
5am to 9pm, closed on Suns and pub hols

CRANE ROAD
Joo Chiat Prawn Noodle
Xin Hua Ji Food House
15 Crane Rd S429812
7am to 3pm, closed on Tues

DUNMAN ROAD FOOD CENTRE
Lau Hong Ser Rojak
(for Chinese rojak)
271 Onan Rd #02-14 S424768
4.38pm to 1.38am, closed on
Suns
63466519

EAST COAST LAGOON FOOD VILLAGE
Cheok Kee Duck Rice
1220 East Coast Parkway
Stall 29 S468960
11am to 10pm, open everyday
67439755

Haron 30 Satay
1220 East Coast Parkway
Stall 55 S468960
2pm to 11pm, closed on Mons
64410495

Hwa Kee BBQ Pork Noodles
(for wanton mee)
1220 East Coast Parkway
Stall 45 S468960
7.30pm to 12.30am, closed
on Weds
64453372

Kampong Rojak
(for Chinese rojak)
1220 East Coast Parkway
Stall 9 S468960
10am till 11pm, open everyday

**Leng Heng BBQ Seafood
& Claypot Deluxe**
(for kiam chye arh)
1220 East Coast Parkway
Stall 51 S468960
3.30pm to 11pm, closed on
Thurs
64450513

Roxy Laksa
1220 East Coast Parkway
Stall 48 S468960
w/days: 10.30am to 9pm,
w/ends and pub hols: 8.30am
to 9pm
96302321

EAST COAST ROAD
328 Katong Laksa
216 East Coast Rd S428914
8am to 10pm, open everyday
97328163

Astons Specialties
(for hawker western food)
119/121 East Coast Rd
S428806
11.30am to 10pm, open
everyday
91474627

Beach Road Prawn Noodle House
370 East Coast Rd S428981
8am to 4pm, closed on Tues
63457196

Boon Tong Kee (Katong)
(for chicken rice)
199 East Coast Rd (opp Holy
Family Church) S428902
11am to 10pm, open everyday
www.boontongkee.com.sg
64781462

Chin Mee Chin Coffee Shop
(for kopi and toast)
204 East Coast Rd S428903
8.30am to 4pm, closed on
Mons
63450419

Empress Place Beef Kway Teow
LTN Eating House
936 East Coast Rd S459129
11am to 11pm, open everyday

Five Stars Chicken Rice
191/193 East Coast Rd
S428897

Mons to Sats: 4.30pm to
1.30am, Suns and pub hols:
11.30am to 2pm
63445911

Fu Lin Tou Fu Yuen
(for yong tau foo)
721 East Coast Rd S459070
8.30am to 8.30pm, open
everyday
64462363

**Geylang Lorong 29
Fried Hokkien Mee**
396 East Coast Rd S428994
11.30am to 9.30pm, closed
on Mons
62420080

Glory Catering
(for popiah)
139 East Coast Rd S428829
8.30am to 8.30pm, closed on
Mons except pub hols
63441749

Katong Durian
227 East Coast Rd
(opp Jago Close) S428924
12.30pm to 10.30pm, open
everyday during durian season
97514828 (Ah Loon)

Marine Parade Laksa
Roxy Square
50 East Coast Rd #01-64
S428769
9.30am to 5pm, open everyday

Yong Huat Hokkien Mee
125/127 East Coast Rd
(junction of Joo Chiat Rd)
S428810
8am to 8pm, open everyday
96301370

EUNOS CRESCENT MARKET &
FOOD CENTRE
Epok Epok Central
(for curry puff and nasi lemak)

4A Eunos Crescent
#01-09 S402004
7am to 7pm, closed on Mons
96958889 (Lokman)

FENGSHAN FOOD CENTRE
Chai Chee Pork Porridge
85 Bedok North St 4 Stall 210
& 250 S460085

Stall 210: 5.30am to 3pm,
open everyday

Stall 250: 5.30pm to 2am,
open everyday
98343113

Seng Hiang Food Stall
(outer stall, for bak chor mee)
85 Bedok North St 4
Stall 8 S460085
Tues to Sats: 6pm to 5am, Suns
to Mons: 6am to 1am
90189846

Xing Ji Rou Cuo Mian
(inner stall, for bak chor mee)
85 Bedok North St 4
Stall 7 S460085
5pm to 1am, closed on Mons
98357884

GEYLANG
Ah Xiao Teochew Braised Duck
Geylang East Industrial Estate
1016 Geylang East Ave 3
S389731
Mons to Fris: 11am to 5pm,
Sats: 11am to 4pm, closed on
Suns and pub hols
91098026

Bali Nasi Lemak
2 Geylang Lor 15 S388596
6pm to 4am, open everyday
67421980

Hong Qin Fish and Duck Porridge
(for fish porridge)
134 Geylang East Ave 1

S380134
5.45am to 3pm, closed on 1st
and 3rd Tues of the month

Hup Kee Oyster Omelette
Sing Lian Eating House
549 Geylang Rd Lor 29
S389504
3.30pm to 10.30pm, open
everyday

Kong Kee Seafood Restaurant
(for hor fun)
611/613 Geylang Lor 31
S389550
11pm to 1am, open everyday
64438221

Koung's Wanton Mee
205 Sims Ave Geylang Lor 21A
S387506
7.30am to 8.30pm, open
everyday
67480305

Kwong Satay
Sing Lian Eating House
549 Geylang Lor 29 S389504
5pm to 11pm, closed on alt Weds
97552771

Lorong 9 Beef Kway Teow
237 Geylang Lor 9 S388756
4.30pm to 2.30am, open
everyday
93880723

Penang Food Restaurant
(for fish head curry)
76 Geylang Lor 25A S388258
11am to midnight, open
everyday
68413002

Putu Piring
Mr Teh Tarik Coffee Stall
970 Geylang Rd
#01-02 S423492
11am to 10pm, open everyday
96883067

Sik Wai Sin (for tofu prawns)
287 Geylang Rd (between
Lor 13 and 15) S389334
11.45am to 2.30pm and
5.45pm to 9.30pm, open
everyday
67440129

Sin Huat Seafood Restaurant
(for crabs)
659/661 Geylang Rd (junction
of Geylang Lor 35) S389589
6.30pm to 1am, open everyday
67449755

Swee Guan (for Hokkien mee)
Sing Lian Eating House
549 Geylang Rd Lor 29
S389504
4.30pm to 11.30pm, closed on
alt Weds
98175652

GEYLANG SERAI MARKET &
FOOD CENTRE
Geylang (Hamid's) Briyani Stall
1 Geylang Serai
#01-327 S402001
9am to 5pm, closed on Mons
98310574

Hajjah Mona Nasi Padang
1 Geylang Serai
#02-166 S402001
8am to 7pm, closed on Weds
82826902

Sinar Pagi Nasi Padang
1 Geylang Serai
#02-137 S402001
9am to 10.30pm, closed every
fortnight on Mons and Thurs
65365302

GUILLEMARD ROAD
Tanjong Rhu Pau & Confectionery
389 Guillemard Rd S399701
12.30pm to 8pm, closed on
Suns
63483817

Putu Piring
14 Haig Rd #01-08 S430014
11am to 10pm, open everyday
96883067

Warong Sudi Mampir
(for satay)
14 Haig Rd #01-19 S430014
w/days: 10.30am to 7pm,
w/ends: 10.30am to 5pm,
closed on Weds or Thurs
64440167

Jalan Sultan Prawn Mee
2 Jalan Ayer S347859
8am to 3.30pm, closed on Tues
67482488

Tanjong Rhu Pau & Confectionery
Chin Huan Eating House
7 Jalan Batu #01-113 S431007
12.30pm to 8pm, closed on
Suns
63483817

Kim's Hokkien Mee
62B Jalan Eunos S419510
11am to 1am, open everyday
67478766

Betel Box: The Living Bistro
(for laksa)
200 Joo Chiat Rd #01-01
S427471
8am to 10pm, open everyday
64405540

D'Bun (for pau)
358 Joo Chiat Rd (junction of
Marshall Lane and Joo Chiat Rd)
S427603
8am to 10pm, open everyday
63458220

Eng Seng Restaurant (for crabs)
247 Joo Chiat Rd S427502
5pm to 10pm, closed on Weds
64405560, 91113564 (Eunice)

Hong Mao Wanton Mee
182 Joo Chiat Rd S427453
7am to 8pm, closed on Mons
98759659

**Kway Guan Huat Joo Chiat
Original Popiah and Kueh Pie Tee**
95 Joo Chiat Rd S427389
10am to 8pm, closed on Mons
(takeaway available on Mons)
63442875, 96773441

Lau Hock Guan Kee
(for fish head curry)
328 Joo Chiat Rd
#01-02 S427585
8.30am to 4pm and 4.30pm to
midnight, closed on Thurs
64404928

**Mr and Mrs Mohgan's Super
Crispy Roti Prata**
Poh Ho Restaurant
7 Crane Rd (off Joo Chiat Rd)
S429356
6.30am to 1.30pm, closed on
Tues or Weds on the 3rd week of
the month
97943124

**Ocean Kingdom
Seafood Restaurant**
(for crabs)
382 Joo Chiat Rd S427622
Noon to 2.30pm and 5pm to
11pm, open everyday
63420382

Sin Heng Claypot Bak Koot Teh
439 Joo Chiat Rd S427652
Tues to Sats: 7.30am to 4am,
Suns: 7.30am to 1am, closed
on Mons
63458754

**Tian Tian Hainanese
Chicken Rice**
443 Joo Chiat Rd S427656
10.30am to 10pm, closed on
Mons
63459443

Xu Jun Sheng Teochew Cuisine
(for Teochew porridge)
121 Joo Chiat Rd S427410
Mons to Sats: 11am to 3.30pm
and 5.30pm to 9pm, Suns:
10.30am to 3pm, closed
on Weds
98472946, 90308600

Hock Lam Street Beef Kway Teow
510 Macpherson Rd S368208
10am to 8pm, open everyday

**Teochew Porridge
(MacPherson Road)**
554 MacPherson Rd S368230
11am to 3.30pm and 5pm to
9pm, closed on Suns
92280828

Roland Restaurant (for crabs)
89 Marine Parade Central
#06-750 S440089
11.30am to 2.30pm and 6pm to
10.30pm, open everyday
64408205

Hilmi Sarabat Stall (for teh tarik)
84 Marine Parade Central
#01-146 S440084
5.30am to 11pm (Presidential
teh tarik is available only till
12.30pm)

Katong Chicken Curry Puff
84 Marine Parade Central
#01-132 S440084
8am to 6pm, closed on Mons
64401998

Mr Wong's Seremban Beef Noodle
(for beef kway teow)
84 Marine Parade Central
#01-184 S440084
Noon to 7pm, open everyday

132 Mee Poh Kway Teow Mee
(for bak chor mee)
MP 59 Food House
59 Marine Terrace
#01-105 S440059
7am to 3.30pm, closed on Mons
and 3rd Sun of the month

Chuan Kee Satay
51 Old Airport Rd
#01-85 S390051
Tues to Sats: 6pm till sold out,
Suns: 1pm till sold out, closed
on Mons and Thurs

Dong Ji Fried Kway Teow
51 Old Airport Rd
#01-138 S390051
8am to 2pm, open everyday

Fatman Satay
51 Old Airport Rd
#01-45 S390051
7pm to 11pm, closed on Tues

**Hwa Kee Hougang Famous
Wanton Mee**
51 Old Airport Rd
#01-02 S390051
11am to 10.50pm, closed on
Mons
96201543

Kallang Wanton Noodle
51 Old Airport Rd
#01-61 S390051
10am to 11.30pm, closed on Tues

Nam Sing Hokkien Fried Mee
51 Old Airport Rd
#01-32 S390051
11am to about 8pm when

everything is sold out, closed as
and when Uncle feels tired
64405340

Mattar Road Seafood BBQ
(for chilli crab)
51 Old Airport Rd
#01-63 S390051
4pm to 11pm, closed on Tues
and Weds
64472798

Meng Kee Foo Chow Fish Balls
(for fishball noodles)
51 Old Airport Rd #01-103
(facing main road) S390051
7am to 11pm, closed on Suns

Toa Payoh Rojak
51 Old Airport Rd
#01-108 S390051
Noon to 8pm, closed on Suns
69589380

To-Ricos Guo Shi (for kway chap)
51 Old Airport Rd
#01-135/36 S390051
11.30am to 4.30pm, closed
on Mons

Western Barbeque
(for hawker western food)
51 Old Airport Rd
#01-53 S390051
11am to 11pm, open everyday
64408934

Xin Mei Xiang (for lor mee)
51 Old Airport Rd
#01-116 S390051
7am to 2.30pm, closed on
Thurs

Dexter Fruits
(for durians)
Blk 441A Pasir Ris Dr 6
#01-74 S511441
6am to 8pm, open everyday
during durian season

Kong Lee Hup Kee Trading
(for durians)
Blk 440 Pasir Ris Dr 6
#01-03 S510440
3pm to 8pm, open everyday
during durian season
98517753

Chye Kee Chwee Kueh
89 Pipit Rd #01-129 S370089
6.30am to 3pm, open everyday

Lian Kee Braised Duck
49 Sims Place #01-73
S380049
10am to 8.30pm, open everyday

Ah Guan Mee Pok
(for bak chor mee)
69 Syed Alwi Rd S207648
7am to 9pm, open everyday
62960069

The Beef House
(for beef kway teow)
Gar Lok Eating House
217 Syed Alwi Rd S207776
8am to 6pm, closed on Fris
96654919, 98215463

Gu Ma Jia
(for fish head curry)
45 Tai Thong Crescent
S347866
11am to 10pm, open everyday
62852023

Lao Zhong Zhong Five Spice Stall
(for ngoh hiang)
Lao Zhong Zhong Eating House
29 Tai Thong Crescent (corner
of Tai Thong Crescent and Siang
Kiang Ave) S347858
11.30am to 11.30pm, closed
on alt Mons

River South (Hoe Nam) Prawn Noodles Eating House
31 Tai Thong Crescent (facing Jackson Centre) S347859
6.30am to 4.30pm, closed once a month on Mons
62819293

Al Mahboob Indian Rojak
(for Indian rojak and sup tulang)
S11 Food Court Blk 506
Tampines Ave 4 S520506
12.30pm to 9pm, closed on alt Weds
67882257, 91322080

Boon Lay Power Nasi Lemak
Blk 474 Tampines St 43
S520474
7am to 3am, open everyday

House of Desserts
137 Tampines St 11
#01-02 S521137
7am to 5pm, closed on Mons

Hong Hakka Yong Tau Foo
137 Tampines St 11
#01-01 S521137
7am to 1pm (when food is usually sold out), open everyday
90932009 (Alan)

Eng's Noodles House
(for wanton mee)
287 Tanjong Katong Rd
S437070
11am to 9pm, open everyday
86882727

Ponggol Nasi Lemak Centre
238 Tanjong Katong Rd
S437026
5.30pm to 2.30am, closed on Thurs
63483303

818 Durian and Pastries
201 Telok Kurau Rd
#01-02 S423910
durian season: 11am to 11pm, open everyday, non-durian season: 11am to 8pm, closed on Mons
96932727

Hong Ho Phang Hong Kong Pau
5 Telok Kurau Rd S423758
7.30am to around 4pm, closed on Mons

Katong Laksa
1 Telok Kurau Rd (opp SPC Petrol Station) S423756
8am to 3.30pm, open everyday
64404585, 98559401

Eng Cheong Pau
416 Upper Paya Lebar Rd
S534995
7am to 7pm, open everyday
68583652

Kay Lee Roast Meat Joint
125 Upper Paya Lebar Rd
S534838
10am to 7pm, closed on Tues
67438778

WEST

Alexandra Village, Ayer Rajah, Boon Lay, Bukit Merah, Buona Vista, Clementi, Dover, Ghim Moh, Holland Road, Lengkok Bahru, Pasir Panjang, Queenstown, Redhill, Telok Blangah, Upper Bukit Timah

Fatty Cheong (for roasted meats)
6 Jalan Bukit Merah
#01-120 S150006
11am to 8.30pm, closed on Thurs
98824849, 94281983

Guang Ji Bao Zai
(for pau)
6 Jalan Bukit Merah
#01-135 S150006
10am to 10pm, closed on Thurs

Jin Jin Dessert
6 Jalan Bukit Merah
#01-20 S150006
Noon to midnight, closed on Weds
90932018

Tiong Bahru Yi Sheng Hokkien Mee
6 Jalan Bukit Merah
#01-13 S150006
3pm to 10.45pm or until food runs out, closed on Weds

Wow Wow West
(for hawker western food)
6 Jalan Bukit Merah
#01-133 S150006
10.30am to 9pm, closed on Suns

Yong Kee Fish Ball Noodle
6 Jalan Bukit Merah
#01-121 S150006
7am to 2am, open everyday
62703956

Depot Road Zhen Shan Mei Claypot Laksa
120 Bukit Merah Lane 1
#01-75 S150120
8.30am to 3.30pm, open everyday
90889203

Lau Phua Chay
(for roasted meats)
120 Bukit Merah Lane 1
#01-20 S150125
11.30am to 3.30pm, closed on Sats
96636862

Abdhus Salam Rojak
Blk 503 West Coast Dr
Stall 73 S120503
10.30am to 11.30pm, open
everyday

Habib's Rojak
Blk 503 West Coast Dr
Stall 68 S120503
Noon to 10.30pm, closed on
alt Mons
93358528

Boon Lay Power Nasi Lemak
221B Boon Lay Place
#01-06 S641221,
7am to 3am, open everyday
90064730

Day Night Fried Kway Teow
Blk 162 Bukit Merah Central
#02-29 S150162
10am to 8pm,
closed on alt Thurs
96404870

**Nan Heng Hainanese
Chicken Rice**
Blk 163 Bukit Merah Central
#02-28 S150163
11.30am to 8.30pm,
closed on Suns
62736993

De Burg (for burgers)
Blk 119 Bukit Merah Lane 1
#01-40 S151119
Tues to Thurs: 11.30am to 3pm
and 6pm to 9pm, Fris to Suns:
11.30am to 3pm and 6.30pm to
9pm, closed on Mons

Hong Kong Street Chun Kee
(for fish soup)
125 Bukit Merah Lane 1
#01-190 S150125
Mons to Sats: 11.30am to
2.30pm and 5pm to 11.30pm,
Suns: 11am to 2pm and
5.30pm to 11pm
62718484, 62728484

Tai Fatt Hau Cuisine
(for beef brisket noodles)
Blk 127 Bukit Merah Lane 1
#01-230 S150127
7am to 4pm, closed on Suns
96405171, 98812393

Tian Tian Hainanese Curry Rice
116 Bukit Merah View
#01-253 S151116
9.30am to 9.30pm, closed on
alt Tues
91096732

Bukit Merah View Carrot Cake
115 Bukit Merah View
#01-279 S151115
7am to 2pm and 6pm to 1am,
open everyday

Bukit Purmei Lor Mee
109 Bukit Purmei Ave
#01-157 S090109
7.30am to 3.30pm, closed on
Mons

Five Stars Chicken Rice
6/7 Cheong Chin Nam Rd
S599732
10am to midnight, open
everyday
64663000

**Chin Huat Live
Seafood Restaurant** (for crabs)

105 Clementi St 12 (Sunset
Way) #01-30 S120105
11.30am to 2.30pm and
5.30pm to 11pm, open everyday
67757348

Balmoral Bakery (for curry puff)
105 Clementi St 12
#01-06 Sunset Way
9am to 9pm, open everyday
67792064

Soon Lee (for porridge)
Blk 448 Clementi Ave 3
#01-50 S120448
Mons to Fris: 6am to 9pm, Sats:
6am to 5pm, closed on Suns

Tan's Tu Tu Coconut Cakes
(for kueh tu tu)
449 Clementi Ave 3
#01-211 S120449
3pm to 9.30pm, open everyday
97372469

Sin Kee Famous Chicken Rice
Blk 38 Commonwealth Ave
#01-02 S149738
11am to 8pm, closed on Mons
64739525

Two Chefs Eating Place
(for butter pork ribs)
Blk 116 Commonwealth
Crescent #01-129 S140116
11.30am to 2.30pm, 5pm
to 11.30pm, closed on Mons
during lunch
64725361, 94379712

Xi Le Ting (for desserts)
40A Commonwealth Ave
#01-70 S140040
Noon to 10pm, closed fortnightly
on Mons and Tues

DOVER CRESCENT
Holland Village XO Fish Head Bee Hoon
Jumbo Coffee Hub
19A Dover Crescent S131019
11.30am to 2pm and 5pm to
11pm, open everyday
98331003

GHIM MOH MARKET & FOOD CENTRE
Ah Seng Durian
20 Ghim Moh Rd
#01-197 S270020
1.30pm to 8.30pm, open everyday

Ghim Moh Chwee Kueh
20 Ghim Moh Rd
#01-31 S270020
6.15am to 6.30pm, open
everyday
64626017

Guan Kee Char Kway Teow
20 Ghim Moh Rd
#01-12 S270020
9.30am to 2.30pm, closed on
Mons and Fris

Heaven's Indian Curry (for appam)
20 Ghim Moh Rd
#01-15 S270020
6am to 1.45pm, open everyday
94837241, 91652868

Jiu Jiang Shao La
(for roasted meats)
20 Ghim Moh Rd
#01-45 S270020
11am to 7.30pm, closed on Weds

Teck Hin Fried Hor Fun
20 Ghim Moh Rd
#01-44 S270020
10am to 3pm, closed on Mons

Tong Fong Fatt (Ghim Moh)
(for chicken rice)
20 Ghim Moh Rd
#01-49 S270020
10am to 8.30pm, open everyday

HOLLAND ROAD
Wan Li Xiang
(for durians)
Holland Rd, Fringe Car Park
Lot 51/53 off Dempsey Rd
3pm till evening, only during
durian season
97562385, 90182853,
84843957

HOY FATT ROAD
Istimewa Nasi Padang
Blk 28 Hoy Fatt Rd S151028
10am to 3pm, closed on Suns
96301272, 97260239

JALAN BUKIT MERAH
Sheng Cheng Char Kway Teow
Blk 132 Jalan Bukit Merah
S160132
Noon to 10pm, closed fortnightly
on an ad hoc basis
92736195

JALAN RUMAH TINGGI
Fook Seng Goldenhill Chicken Rice
Blk 37 Jalan Rumah Tinggi
#01-415/417 S150037
8am to 4pm, open everyday
97773318

JURONG EAST
Zai Shun Curry Fish Head
Blk 253 Jurong East St 24
#01-205 S600253
7am to 3pm, closed on Weds
65608594

KIM TIAN ROAD
Soon Soon Huat 1A Crispy Curry Puff
Blk 127 Kim Tian Rd
#01-01 S160127
8am till sold out, closed on Mons
68415618

LENGKOK BAHRU
Seng Hong Coffeeshop
(for kopi and toast)

58 Lengkok Bahru S150058
6am to 6pm, closed on alt
Suns

Tom's Citizoom Mee Pok Tar
Blk 57 Lengkok Bahru S151057
8.30am to 3pm, closed on alt
Suns and pub hols
97420854

MEI CHIN FOOD CENTRE
Shi Hui Yuan Hor Fun Specialty
(for Ipoh hor fun)
159 Mei Chin Rd
#02-33 S140159
7.30am to 2pm, closed on Mons
and Tues

PASIR PANJANG FOOD CENTRE
Heng Huat Fried Kway Teow
121 Pasir Panjang Rd
#01-36 S118543
Noon to 10pm, closed on Suns
and pub hols
97355236

PASIR PANJANG ROAD
Soon Heng Noodle
(for wanton mee)
114 Pasir Panjang Rd S118539
5.30am to 2.45pm, closed on
Suns and pub hols

Tong Lok Kway Chap
114 Pasir Panjang Rd S118539
7am to 3pm, closed on Suns,
Mons and pub hols

QUEENSTOWN
No Name Nasi Padang
Khong Guan Restaurant
Blk 49 Stirling Rd S141049
7am to 5pm, closed on Suns
and pub hols

Marine Parade Laksa
Queensway Shopping Centre
1 Queensway #01-59 S149053
10am to 9.15pm, open
everyday

Redhill Curry Rice
(for Hainanese curry rice)
85 Redhill Lane #01-95
(facing main road) S150085
10.30am to 9.30pm, closed
on Suns
96523471

Redhill Lor Duck Rice and Noodles
85 Redhill Lane
#01-79 S150085
9am to 2.30pm, closed on
Thurs and Fris

SILAT AVENUE
Yee Kee Specialist Roasted Duck
Blk 148 Silat Ave
#01-14 S160148
11am to 4pm, closed on Suns
96977083

Zhong Xing Foo Foochow Fishballs
(for fishball noodles)
Blk 148 Silat Ave
#01-14 S160148
7.30am to 5pm, closed on Tues
93675420

SOUTH BUONA VISTA ROAD
Lim Seng Lee Duck Rice
38 South Buona Vista Rd
S118164
10.30am to 8.30pm, closed
on Suns
64759908

TANGLIN HALT MARKET
Delicious Duck Noodles
(for braised duck)
48A Tanglin Halt Rd
#01-23 S148813
4am to 2pm, closed on Sats
97829210

Tanglin Halt Original Peanut Pancake
48A Tanglin Halt Rd
#01-16 S148813

5am to 11am, closed on Mons
and Fris
97123653

Tian Shui Chicken Rice
48A Tanglin Halt Rd
#01-21 S148813
9am to 8pm, closed on Mons
97575532

TELOK BLANGAH CRESCENT
MARKET & FOOD CENTRE
**Hai Kee Teochew
Char Kway Teow**
11 Telok Blangah Crescent
#01-102 S090011
5pm to 10pm, closed on Suns

TELOK BLANGAH DR FOOD CENTRE
Hong Ji Mian Shi Jia
(for wanton mee)
79 Telok Blangah Dr
#01-05 S100079
7am to 7pm, closed on Fris

CENTRAL

Adam Road, Ang Mo Kio, Balestier,
Braddell, Newton, Novena, Sin Ming,
Toa Payoh, Whampoa

ADAM ROAD FOOD CENTRE
**Noo Cheng Adam Road
Prawn Noodle**
2 Adam Rd #01-27 S289876
9.15am to 4pm and 6.30pm to
2am, open everyday

Selera Rasa Nasi Lemak
2 Adam Rd #01-02 S289876
7am to 6pm, closed on Fris
98434509

Taj Mahal (for teh tarik)
2 Adam Rd #01-15 S289876
Open 24 hours daily

ANG MO KIO
Chia Keng Kway Teow Mee
(for mee pok tar)

Chong Boon Food Centre
Blk 453A Ang Mo Kio Ave 10
#01-11 S561453
5am to 2pm, closed on Mons
and Fris
96446338, 93591838

Economic Mixed Vegetable Rice
(for Teochew porridge)
Teck Ghee Court
Blk 341 Ang Mo Kio Ave 1
Stall 13 S560341
11.30am to 2pm and 6.45pm to
10pm, closed on Mons

Hong Heng Beef Noodle King
Kebun Baru Mall Food Centre
Blk 226H Ang Mo Kio St 22
#01-16 S568226
7.30am to 3pm, closed on Mons
64524017

Lao San Kway Chap
Blk 232 Ang Mo Kio Ave 3
S560232
6am to midnight, closed on
Mons

Tip Top Curry Puff
Hiap Hwa Coffeeshop
Blk 722 Ang Mo Kio Ave 8
#01-2843 S560722
9.30am to 9.30pm,
closed on Weds

Shanghai Renjia
(for xiao long bao)
Blk 151 Ang Mo Kio Ave 5
#01-3046 S560151
11am to 3pm and 6pm to 10pm,
closed on Mons
63686927

ANG MO KIO CENTRAL FOOD CENTRE
Ang Mo Kio Char Kway Teow
724 Ang Mo Kio Ave 6
#01-28 S560724
11.30am to 8pm, open everyday
97298273

Lim Hai Sheng Cooked Food
(for carrot cake)
724 Ang Mo Kio Ave 6
#01-09 S560724
7am to 10pm, open everyday

Xi Xiang Feng Yong Tau Foo
724 Ang Mo Kio Ave 6
#01-23 S560724
7am to 7pm, closed on Suns
96353203

ANG MO KIO MARKET &
FOOD CENTRE
**Joo Heng Mushroom
Minced Pork Mee**
(for bak chor mee)
628 Ang Mo Kio Ave 4 St 61
#01-86 S569163
7am to 2pm, open everyday

BALESTIER ROAD
Combat Durian
Balestier Point
279 Balestier Rd S329727
3pm to midnight, open everyday

Founder Bak Kut Teh Restaurant
New Orchid Hotel
347 Balestier Rd S329777
Noon to 6pm, closed on Tues
63526192

**Whampoa Keng Fishhead
Steamboat**
556 Balestier Rd
S329872
w/days: 11am to 3pm and 5pm
to 11pm, w/end and pub hols:
11am to 11pm
91276550

BRADDELL ROAD
**Yeo Keng Nam (Traditional)
Hainanese Chicken Rice**
8 Braddell Rd S359898
10.30am to 10pm, open
everyday
62854261, 62854153

BUKIT TIMAH FOOD CENTRE
& MARKET
He Zhong Carrot Cake
116 Upper Bukit Timah Rd
#02-185 S588172
7am to 10pm, open everyday
64685398

Seng Kee Carrot Cake
116 Upper Bukit Timah Rd
#02-182 S588172
7.30am to 11pm, closed on
Thurs

CAMBRIDGE ROAD
Choon Seng Teochew Porridge
Blk 43 Cambridge Rd
#01-09 S210043
11am to 2.30pm, closed on
Suns and pub hols
62930706, 96788458

JALAN DATOH
Tiong Bee Bah Kut Teh
588F Jalan Datoh (off
Balestier Rd) S329899
7am to 3pm, closed on alt Mons

**Noi's Mushroom
Minced Meat Noodles**
(for bak chor mee)
588F Jalan Datoh (off
Balestier Rd) S329899
8.30am to 4pm, open everyday

KIM KEAT PALM MARKET
& FOOD CENTRE
Ah Chuan Oyster Omelette
22 Toa Payoh Lor 7
#01-25 S310022
3pm to 9pm, closed on Tues

Dove Desserts
22 Toa Payoh Lor 7
#01-21 S310022
Mons to Thurs and Sats: 11am
to 8pm, Fris: 11am to 6pm,
closed on Suns
92725712

Hai Nan Xing Zhou Beef Noodles
22 Toa Payoh Lor 7
#01-06 S310022
8am to 7pm, closed on Mons
63543397

Old Long House Popiah
22 Toa Payoh Lor 7
#01-03 S310022
6am to 4pm, closed on Mons
91717157

KINTA ROAD
Soon Heng Restaurant
(for fish head curry)
39 Kinta Rd S219108
w/days: 10.30am to 8pm,
w/ends and pub hols: 10.30am
to 5pm
62947343, 62946561

NEWTON FOOD CENTRE
Heng Carrot Cake
500 Clemenceau Ave North
#01-28 S229495
6pm to 1.30am, open everyday

Thye Hong (for Hokkien mee)
500 Clemenceau Ave North
#01-69 S229495
5pm to 1am, open everyday
96181221

OWEN ROAD
Heng Heng Bak Kut Teh
107 Owen Rd S218914
7.30am to 2.30pm, closed on
Tues
62924913

QUEEN'S ROAD
Westlake (for pau)
Blk 4 Queen's Rd #02-139
Singapore 260004
11am to 2.30pm and 6pm to
10pm, open everyday
64747283, 64711441

SHUNFU MART FOOD CENTRE
Fu Shi Traditional Roasted
(for roasted meats)
Blk 320 Shunfu Rd
#02-25 S570320
9am to 2pm, closed on Mons
and Tues
92378157

Lai Heng Fried Kway Teow
Blk 320 Shunfu Rd
#02-20 S570320
11am to 8pm, closed on Mons

SIN MING
Hooked on Heads
(for fish head curry)
Sin Ming Plaza
6 Sin Ming Rd Tower 2
#01-01/02 S575585
11am to 2.30pm and 5.30pm to
9.30pm, open everyday
64554948

Rong Cheng Bak Kut Teh
Eng Ho Hup Coffeeshop
22 Sin Ming Rd S570022
7am to 4pm, open everyday

Mid View City
Blk 26 Sin Ming Lane
#01-114/117 S573791
7am to 9pm, open everyday
96681412

Sin Ming Roti Prata
24 Sin Ming Rd
#01-51 S570024
6am to 7pm, open everyday
64533893

SIXTH AVENUE
Tao Xiang Kitchen
(for chicken rice)
10E Sixth Ave #01-01/02
S276474
8.15am to 8.30pm, open
everyday

THOMSON ROAD
Penang Road Café
(for prawn noodles)
Novena Ville
275 Thomson Rd
#01-08 S307645
11.30am to 2.30pm and 5.45pm
to 9.15pm, closed on Mons
62563218, 97862079

Tanjong Rhu Pau & Confectionery
72 Thomson Rd S307589
12.30pm to 8pm, closed on
Suns
62536942

**Wee Nam Kee Hainanese
Chicken Rice**
Novena Ville
275 Thomson Rd
#01-05 S307645
10am to 12.30am, open
everyday
62556396

TOA PAYOH
Ah Chiang's Porridge
Blk 190 Lor 6 Toa Payoh
#01-526 S310190
7am to 9.30pm, open everyday
63566009

Hua Fong Kee Roast Duck
Blk 116 Toa Payoh Lor 2
#01-140 S310116
8am to 8pm, open everyday
62532884

Blk 128 Toa Payoh Lor 1
#01-811 S310128
8am to 8pm, closed on Thurs
62515192

Hup Chong Hakka Niang Dou Foo
(for yong tau foo)
Blk 206 Toa Payoh North
S310206
6.30am to 3pm and 5pm to
8.30pm, closed on Suns
90932009

**Lai Heng Mushroom Minced Meat
Mee** (for bak chor mee)
Blk 51 Toa Payoh Lor 6
S 310051
8.30am to 4pm, closed on Weds
96202074

Wok Inn Fish and Chips
(for hawker western food)
Blk 125 Toa Payoh Lor 2
11.30am to 9.30pm, closed
on Tues
98976048

Song Kee Fishball Noodle
Blk 75 Toa Payoh Lor 5
#01-354 S310075
10.30am to midnight, closed on
alt Weds
96776979

TOA PAYOH HDB HUB
Soon Heng Silver Stream Rojak
HDB Hub
480 Toa Payoh Lor 6
#B1-23 S310480
11am to 8pm, open everyday

TOA PAYOH LORONG 4
93 Wu Xiang Xia Bing
(for ngoh hiang)
Blk 93 Food Centre
93 Toa Payoh Lor 4
#01-33 S310093
Noon to 9pm, closed on Thurs

Gen Shu Mei Shi Shi Jia
(for porridge)
Blk 74 Food Centre
Toa Payoh Lor 4
#01-03 S310074
6am till sold out around lunch
time, closed on Mons

TOA PAYOH WEST MARKET
& FOOD COURT
Chey Sua Carrot Cake
127 Toa Payoh Lor 1
#02-30 S310127
6am to 1pm, closed on Mons

Teochew Handmade Pau
127 Toa Payoh Lor 1
#02-02 S310127
Tues to Sats: 6am to 2pm,
Suns: 6am to noon, closed on
Mons and alt Tues
62542053, 66595786

Tian Tian Lai (Come Everyday)
Fried Hokkien Prawn Mee
127 Toa Payoh Lor 1
#02-27 S310127
9.30am to 9pm, closed on Mons
62518542, 96717071

UPPER BUKIT TIMAH ROAD
Karu's Indian Banana Leaf
Restaurant (for fish head curry)
808/810 Upper Bukit Timah Rd
S678145
10.30am to 10pm, closed on
Mons
67627284, 83859511

WHAMPOA DRIVE MAKAN PLACE
(Whampoa Food Centre)
Ah Hock Fried Oyster Hougang
(for oyster omelette)
90 Whampoa Dr
#01-54 S320090
Noon to 11pm, closed on alt
Weds

Hoover Rojak
90 Whampoa Dr
#01-06 S320090
Mons, Weds to Suns: 10.30am
to 9.30pm, Tues: 10.30am
to 6pm
90214593

Nan Xiang Chicken Rice
90 Whampoa Dr
#01-21 S320090
11am to 10pm, open everyday
90906342

Rabiah Muslim Food Nasi Melayu
(for nasi padang)
90 Whampoa Dr

#01-34 S320090
10am to 6pm, closed on Suns

Singapore Fried Hokkien Mee
90 Whampoa Dr
#01-32 S320090
4pm to 1.30am, open everyday
62512857

Whampoa Soya Bean and Grass
Jelly (for beancurd)
Blk 91 Whampoa Dr
#01-52 S320090
6.30am to 4.30pm, closed on
Mons

Xin Heng Feng Guo Tiao
Tan (Whampoa Fish Head
Steamboat)
(for fish head steamboat)
Blk 91 Whampoa Dr
#01-14/15 S320091
5pm to 9.30pm, closed on Tues

DOWNTOWN/CITY

Beach Road, Central Business
District, Chinatown, Esplanade,
Lau Pa Sat, Lavender, Little India,
Mohammed Sultan, North Bridge
Road, River Valley, Rochor, Seah Im
Road, Tanjong Pagar, Tiong Bahru

AMOY STREET FOOD CENTRE
Han Kee Fish Porridge
(for fish soup)
7 Maxwell Rd
#02-129 S069111
10am to 3pm, closed on Suns

Hong Kee Beef Noodle
(for beef kway teow)
7 Maxwell Rd
#01-42 S069111
w/days: 11am to 7.30pm,
w/ends: 9am to 2.30pm, closed
on pub hols
63231679

Piao Ji Fish Porridge
(for fish soup)
7 Maxwell Rd
#02-100/103 S069111
10.30am to 3pm, closed on
Thurs

Rafee's Corner (for teh tarik)
7 Maxwell Rd
#02-85 S069111
Mons to Fris: 6.30am to 6pm,
w/ends: 6.30am to 2pm,
62214978, 90275153

Yuan Chun Famous Lor Mee
7 Maxwell Rd
#02-79/80 S069111
8.30am till around 4pm when
sold out, closed on Mons and
Tues

BAGHDAD STREET
No Name Sarabat Stall
(for teh tarik)
21 Baghdad St S199660
6.30am to midnight, open
everyday

BEACH ROAD
Alex Eating House
(for roasted meats)
Chye Sing Building
87 Beach Rd #01-01 S189695
9am to 6pm, open everyday
63340268

Blanco Court Prawn Noodles
(for prawn mee and ngoh hiang)
243/245 Beach Rd
#01-01 S189754
7.15am to 4pm, closed on Tues
63968464

Chao Shan Cuisine
(for oyster omelette)
85 Beach Rd S189694
11.30am to 2.30pm and 6pm to
10pm, open everyday

Leong Kee (Klang) Bak Kut Teh
321 Beach Rd (Jalan Sultan
Gate and Beach Rd) S199557
11am to 9pm, closed on Mons
93801718

Prince Coffee House
(for hor fun and hawker
western food)
249 Beach Rd
(opp Park Royal) S189757
11am to 9pm, open everyday
64682088

BENCOOLEN STREET
Oven Marvel (formerly known as
Delicious Muffins, for curry puff)
Sunshine Plaza
91 Bencoolen St
#01-51 S189652
11.30am to 8pm, closed on 8th,
18th and 28th of every month
96361503

BEO CRESCENT
No Name Hainanese Curry Rice
40 Beo Crescent S160040
6.30am to 3pm, closed on
Weds

Yang Zhou (for Hokkien mee)
40 Beo Crescent
#01-16 S160040
10am to 8pm, closed on Fris
62730429, 97400653

BERSEH FOOD CENTRE
Coffee Hut (for kopi and toast)
166 Jalan Besar
#02-43 S208877
w/days: 7am to 3pm, w/ends:
7am to noon
90108311

Mei Xiang Fish Soup
166 Jalan Besar
#02-44 S208877
11am to 2pm, closed on w/ends
and pub hols
97896686

BUFFALO ROAD
Blue Diamond Restaurant
(for biryani)
24-26 Buffalo Rd S219791
10am to 10pm, open everyday
62911629

CHINATOWN COMPLEX
FOOD CENTRE
Chai Wee Cuttlefish (for pig's
ears biscuits and cuttlefish)
335 Smith St
#02-59/65 S050335
Suns through Fris: 10am to 3pm
and 6pm to 8.30pm, closed
on Mons
97511986

Heng Ji Chicken Rice
335 Smith St
#02-131 S050335
3pm to 9pm, open everyday

Hong Kong Soy Sauce Chicken
335 Smith St
#02-127 S050335
10am to 8pm, closed on Weds

Ma Li Ya Virgin Chicken
(for soya sauce chicken)
335 Smith St
#02-176 S050335
7am to 4pm, closed on Mons
81637726

**Teochew Street Mushroom
Minced Meat Noodle**
(for bak chor mee)
335 Smith St #02-23 S050335
12.30pm to 9pm, closed on
Mons and Tues

Xiu Ji Ikan Bilis Yong Tau Foo
335 Smith St #02-88 S050335
6am to 3pm, open everyday

Yuet Loy (for hor fun)
335 Smith St
#02-151 S050335
12.15pm to 2pm and 6.15pm to
9pm, closed on Thurs
91704152

CRAWFORD LANE
Happy Chef Western Food
Tai Hwa Eating House
466 Crawford Lane
#01-12 S190466
11am to 10pm, open everyday
92749591, 96827000,
63980773

Hill Street Tai Hwa Pork Noodle
(for bak chor mee)
Tai Hwa Eating House
466 Crawford Lane
#01-12 S190466
9.30am to 9pm, closed on 1st
and 3rd Mons of the month
62927477

DUNLOP STREET
Bismillah Biryani Restaurant
50 Dunlop St S209379
11.30am to 3pm and 5.30pm to
10pm, closed on Tues
93827937

ENG HOON STREET
Loo's Hainanese Curry Rice
Blk 57 Eng Hoon St
#01-88 S160057
8am to 2pm, closed on alt Tues
62253762

FAR EAST SQUARE
Hock Lam Street Beef Kway Teow
22 China St #01-01 S049564
10am to 9pm, open everyday
www.hocklambeef.com
62209290

Nam Seng Wanton Mee
(for wanton mee and hor fun)
25 China St #01-01 S049567
8am to 8pm, closed on Suns
64385669, 96896288

Mr Teh Tarik Cartel
135 Amoy St #01-01 S049964
7am to 9.30pm, open everyday
www.mrtehtarik.com.sg

Puay Heng Bak Chor Mee
23/24 China St
#01-01 S049565
9.30am to 9.00pm, closed on
alt Suns
65366707

Ya Kun Kaya Toast
(for kopi and toast)
18 China St #01-01 S049560
w/days: 7.30am to 7pm,
w/ends: 8am to 5pm
www.yakun.com
64383638

GOLDEN MILE FOOD CENTRE
Golden Mile Special Yong Tau Foo
505 Beach Rd
#01-44 S199583
11am to 2.30pm, closed on
Suns
62985908

Haji Kadir (for sup tulang)
505 Beach Rd
#B1-13/15 S199583
12.30pm to 1.30am, open
everyday
62940750

Hainan Fried Hokkien Prawn Mee
505 Beach Rd
#B1-34 S199583
11am to 2pm and 3pm to 9pm,
closed on Weds
62946798

Rosraihanna Soto and Satay
505 Beach Rd
#B1-19 S199583
Noon to 10pm, closed on Suns
92371199

Zhao An Granny Grass Jelly
(for desserts)
505 Beach Rd #01-58
S199583
11am to 7pm, closed on alt Suns

HAVELOCK ROAD
Lim Joo Hin Eating House
(for Teochew porridge)
715/717 Havelock Rd S169643
11am to 5pm, open everyday
62729871

Meng Kee Char Kway Teow
Wei Xuan Eating House
22 Havelock Rd
#01-669 S160022
Mons to Sats: 10.30am to 7pm
Suns: 10.30am to 4pm

Tan's Tu Tu Coconut Cakes
(for kueh tutu)
Blk 22B Havelock Rd
#01-25 S162022
9am to 3pm, open everyday
97372469

HONG LIM FOOD CENTRE
**Ah Kow Mushroom
Minced Pork Mee**
(for bak chor mee)
531A Upper Cross St
#02-42 S510531
9am to 7pm, open everyday

Cantonese Delights (for laksa)
531A Upper Cross St
#02-03 S510531
9am to 3pm, closed on w/ends
91051904

**Famous Sungei Road
Trishaw Laksa**
531A Upper Cross St
#02-67 S510531
10.30am to 6.30pm, closed
on Suns

Lee Kheong Roasted Delicacy
(for roasted meats)
531A Upper Cross St
#02-15 S510531
10am to 6pm, closed on Suns
93804854

**Old Stall Hokkien Street
Famous Hokkien Mee**
531A Upper Cross St
#02-67 S510531
9.30am to 4pm, closed on Thurs
98539630, 97411849

**Outram Park Fried
Kway Teow Mee**
531A Upper Cross St
#02-17 S510531
6am to 4.30pm,
closed on Suns and pub hols

**Shan Zai Ding Ji Ji
Wanton Noodle Specialist**
531A Upper Cross St
#02-49 S051531
10.30am to 8pm, open everyday
65322886

Teo Heng Porridge Stall
(for Teochew porridge)
531A Upper Cross St
#01-125 S051531
8am to 1.30pm, closed on
w/ends and pub hols

Tuck Kee (Ipoh) Sar Hor Fun
531A Upper Cross St
#02-41A S051531
11am to 3pm, closed on Suns

JALAN BERSEH
Sungei Road Laksa
Jalan Shui Kopitiam
27 Jalan Berseh
#01-100 S200027
9am to 6pm, closed on the first
Wed of the month

Beach Road Scissor Cut Curry Rice (for Hainanese curry rice)
Lao Di Fang Restaurant
229 Jalan Besar S208905
11am to 3.30am, open everyday
62923593

Beancurd City
133 Jalan Besar
(after Desker Rd) S208851
10.30am to midnight, open everyday
62969058

Da Jie Famous Wanton Mee
209 Jalan Besar S208895
7am to 2pm, closed on Suns and pub hols
96670087

Hainan Chicken Rice Ball
Shin Boon Hwa Food Centre
43 Jalan Besar
(Dickson Rd) S208804
8.30am to 9.30pm, open everyday
81338287, 63965191

Oriole Coffee Roasters
(for kopi and toast)
10/10A Jiak Chuan Rd S089264
Mons to Sats: 8.30am to 10pm
Suns and pub hols: 8.30am to 6pm
62248131

Rumah Makan Minang
(for nasi padang and teh tarik)
18 Kandahar St S198884
8am to 6pm, open everyday
62944805

Foong Kee Coffee Shop
(for wanton mee and roasted meats)
6 Keong Saik Rd S089114

11am to 8pm, closed on Suns and pub hols
96953632

Kok Seng Restaurant
(for fish head curry)
30-32 Keong Saik Rd S089137
11.30am to 11.30pm, open everyday
62232005

Tong Ya Coffeeshop
(for kopi and toast)
36 Keong Saik Rd S089143
w/days: 11am to 2.30pm and 5.30pm to 10.30pm, w/ends: 11am to 2.30pm and 5.30pm to 11pm, closed on alt Weds
62235083

Killiney Kopitiam
(for kopi and toast)
67 Killiney Rd S239525
Mons, Weds to Sats: 6am to 11pm, Tues, Suns and pub hols: 6am to 6pm
www.killiney-kopitiam.com
67349648

Teck Kee Tanglin Pau
83 Killiney Rd S239531
9am to 10.30pm, closed on Mons
www.teckkeepau.com
67349253

Killiney Curry Puff
93 Killiney Rd S239536
7am to 7.30pm, open everyday
67262011

Fatman Satay
Lau Pa Sat Festival Market
18 Raffles Quay
Stall 1 S048582
5.30pm to 12.30am, open everyday

Bugis Street Ngak Seah Beef Kway Teow
380 Jalan Besar
#01-28/29 S209000
9am to 9pm, closed on alt Weds

Kok Kee Wanton Mee
380 Jalan Besar
#01-06 S209000
Noon to 2am, closed every three weeks on Weds and Thurs

Miow Sin Popiah and Carrot Cake
(for carrot cake)
380 Jalan Besar
#01-04 S209000
9am to midnight, closed on alt Weds
62928764

Wei Nan Wang Hock Kian Lor Mee
50 Market St #03-03 S048940
9.30am to 3.30pm, open everyday

Funan Weng Ipoh Hor Fun
32 Maxwell Rd
#01-07 S069115
w/days: 11am to 9pm, w/ends: noon to 8.30pm, closed on pub hols
www.funanweng.com
62385038

China Street Fritters
(for ngoh hiang)
1 Kadayanallur St
#01-64 S069184
Noon to 8pm, closed on Mons
92386464

Hoe Kee (for porridge)
1 Kadayanallur St
#01-45 S069184
Mons to Thurs: 6.30am to

2.30am, Fris to Suns: 6.30am
to 4am

Hup Kee Wu Siang Guan Chang
(for ngoh hiang)
1 Kadayanallur St
#01-97 S069184
Noon to 8pm, closed on Mons
90040618

Jing Hua Sliced Fish Bee Hoon
(for fish soup)
1 Kadayanallur St
#01-77 S069184
11am to 8.30pm, closed on
Thurs

Peanuts Soup
1 Kadayanallur St
#01-57 S069184
7.30am to 4pm, closed on Mons

**Tian Tian Hainanese
Chicken Rice**
1 Kadayanallur St
#01-10 S069184
11am to 8pm, closed on Mons
www.tiantianchickenrice.com
96914852

**Xin Jia Po He Pan
Teochew Rice and Porridge**
1 Kadayanallur St
#01-98 S069184
10.30am to 8.30pm, open
everyday

Zhen Zhen (for porridge)
1 Kadayanallur St
#01-54 S069184
5.30am to 2.30pm, closed
on Tues

NEW BRIDGE ROAD
Le Chasseur
(for claypot rice)
31 New Bridge Rd S059393
11am to 11pm, open everyday
63377677, 91440322

Song Fa Bak Kut Teh
11 New Bridge Rd
#01-01 S059383
7am to 10pm, closed on Mons
65336128

NORTH BRIDGE ROAD
Islamic Restaurant
(for biryani)
745 North Bridge Rd S198713
10am to 10pm, open everyday
62987563

**Nam Wah Chong Fish Head
Steamboat Corner**
814/816 North Bridge Rd
S198779
5pm-1am, open everyday
62979319

Nasi Padang Sabar Menanti II
747 North Bridge Rd S198715
6am to 5pm, closed on Suns
and pub hols
62981389

Qi Ji Poh Piah
Funan DigitalLife Mall
109 North Bridge Rd
#01-17 S179097
9am to 8.30pm, open everyday
www.qiji.com.sg
62838572

Seng Huat Eating House
(for bak chor mee)
492 North Bridge Rd
(opp Parco Bugis Junction)
S188737
Open 24 hours everyday

Singapore Zam Zam Restaurant
(for murtabak)
697 North Bridge Rd S198675
8am to 11pm, open everyday
62987011

Warong Nasi Pariaman
(for nasi padang)
738 North Bridge Rd S198706

7.30am to 3pm, closed on Suns
and pub hols
62925958

ORCHARD TURN
Li Xin Chao Zhou Fish Ball
(for fishball noodles)
ION Food Opera
Orchard Turn Basement 4
S238801
Mons to Thurs: 8am to 10pm,
Fris, Sats and eve of pub hols:
8am to 11pm, Suns: 10am to
10pm

PEK KIO MARKET & FOOD CENTRE
Tong Siew Fried Rice
(for oyster omelette)
41A Cambridge Rd
#01-23 S211041
11am to midnight, closed on
Weds
96939599

Wah Kee Prawn Noodles
(for prawn mee)
41A Cambridge Rd
#01-15 S211041
7.30am to 2pm, closed on Mons
96883633

PEOPLE'S PARK COOKED
FOOD CENTRE
Poy Kee Yong Tau Foo
32 New Market Rd
#01-1066 S050032
11am to 7pm, open everyday

Toh Kee (for roasted meats)
32 New Market Rd
#01-1014 S050032
Noon to 7.30pm, closed on Mons
63233368

Yong Xiang Xing Yong Tau Foo
32 New Market Rd
#01-1084A S050032
1pm till sold out (4pm latest),
open everyday

PURVIS STREET
Chin Chin Eating House
(for chicken rice)
19 Purvis St S188598
7am to 9pm, open everyday
63374640

Yet Con Hainanese Chicken Rice
25 Purvis St S188602
10am to 10pm, open everyday
63376819

QS269 FOOD HOUSE QUEEN STREET
Eleven Finger (Eu Kee) Curry Rice
(for Hainanese curry rice)
Blk 269B Queen St
#01-235 S180269
10am to 6pm, closed alt Fris

Fragrant Sauce Chicken
(for chicken rice and soya
sauce chicken)
Blk 269B Queen St
#01-236 S182269
10.30am to 8pm, closed on
Thurs
98522245

**New Rong Liang Ge Hong Kong
Roast** (for roast duck)
Blk 269B Queen St
#01-235 S182269
9am to 8pm, closed on the first
Wed of every month

QUEEN STREET BLK 270
MARKET & FOOD CENTRE
**Siraj Famous Waterloo Street
Indian Rojak (Bugis)**
270 Queen St
#01-120 S180270
9am to 7pm, closed last Mon of
every month

RANGOON ROAD
Founder Bak Kut Teh Restaurant
154 Rangoon Rd S218431
9am to 3pm and 5.30pm to
10.30pm, closed on Weds
62920938

**Ng Ah Sio Pork Ribs Soup
Eating House**
208 Rangoon Rd S218453
7am to 10pm, closed on Mons
www.ngahsiobkt.com
62914537

**Whampoa Keng Fishhead
Steamboat (Rangoon Road)**
116/118 Rangoon Rd
S218396
11am to 11pm, open everyday
90232854

RIVER VALLEY ROAD
Five Stars Chicken Rice
419 River Valley Rd S248318
11am to 5am, open everyday
62356760

SEAH IM FOOD CENTRE
Ichiban Fish Soup
2 Seah Im Rd #01-18 S099114
8am to 8pm, closed on Sats

SELEGIE ROAD
Sri Vijaya Restaurant
(for teh tarik)
229 Selegie Rd S188344
6am to 10pm, open everyday
63361748

SHORT STREET
Eryimin (for beancurd)
4 Short St S188212
Noon to midnight, open everyday
63366394

Rochor Original Beancurd
2 Short St S188211
Noon to midnight, open everyday
63341138

SOUTH BRIDGE ROAD
Lee Tong Kee Ipoh Sar Hor Fun
278 South Bridge Rd S058827
10am to 9pm, open everyday
62231896

TANJONG PAGAR COMPLEX (PSA)
Ali Nachia Briyani Dam
(for biryani)
7 Keppel Rd
#01-16/17 S089053
10.30am to 2.30pm, open
everyday
93546363

Outram Park Ya Hua Rou Gu Char
(for bak kut teh)
7 Keppel Rd
#01-05/07 S089053
6am to 3pm and 6pm to 4am,
closed on Mons
62229610, 98241066

TANJONG PAGAR MARKET
& FOOD CENTRE
Annie's Peanut Ice Kachang
(for desserts)
6 Tanjong Pagar Plaza
#02-36 S081006
w/days: 10.30am to 7.15m,
w/ends: 10.30am to 6pm
81635678

Rong Xing Cooked Food
(for yong tau foo)
6 Tanjong Pagar Plaza #02-04
& #02-01 S081006

Older Sister Stall #02-04:
7am to 2.30pm, closed on Suns
and pub hols

Younger Sister Stall #02-01:
8.30am to 2.30pm, closed
on Sats

TANJONG PAGAR PLAZA
Five Spice Prawn Fritter
(for ngoh hiang)
Teck Kee Coffeeshop
Blk 5 Tanjong Pagar Plaza
#02-04/05 S081005
11.00am to 1.00pm, closed
on Suns

Allauddin's Briyani
665 Buffalo Rd
#01-297 S210665
10am to 7pm, open everyday
62966786

AR Rahman Cafe & Royal Prata
(for teh tarik)
665 Buffalo Rd
#01-247/248 S210665
7am to 10pm, open everyday
91899420, 98554210

Heng Gi Goose and Duck Rice
(for braised duck)
665 Buffalo Rd
#01-335 S210665
8.30am to 2.30pm, closed on
Mons
63960969

Temasek Indian Rojak
Blk 665 Buffalo Rd
#01-254 S210665
9am to 9pm, closed on alt Mons
93350957

Rendezvous Restaurant
(for nasi padang)
6 Eu Tong Sen St
#02-72/73 S059817
11am to 9pm, open everyday
63397508

Ah Chiang's Porridge
Blk 65 Tiong Poh Rd
#01-38 S160065
7am to 2pm and 6pm to
midnight, closed on alt Mons
65570084

Old Tiong Bahru Bak Kut Teh
Blk 58 Seng Poh Rd
#01-31 S160058
6.30am to 9pm, closed on Mons
62244990

Sum Long Teochew Braised Duck
Blk 57 Eng Hoon St
#01-88 S160057
Mons to Fris: 7am to 8pm, Sats:
7.15am to 4pm, Suns: 7.15am
to 3pm

**Hui Ji Fishball Noodles and Yong
Tau Foo** (for fishball noodles)
30 Seng Poh Rd
#02-44 S168898
7am to 2pm, open everyday

Jian Bo Shui Kweh
(for chwee kueh)
30 Seng Poh Rd
#02-05 S168898
6.30am to 10.30pm, open
everyday
90223037

Lor Mee 178
30 Seng Poh Rd
#02-58 S168898
6am to 9.30pm, closed on Weds

Tiong Bahru Pau
30 Seng Poh Rd
#02-18/19 S168898
7.30am to 9pm, closed on Mons
64381663

Wanton Noodle (for wanton mee)
30 Seng Poh Rd
#02-30 S168898
10.30am to 3pm, closed on Fris

Chew Kee Eating House
(for soya sauce chicken)
8 Upper Cross St S058327
9am to 7pm, closed on Fris
except on pub hols
62220507

Chiew Kee Chicken Noodle House
(for soya sauce chicken)
32 Upper Cross St S058339

8am to 7pm, closed on alt Weds
62213531

Good Morning Nanyang Café
(for kopi and toast)
Telok Ayer Hong Lim Green
Community Centre
20 Upper Pickering St S058284
w/days: 7.30am to 7.30pm,
w/ends and pub hols: 8.30am
to 5.30pm
81331882

**Johore Road Boon Kee
Pork Porridge**
Blk 638 Veerasamy Rd
#01-101 S200608
Tues to Suns: 7am to 3.30pm,
closed on Mons
62969100

Nasi Padang River Valley
54 Zion Rd S247779
11am to 8.30pm, closed on
Mons and pub hols
67343383

**Lau Goh Teochew Chye
Thow Kway** (for carrot cake)
70 Zion Rd Stall 26 S247792
Mons to Sats: noon to 2.30pm
and 5pm to 11.45pm, Suns:
10am to 3pm and 5pm to 11pm,
closed on Tues
96745483 (SMS only)

**No. 18 Zion Road Fried
Kway Teow**
70 Zion Rd Stall 17 S247792
Noon to 2.30pm and 6pm to
11pm, closed on alt Mons

**Noo Cheng Adam Road
Prawn Mee**
70 Zion Rd Stall 4 S247792
Noon to 3pm and 6pm to
11.30pm, closed on Mons

ACKNOWLEDGEMENTS

I would like to thank God for His bountiful blessings. Above all, for the gift of His Son Jesus Christ, who loved me and gave Himself for me. In Him, I live and breathe and have my being. In Him, I find meaning and purpose in all I do. I have seen Him do exceedingly, abundantly, above all that I can ever ask for or dream of.

Among His many blessings is the gift of my beautiful wife Lisa who is the embodiment of Proverbs 31:10—A wife of noble character, worth far more than earthly riches. I truly lack nothing. My two wonderful kids, James and Megan, who patiently put up with Daddy's insistence on getting that perfect shot before eating.

Over the years, I have relied on many makan kakis to suggest new places to eat, run the forum, organise makan sessions and basically be my sounding board on many issues. Many have come and gone. Their contribution to the blog has been invaluable. My current committee consists of Cactuskit, Soundman, OMark,

Liverpool, Damien and Holydrummer. These are the guys who are my arms, legs, eyes, ears and palate and are the people I most frequently turn to for help. Thanks also to my durian expert, Tommy, who inspired me to write about durians!

The person who kept insisting that I had to write another book even though I kept telling her I had no time was my editor, Ruth Wan. She and her editorial team went through all my blog posts, handed the manuscript to me to edit, and said we are going to press within two months! She's worse than my mom! But looking at the final product, I have to thank her for her vision. Thanks very much to her and her wonderful team at Epigram Books who worked so hard to put this book together: Ruth, Josephine, Sasha, Aditi, and most of all, Siew Huey, my designer, whom I have worked to the bone with my exacting standards and constant revisions, all for the sake of putting out only the best for the reader. Thanks guys!

Finally, thank you for buying this book! Just as a hole-in-one is worthless unless someone sees it, so a book is useless unless someone reads it! So thank you for reading and allowing me to share a fascinating facet of Singapore life with you!

ABOUT THE AUTHOR

Singapore's most talked-about food blogger is a doctor. Dr Leslie Tay is the winner of Asia Pacific's Best Food Blog Award. His first book, *The End of Char Kway Teow and Other Hawker Mysteries*, is a national bestseller and won the Best Food Literature Award for Singapore at the Gourmand World Cookbook Awards in 2011. He continues to eat his way through Singapore's cornucopia of hawker stalls. He specialises in street food photography, where all shots are taken without the use of props or studio lighting. More of his work can be found on *ieatishootipost.sg*.